Looking Backwards

COLETTE

Looking Backwards

TRANSLATED FROM THE FRENCH BY

DAVID LE VAY

WITH AN INTRODUCTION BY

MAURICE GOUDEKET

INDIANA UNIVERSITY PRESS

BLOOMINGTON & LONDON

Translated from the French *Journal à rebours* and *De ma fenêtre*
© *Journal à rebours,* Fayard 1941, *De ma fenêtre,* Hachette 1942, 1944
English translation © Peter Owen 1975
Indiana University Press edition published
by arrangement with Peter Owen, 1975

Published in Canada by Fitzhenry & Whiteside Limited,
Don Mills, Ontario
Manufactured in the United States of America

Library of Congress Cataloging in Publication Data
Colette, Sidonie Gabrielle, 1873-1954.
    Looking backwards.

    Translations of Journal à rebours and De ma fenêtre.
    1. Colette, Sidonie Gabrielle, 1873-1954—Biography.
I. Colette, Sidonie Gabrielle, 1873-1954. De ma
fenêtre. English. 1975. II. Title.
PQ2605.028J613 1975   848'.9'1209 [B]   74-29051
ISBN 0-253-14900-2   75 76 77 78 79 1 2 3 4 5

CONTENTS

FOREWORD

Few writers, I imagine, have observed everyday happenings more keenly than Colette, but her impressions, however vivid, were often stored in her mind for many years before being written down. *Journal à rebours* and *De ma fenêtre*, on the contrary, contain many pages that were set down quite rapidly, generally because they were intended for daily newspapers or periodicals and a copy date had to be met. It is interesting to compare these hasty articles with Colette's other works, some of which were long in maturing : the more elaborate ones do not always deserve the laurels.

The two works brought together in this edition have been arranged in three parts, entitled 'Pre-War', 'The Flight from Paris' (both from *Journal à rebours**) and 'Occupation' (*De ma fenêtre*). The second of these describes briefly *'l'exode'* of late June 1940, when the Germans were invading France and practically the whole of the North was moving southwards to avoid them. I shall always remember these tragic days. Colette and I were not residing in Paris but at Méré, near Montfort l'Amaury, about thirty-five miles away. I had, however, to come to Paris twice a week on business for two French newspapers. On 11 June, entering Paris, I found the city at once febrile and exceptionally silent. Cars were being loaded hastily. Documents were burning in official places. At *Paris Soir*, one of the papers for which I worked, they were moving out fast. In fact, the Germans were very near.

I returned to Méré at once and informed Colette of the situation.

'We'd better move,' I told her.

'Oh no,' she answered. 'All is quiet here, and this is my vacation.'

'But the place may become a battlefield at any moment, and I'm not sure a vacation on a battlefield is good for one's health.'

She still refused to move.

---

* Some of the pieces in *Journal à rebours* had appeared in other publications before its first appearance complete in 1941 (ed.).

7

'Very well,' I said, 'then let's go for a ride.'

I took her to the main road without preparing her for the scene she now witnessed and which she describes in the opening lines of *Journal à rebours* with the phrase, 'France glissant sur elle-même'. She remained silent for a while.

'When do we leave?' she said finally.

'At four tomorrow morning,' was my reply.

She looked at me, knowing that I was right, not only for our safety but because the newspapers upon which we both depended for a living had moved away.

By the time we were ready to go, the traffic had greatly increased. We had decided to take refuge at Colette's daughter's residence in central France. It took us six hours to do the first hundred miles.

At Curemont, Colette de Jouvenel's home, the first part of *Journal à rebours* was written. But soon Colette began to sigh every time the name of Paris was mentioned. She finally said to me:

'We are perfectly quiet and comfortable here, but I cannot bear such quietness when so many people are so anxious. I am used to spending my wars in Paris. I want to go back there, and share with others what there is to be shared.'

We returned to Paris quite soon. Colette began to watch the war through her window, and to this long contemplation we owe *De ma fenêtre*.

MAURICE GOUDEKET

Pre-War

SIDO AND I

'Minet-Chéri, you've thrown another chestnut skin in the fireplace.'

'No, mummy.'

'Yes, daughter.'

And Sido, my mother, brandished at the end of the tongs, under my nose ('and why did you choose to take after my nose, little nuisance?') the *corpus delicti*.

'My ashes! Soiling my precious ashes of apple, poplar and elm! What about the washing, eh? I've told you twenty times . . .'

It was not from irreverence that I did not listen to what followed, which was familiar to me. A child's attention obeys the most alert of its senses. Already mine was that of smell. My mother had barely uttered the word 'washing' than I imagined myself inhaling the sweetish smell of the ashes, spread out on the hempen sheet which covered the great vat in the wash-house. At regular intervals the washerwoman would pour on the bed of ashes a pitcher of boiling water which filtered through into the mass of linen. . . . The murky air, blue with steam, surged in distinct clouds, veiled the great rounded copper, with its pipe which pierced the ceiling. Enormous, padded out with cloth, the washerwoman went floating from one wall to the other in defiance – so it seemed – of the laws of gravity. A bundle of iris roots, white as bones, hung from a nail. . . . A smooth and smoking lava, the layer of ashes retained a few black cinders – currants in the cake, truffles in the *foie gras* – and I would extract these, scalding my fingers.

'You're not to touch that, my little servant,' said the washer-woman.

For the nicest names that a nurse, a domestic or a mother can bestow in my part of the world on the child they have seen born are 'my little servant', 'my little companion'.

'I've told you twenty times', continued Sido, 'that the tannin contained in the chestnut skins stains the linen yellow. . . . When will you learn, if not now, the things a woman has to know?'

'When I am married,' I replied stupidly.

The effect of such a reply on my mother exceeded my expectations. Her spectacles (for seeing at a distance) fell from her eyes. She seized her lorgnette, mended with iron wire, fixed it on me as if to be assured that no evil spell resulting from this reply had not already delivered me, aged only fifteen years, into the arms of a ravisher. Her eyebrows became joined from side to side by a short vertical crease and, tugging at their lids, inflicted on her eyes the shape of a lozenge.

'Charming!' she exclaimed. 'You take after your father with this taste for delicate witticisms!'

'But it's not a witticism, mummy. I think I shall get married. Why, you've been married twice, you have.'

'Do what I say and not what I do,' quoted Sido sententiously.

'If daddy heard you . . .'

'I do hear her,' said a magnificent male voice from behind a spread copy of *Le Temps*.

'And he dares to pretend that he's getting deaf,' murmured my mother indignantly.

But she had blushed; her young girl's cheeks, still pink at over fifty, became empurpled twenty times a day whenever she became embattled with her children, broke a blue cup, or allowed herself to be caught in the act of being in love with my father.

Did I cause her much concern? Maybe yes, maybe no. She relied on me and took me seriously, provided it was not to do with practical matters or household affairs. I listened and retained what she taught me; I have still forgotten none of it. But if I knew how to carve a rose out of a radish, if I had no equal in making a grass flute, changing an old ten centime piece into gold, skimming off for my own benefit the pink froth that rose from the strawberries and gooseberries in the jam-making pan, on the other hand I let the butter burn, I sewed more clumsily than a soldier and, in process of cleaning the mirror over my fireplace, would stop to read, standing, a book open on the mantelpiece. . . .

'If it were only the washing!' continued Sido. 'But the ashes for the potatoes, you must know that absolute purity is essential. . . .'

The ashes for the potatoes reposed, as if they were those of a hero, in an urn. By urn, I mean a black cast-iron cauldron with three long divergent legs, covered with a convex lid which had only one handle. Seen from a distance, and in the shadow, one thought: 'What's this strange animal?' Its content of fine, whitening, sieved ashes delicately inhumed several large unpeeled potatoes, then the lot was planted right in the embers and packed round with ashes. Cooked without water, without steam, the potatoes became marvellously floury, needing only fresh butter on the plate and a pinch of salt. Beneath their dusty skin I found both main course and dessert, for I also mixed their friable flesh with some very sugary apple marmalade. The ashes would also soften red beetroots, which went well with lamb's lettuce in a salad.

'As all you can think about is leaving me,' said Sido, 'you can go and find me some lamb's lettuce. Take the round-ended knife.'

She did not have to tell me twice. I was already running down the street when Sido, on the doorstep, shouted her last urgent warnings:

'Don't go by the fields of the Petit-Moulin, they're under water! Don't go round by Thury, there are some gipsy waggons there! Mind you're back before dark! Don't eat the sloes on the hedges or the haws! And don't fill your pockets with salad full of earth! ...'

Out of sight, I shrugged my shoulders furiously and asked myself what kind of idea – 'no, there, really, all the same!' – parents have of their children, and if my mother – 'there, really, oh dear, let's see now!' – would one day recognize the fact that I was practically fifteen.

Beyond the limit which the maternal voice – a modulated soprano of good compass which was never discordant – could reach, I proceeded with determination towards the Petit-Moulin and its submerged fields. Five hundred steps further I feasted on sloes and haws, the latter insipid, the former bitter enough to rasp the mucous membranes. After which I was all set for the salad harvest. And as, from one head of lettuce to the next, I moved away from the old holed basket, I accumulated my harvest in my pockets. . . .

Ritual gestures, in which calculated disobedience played no part. Ever since I learned to walk, the deserted countryside constituted my limitless domain. Who would have determined, if not I, that the sloe, the wild strawberry, the hazelnut were ripe? Who but I knew the secrets of the favourite places of the lily of the valley, the white narcissi, the squirrels? . . . To each his domain. Did I dispute with Sido the sovereignty of the family home? The discovery of a ring of mushrooms led me on to look for another, and another. . . . The mauve colchicums, the 'night-lights' of the meadows, I gathered in a bouquet, mixed with the last scabious. The autumn twilight descended with its intoxicat-ing smell of rotting oak-leaves and fertile marshland. It was the time when Sido would stand on the door-step and look out for my return. Would I arrive by the bottom of the road, or the top? She would turn her head from right to left, like a broody hen on the edge of the nest. It was the hour of her great torment. Waiting for me she'd throw over her head and shoulders any old garment snatched in passing from the coat-rack in the passage. So that I saw her at various times with an overcoat of my father, my little old cloak, fit at best for the garden, and even a blue apron whose strings she tied under her chin. She was Anxiety itself, in its varied forms. . . . Other symbols – pince-nez, two pince-nez, a pair of spectacles, a magnifying-glass – proclaimed that she was also Discovery. Her great word 'Look!' meant: 'Look at that hairy caterpillar, like a little golden bear! Look at the first shoot of the haricot bean, the cotyledon which lifts a little hat of dry earth on its head. . . . Look at the wasp cutting a fragment of raw meat with its shears of mandibles. . . . Look at the colour of the sky at sunset, which foretells high winds and storm. What does tomorrow's high wind matter so long as we admire this furnace today? Look, quick, the bud of the black iris is about to open! If you don't hurry, it will be quicker than you. . . .'

But as soon as I turned the corner of the street, whether from above or below, Sido would disappear, not to seem to have been waiting for me. For my part, I pretended not to know that she had followed from afar my fifteen years, endowed with long hair, a slim figure, a small cat's face with wide temples and pointed chin, my fifteen years and their trust in a native country where they had never had an unfortunate encounter. . . . Under the pale green dome of the hanging lamp a grey gaze, almost hard in its sharpness, swept all over me, scrutinized me from my scratched cheek to my muddy shoes, listed the damage: 'A streak of blood on the cheek, a tear by the shoulder, the hem of the skirt unstitched and damp, shoes and stockings like sponges . . . That's all. That's all there is; thank God, once more, that's all there is. . . .'

THE FOOT-WARMER

Vocation, holy signs, childhood poetry, predestination? . . . I can find nothing of the sort in my recollections. At the beginning of my career was a foot-warmer. . . . Foot-warmer! To make myself clear it will immediately be necessary to describe an accessory which no longer exists. Allow me to open a dictionary: 'Foot-warmer, metal box in which were enclosed glowing embers mixed with ashes, and on which the feet were placed to keep them warm.' Already the dictionary speaks of it in the past. . . . A foot-warmer, then, reigns over the début of my intellectual – let's say my scholarly life. In the vast and glacial residences of the country, among the blasts of north wind, the foot-warmer was an object of prime necessity in winter. At my parents' house there was the foot-warmer of the cook, that of the visiting dressmaker, my mother's foot-warmer and, finally, mine, the one I used to take to school filled with poplar embers covered with fine ashes. . . . I was given the finest because it was the most solid, a magnificent object in wrought iron, indestructible, which weighed as much as a full suitcase. Have you any idea of the power of my wrought-iron foot-warmer used as an offensive or defensive weapon at play-time? I bear the ineffaceable evidence of one of these fights with blows from a foot-warmer; a broken cartilage in the left ear. Foot-warmer, shield, projectile, heater, primitive comfort of a small region which ignored every kind of comfort for so long! In the first form – six to eight years – of that poor bare school, each small girl had her own. Massive emanations of carbon monoxide rose from all these braziers. Children went off to sleep, vaguely asphyxiated. . . .

My first school winter was severe; I went to school between two walls of snow taller than myself. . . . What has happened to those great winters of yesteryear, white, solid, enduring, embellished with snow, fantastic stories, pines and wolves? Having been as real as my childhood, are they now as lost as that is? As lost as old Mlle Fanny, insubstantial phantom teacher, who subsisted on novels and privations? Sometimes Mlle Fanny would emerge from her romantic dream and utter a neighing which announced the reading lesson. . . . That year we learned to read in the New

Testament. Why the New Testament? Because there was one there, I suppose. And the old maid phantom teacher, with blows of a ruler on her desk, scanned the rhythm of the sacred syllables chanted in chorus: '*In! – that! – time! – Je! – sus! – said! – to! – his! – dis! – ci! – ples!* . . .' Sometimes a baby pupil, who was sitting on her foot-warmer to warm herself, uttered a shrill scream because she had just burned her small backside. Or perhaps a column of smoke rose from a foot-warmer, spreading the smell of a chestnut, a potato, a winter pear, that one of us was trying to cook in the foot-warmer. . . . All around us was the winter, a silence broken by rooks, the wind's howls, clattering sabots, the winter and the ring of woods round the village. . . . Nothing else. Nothing more. A humble, a rural image. . . .

But I believe that if a little harmless magic could restore to me the aroma of the potato oozing in the embers and the charred chestnut, and especially of the extraordinary old tome of the New Testament, nibbled, tattered, musty, between the pages of which Mlle Fanny preserved dried tulip petals, transparent as red onyx, little grey corpses of violets, the square bearded faces of springtime pansies, I really believe that I should be content. I believe that I should bear off, inhale, that spell to unveil the past, that key which reopens childhood, and that it would restore to me my age of six years which knew how to read but did not wish to learn to write. No, I did not wish to write. When one can enter the enchanted kingdom of reading, why write? Was not this repugnance, inspired by the action of writing, a providential piece of advice? It is a little too late to cross-examine myself on this. What's done is done. But in my youth I never, *never* wanted to write. No, I did not get up at night in secret to write verses in pencil on the lid of a shoe-box! No, I did not get nineteen or twenty for style in an exercise between the ages of twelve and fifteen! For I felt, more so every day, I felt that I was made precisely *not* to write. I never sent essays promising a pretty amateur talent to a famous writer; yet today everyone does, since I never cease to receive manuscripts. I was, then, the only one of my kind, the only one brought into the world not to write. What pleasure I enjoyed at such a lack of literary vocation! My childhood, my free and solitary adolescence, both preserved from the cares of self-expression, were both uniquely occupied with directing their subtle antennae towards whatever contemplates and listens to itself, probes itself and breathes. Limited deserts, without dangers; imprints of bird and hare on the snow; lakes covered with ice or veiled with warm summer mist; assuredly, you gave me as many joys as I could contain. Must I call my school a school? No, but a sort of rude paradise where ruffled angels broke the wood in the morning to light the stove and ate, in the guise of heavenly manna, thick *tartines* of red haricot beans, cooked in a wine sauce, spread on the grey bread kneaded by the farmers' wives. . . . No railway in my parts, no electricity, no nearby college or large town. In my own family, no money, but books. No gifts, but tenderness. No comfort, but freedom. No voice borrowed the sound of the wind to whisper in my ear, with a small chill breath, the advice to write and to write again, to tarnish, in writing, my soaring or tranquil perception of the living universe. . . .

I thought originally that I might cause amusement by relating the adventure of the writer who did not want to write. And, now that I am concluding, I am aware that it is a sad story. For when, at seventeen, love arrived in my life, despite the love and despite the seventeen years, I had neither desire to write about it nor to describe it, and I felt that love can dispense with love-letters, reflect on itself in silence, and satisfy itself with a sovereign presence instead of writing its own novel.

Yet my life turned towards writing. . . . Born into a family without money, I had learned no calling. I knew how to climb, whistle, run, but no one came to propose a career as a squirrel, a bird or a hind. The day when necessity put a pen in my hand and I was given a little money in return for the pages I had written, I understood that I should have to write slowly, submissively, each day, patiently reconcile sound and number, rise early by preference, retire late from duty. A young reader, male or female, need not know more about the stay-at-home and sensible writer hidden behind a sensual novel. French is quite a difficult language. After forty-five years of writing one just begins to appreciate this.

A SALON IN 1900

Can I say that I really knew him, my illustrious collaborator, the author of *L'Enfant et les sortilèges*? I met Maurice Ravel for the first time at Mme de Saint-Marceaux's, who used to receive on Friday evenings after dinner. Forty years ago, the gatherings at the Saint-Marceaux mansion, rather than a worldly curiosity, were more a reward accorded to the musical faithful, a sort of elevated recreation, the bastion of artistic intimacy. Two drawing-rooms of modest dimensions joined into one were, over a long period, the place which consecrated the reputations of composers and virtuosi under the aegis of a good female musician. In fact, Mme de Saint-Marceaux did not appear to seek anyone out and the favour of becoming a familiar of those Fridays had to be solicited.

A dinner, always excellent, preceded these reunions, where the mistress of the house maintained an atmosphere of 'ordered liberty'. She did not insist that one listened to the music but suppressed the slightest whisper. Everyone was free to arrive whenever he wished, provided that the men were in lounge-suits, the women in the equivalent. 'My Fridays', explained Mme de Saint-Marceaux, 'welcome hardworking friends, tired after their day's endeavours, neighbours who decide at the last moment to desert their fireside to come and sit at mine, painters attached to their undress. I've spent twenty years ridding them of all distrust, accustoming them to comfort without affectation. If Fauré, leaving his duchesses in evening-dress, comes to swagger at my house, Messager, who is affectation itself, will feel humiliated and assume his sad *palikare* face.* No, no, no more *panache*!'

Princess Edmond de Polignac always appeared in a high-necked dress. I admired, intimidated and from a little distance, the character of indestructibility bestowed by her intense blue gaze and her conqueror's chin. Her husband never quitted a light beige vicuna shawl which sometimes draped his chilly shoulders, sometimes warmed his knees. He was charming, young in heart, and resembled a great ironic bird. To listen to Fauré

* (Greek) Heroic. (This and all subsequent notes are the translator's.)

18

at the piano, or Edouard Risler, or Bages who sang Schumann, or the brief melodies of Pierre Bréville, the Prince de Polignac installed himself at the end of one of the sofas and sketched. How did the pretty little caricature, so flattering, that he did of me, get mislaid? I miss it.

Large shaded lamps, accessible tables well strewn with reviews, newspapers and cigarettes, warmth in winter, cool drinks and *petits fours* in the adjacent dining-room. . . . No one was distressed because Saint-Marceaux buried himself in a book, because the three Baugnies brothers, sons of Mme de Saint-Marceaux, retired to the top floor, because the painters Clairin, Billotte, Besnard, Jeanniot were absorbed in a painters' argument, because Gabriel Fauré preferred to music the pleasure of drawing in three strokes of the pen a portrait of Koechlin, long and bearded, or one of Henri Février, father of Jacques. Sometimes the phalanx of musicians threw themselves on the music-books, played, sang with spirit the melodies of Loisa Puget, ransacked a repertory of 1840 haunted by madmen on the heath, Breton fiancées leaning on harbour walls, young girls intoxicated by the waltz. . . . A fine basset bitch, Waldine, gave ear. A delightful female marmoset came to eat the cake crumbs and a small banana, wiped its fingers delicately with a handkerchief, fastened its alert, golden, unfathomable eyes on ours. . . . Such discreet, almost familial, liberties gave us much pleasure. Yet we felt ourselves to be governed by a hostess quick of wit and tongue, basically intolerant, with beaked nose and roving eye, who fought for music and became tipsy with it.

It was there that I saw the score of *Pelléas et Mélisande* arrive one evening. It came in Messager's arms, clasped to his heart, as if he had stolen it. He began to read it at the piano, to hum it with passion in a rusty zinc voice. He stopped, resumed : 'And this? . . . And this? . . .' and singing Mélisande's part he almost closed his eyes. . . .

Often, side by side on one of the piano-stools, Gabriel Fauré and Messager improvised with four hands, competing in sudden modulations and departures from the key. They both enjoyed this game, during which they would exchange duellers' ripostes : 'Take that! . . . And that, were you ready? . . . All right, I'll catch you out. . . .' Fauré, a swarthy emir, tossed his silver crest, smiled at these ambushes and went one better. . . . Chabrier's parody quadrille for four hands, containing the themes of the *Tétralogie*, often sounded the curfew. . . .

It was in this setting, echoing but responsive to meditation, jealous of its prerogatives but capable of gentleness, that I first met Maurice Ravel. He was young, this side of the age whence comes simplicity. Side-whiskers – yes, side-whiskers! – of voluminous hair exaggerated the contrast between his imposing head and tiny body. He loved striking cravats, linen with ruffles. Seeking attention, he feared criticism; that of Henry Gauthier-Villars was cruel. Perhaps inwardly shy, Ravel maintained a distant air, a dry manner. Apart from listening to his music, which I undertook initially from curiosity, then from an atttachment to which the slight unease of surprise, the sensual and malicious attraction of a new art, added their charms, that was all I knew of Maurice Ravel for many years. I cannot recall any particular encounter with him, any friendly abandon.

Came the day when M. Rouché asked me for a libretto for a fantasy-ballet for the Opéra. I still don't know how I was able to give him – I who work slowly and with difficulty – *L'Enfant et les sortilèges* in less than a week. . . . He liked my little poem and suggested composers whose names I greeted as politely as I could.

'But,' said Rouché after a pause, 'suppose I suggested Ravel?'

I emerged clamorously from my politeness and expressed my hopes in no niggardly fashion.

'We must face the fact,' added Rouché, 'that it may take a long time, even if Ravel accepts. . . .'

He did accept. It *was* long. He went off with my libretto and we heard no more of Ravel, nor of *L'Enfant*. . . . Where was Ravel working? Was he working? I did not realize what the creation of a work demanded of him, the slow frenzy which possessed and isolated him, heedless of hours and days. The War took Ravel, silenced his name with a hermetic seal, and I lost the habit of thinking about *L'Enfant et les sortilèges*.

Five years passed. The finished work and the author emerged from the silence, escaped the blue, day-blind eye of the Siamese cats who were Ravel's confidants. But he did not treat me as a privileged person, granted me no commentary, no preliminary audition. He seemed concerned only with the 'duo miaow' between the two Cats, and asked me gravely if I saw any problem in his replacing the 'mouao' by 'mouain', or possibly the other way round. . . .

The years had deprived him, not only of the ruffled shirt and side-whiskers, but also of the arrogance of a short-statured man. Mingled white and black hair crowned him with a sort of plumage and as he spoke he crossed his delicate rodent hands, touched everything with his squirrel's glance. . . .

The score of *L'Enfant et les sortilèges* is famous now. How can I express my emotion at the first drum-roll which accompanies the procession of the Shepherds? The moonlight dazzle of the garden, the flight of the dragonflies and the bats . . . 'It's amusing, isn't it?' said Ravel. But I was choked with unshed tears : the Beasts, with an urgent, barely articulated whispering, bent over the child in reconciliation. . . . I had not conceived that an orchestral swell, spangled with nightingales and fire-flies, could raise my modest work so high.

I did not have the distress of witnessing Ravel's decline. At Montfort-l'Amaury his solitude and his strange 'belvedere' preserved him from a public downfall. When Hélène Morhange returned to Paris, worried because 'Ravel is very, very ill,' we did not yet see much difference between the Ravel shyly ensconced in the midst of his work, evasive, silent, and the Ravel who was being dragged down. But his *confidante*, the great violinist to whom he dedicated the Sonata for violin and piano and entrusted the honour of realizing it, Hélène Morhange, was not deceived. The hand that forgot musical writing and other graphisms, the lips that speech deserted, all the vain selfconscious efforts, all these Morhange witnessed. She saw, as he drew away from music, one who, in 1907, said to Jules Renard with a sort of ingenuousness : 'It is not my intention to add, through my music, to the value of the words, I wish only to interpret them. I feel and think musically and I should like to think the same things as yourself. There is intellectual music : d'Indy. There is sentimental instinctive music : my own.'

Before the end of his life Ravel suffered a period of the worst mental confusion. I gather that his disease granted him remissions, the gleams of light and the relapses which alternately delude and desolate a condemned genius. One Sunday, his steps found without effort the little road which connects Montfort to the hamlet of Mesnuls, and he arrived at Luc-Albert Moreau's after lunch. Thin, greyish-white like the mist, he could still smile. Seeing me, he said : 'Hullo Colette . . .' in a normal voice. But he made no effort to say any more and, seated among us, had rather the appearance of a being who risks dissolution from one moment to the next. He resembled the living Ravel as Luc-Albert's portrait resembles the dead Ravel : a large nose, already remodelled by the invisible hand, the chin of Dante, the vigorous badly-shaven beard of the dead, a spreading shadow under the orbit and at the root of the nose. . . . I think it was on that day that Ravel pronounced my name for the last time.

AUTUMN

Imaginative; but one detects a determination to show off.

It has stayed in my memory, this note written in red ink in the margin of a French essay. I was eleven, twelve years old. In thirty lines I declared myself in disagreement with those who called autumn a decline; *I* called it a beginning. No doubt I did not make my thoughts plainly understood; they have not changed; I meant that the vast autumn, insidiously conceived, issue of the long days of June, was perceived by me through subtle signs, with the especial aid of the most primitive of the senses, that of smell. But a child of twelve is rarely equipped with a vocabulary capable of translating what she thinks and feels. For not having chosen the dappled spring and its nests, I received only a middling mark.

The fury of growth, the passion of flowering, subside in nature at the end of June. Then the universal green darkens, the forest's brow assumes the colour of shallow seaweed meadows. Alone in the garden the rose, managed by man rather than the seasons, some large peonies, aconites, continue the spring, typify the summer. The elders have declined from flower to seed and the harvested fields await the next crop.

All the scattered yellows, which in April repeated the colour

of young chicks, have passed. Wild chicory, cornflower, self-heal:
these are the last blues of the season, among the waves of paling
corn. But already the wild campanula, the knapweed, the
scabious, suggest the mauve of the colchicum – night-lights born
of the first cool nights. Thick verdure, illusion of stability, imprudent undertaking to survive! Contemplating it, we say, 'It's
really summer,' while, in a breezeless dawn, a passage of discreet
humidity, a circle of vapour over a meadow which betrays water
underground, while, predicted by a bird, by a worm-eaten apple
brilliant with hectic colouring, by a smell of burnt brushwood,
of mushrooms and half-dry mud, autumn emerges through
impassive summer. It is only a moment. July resumes its torrid
avarice. The apple and the pear are as bitter as the green walnut.
A residue of whiteheart cherries hang from a few cherry-trees;
the strawberries, gooseberries and blackcurrants have melted into
jam. . . . When, oh when will full-handed autumn come? . . .

It is already here, if you only knew how to interpret, on the
back of the leaf that has fallen for no obvious reason, a glittering
transpiration, how to read the sparkling zigzag traced by the
spider on the tops of the box-trees. At the two ends of a still limitless day, the dawn and the sunset suffer the same fires, the
drought is upon us, and only the storm provides a heavy dew;
yet the crab reddens, no longer is there the small voice of the
fledgling bird, a few oval coins separate from the acacias and
plane uncertainly before falling withered. Two months earlier
the lemon-yellow butterfly was on the wing, the same pale yellow
colour as the decayed leaves. . . . But the fate of the yellow butterfly is already settled. In its place are to be found the marvellous
peacock butterfly dotted with bluish planets, the wary vulcan
for which it is never too hot, and the beautiful silver, for these
stay on until the frosts.

We have still to traverse a long corridor of dark verdure. We
like to call it the height of the summer. Grave and beautiful,
fleecy, temperate where it adjoins the sea and the lakes, it has,
even in France, its terrible zones and the wild game wastes under
its oppression. The flanks of the hares, flattened to the ground,
heave. Where will the sandpiper with the broken stilt find some
moist clay to dress its wound?

Over the lakes of my own country, as the water-level fell,
August the harbinger spread a film of tin. When a grass-snake,

long and vigorous, crossed the lake, its tiny nostrils at the surface
of the water, accompanied by a triangular wake, I hesitated as a
child to bathe. So much secret life rose in circles, as watered silk,
in bubbles, haunted slime, so many springs erupted, stalks waved
languidly. . . . Yet the tree-frog, green on its green raft, the brutal
and doubtless myopic dragonfly, tempted me. Even a child cannot respond to everything; but his antennae quiver at the least
stimulus and he prefers above all else that which is closed, misty,
unnamed, impressive. It is to my lakes, thickened by summer,
stirred by the autumn, that I owe my love for a little Mediterranean marsh whose red waters were salted by the equinoctial gales
around mid-September. Meadow, moor and underwood are less
alive than a marsh. From the foraging swallow, snapper-up of
morning mosquitoes, to the last glissades of the warbler on the
reed-stalks, what gaiety! . . . Birds, yellowish rats and fieldmice,
ponderous butterflies supported on the layer of overheated air
which trembles like a feverish mirage, the leaps of great toads
which bathe only briefly because they fear the salt, the slow twists
and turns of a strange black and white water-snake, finally the
uncertain departure of the first bat and the mewing of the
sparrow-owl which upsets the cats, what gaiety on the little
Cannebiers marsh! . . . No time is wasted when the hours flow
by quietly beside this near-hidden stretch of water, neither sweet
nor altogether bitter, deceptive meadow of reeds with edible
seeds, sedge, yellow St John's wort. . . . From August on the sea-
lavender covers my marsh with its unfading mauve florescence.
When you want to gather the sea-lavender you must fear neither
the invisible water which clutches at the foot and leaves it
enslimed, nor the flight of the swarms which were sleeping in the
tepidity and now jump, writhe, swim, fly off. The stalk of the
freshly-cut false bamboo cuts the flesh with its keen bevelled
edge. . . .

August, in my northern country, was a month for long
patience. Like me deprived of school, the children found the
days long. They crowded together during their interminable
leisure in the shade at the foot of the houses, for they were tired
of the shorn stubble and the silent woods. As the sun rotated they
folded up their dusty legs to shield them from it. They played, we
played, at spinning the knife, three pebbles, knuckle-bones. They
bit into the first half-green peaches – I don't write 'we bit'

because, as always, I was an expert on the taste of ripe juicy fruit. We watched the upward growth on the waste land of those thistles, fit for carding, whose flower, armed overall, takes fire with a violet flame just before the expiration of summer. Mulleins also climbed there, all covered – hairy leaves, buff-coloured flower – with the dustiness of those sultry days. Sated with idleness, listless from missing school and from concealing it, we counted the days and lied : 'My word, doesn't it go quickly!'

Nothing goes quickly in summer, except the summer. An abrupt August squall got up in the stony dryness, lifted columns of white dust to the skies, fell again in a deluge whose first showers set the teeth on edge, tore from the dried-up ponds hosts of little frogs which fell with a 'floc!' which quite knocked them out. The storm departed and behind it its great trail of vertical rain lasted the whole night. In the morning we noticed that everything had changed, also that the cats were plump. . . . September! September! It hadn't actually arrived but already it breathed its strong breath of delicate corruption, a renewal which smelled of plums, smoke and walnut-shells. Soon September! The children revived under the rain, the swollen west shed a blue, spare, abbreviated light. 'But it's evening!' cried my mother. 'The lamp already!' To myself I said : 'The lamp at last . . .' Another week and the ripe peaches fell, and the red sage extended its spikes, and the sour opaque grape turned to transparent agate. . . . Another fortnight, and the two punctual cats gave birth on the same day, attesting the actual presence, this time, of September.

The fire, the wine, the red and windy skies, the flesh of fruits, the rich game, the barrels, the pulpy spheres, all roll before it. Chestnut husks, bletted medlars, pink service-berries, tart sorb-apples : autumn chases before its steps a profusion of modest fruits which do not have to be picked but which drop into the hand, which patiently wait at the foot of the tree until man condescends to gather them. He has eyes and thoughts only for his last crop and the grape-harvest.

Above the Loire he has an austere enough vintage, this poor man of the soil, under fire at every moment in his work, hailed on, drowned, numbed with cold, attacked by the invisible. The very day of the harvest is a day already curtailed, a task pursued by October's ill-humour, a task for which the vinearoon buttons his woollen coat. Only the South knows, while he is at work on the vintage, the expression of a joy which derives from the climate, the unimpaired season, the prompt and perfect maturity of the grape, sometimes so caressed by the sun as to call the gossiping hosts to the vines at the end of August. Some years ago the entire *département* of the Var – and, I believe, its neighbours – had to strip its laden vine-stocks from the twenty-sixth of August to save the long and heavy grapes, which were dragging and scorching on the ground. What sugar and flame, what a bloom of blue on those bulging grapes, what a violet-mauve on the skin of the violet berry that is called *olivette*! . . . The *clairette* is rosy and round, the rich *picardan* burdens the stock, the golden-white *muscat* and a very black little *pineau* burst their delicate skin and lose their richness if there is any delay. A wildly abundant year offers the grapes of Canaan. The little vine which is no longer mine prided itself, that year, on a cluster which someone brandished, crying: 'Not bad, eh! Not less than eight pounds, that one!'

Down there the pale, blackhaired women grape-harvesters put on large hats, turn down their sleeves to the wrists, and affect fearfulness: 'Oh, there's a spider! Holy Mother, a snake!' With equal affectation the men shed their coats and throw off their shirts. While the men go handsomely half-naked, the women laugh freely and sing on the paths. Fine high voices, which the west wind carries from one bay to the next. . . . The wasps, drunk and defenceless, adhere to the sticky tubs; the September sun is as good as August's. . . . Only privileged climates paint such pictures, retain such pagan pleasures on their easy shores. The old hand wine-press still visits Saint-Tropez, stops from door to door surrounded by its swarms of children and blonde flies. From its purple straps, from its indelibly violet-stained wood there flows, choked with *débris*, the new wine for which each may hold out his glass. . . . From then on they make the *vin marquis* in the kitchens. Do you prefer it simple – new wine boiled, reduced to one-third – or refined, improved with spices and filtered, then bottled? The one for Sundays, the other for workdays, that's the best you can do. . . .

After the grape, in those parts, there comes the 'second fig', which is all honey. Its pink heart is like that of the strawberry called 'June beauty'. After the second fig the last hard peaches come down from the lower slopes. Walnuts and hazels are already heaped on echoing floorboards. Then there begins a kind of agrarian idleness, a local leisure during which the fig on the fruit-trays contracts, sweats a dry sugary sweat. . . . If I had to choose, I'd take my holidays at the same time as Provence itself.

Then I should reascend France 'from bottom to top' as children say. Such a trip is not accomplished without melancholy. But I have never been in the habit of enjoying what is gayest, preferring that which is free from bitterness. To leave the Midi in September means to leave behind a fête which continues pleasantly in one's absence, convoking naked youths, women in fancy-dress, bands playing the same tunes over and over again. After Avignon the summer yellows, the vine-stalks are mouldy, the sky descends and a vague aurora rises from the earth; France regains its four seasons, its jealously-defined and glorious wine-producing areas, and its migratory birds.

O long-nuanced autumn, prolonged fruitfulness . . . It is the perfected, the strong, the fragrant which has for so long brought the starlings about my head, their whistlings of icy winds and ripped silk, which has for so long stretched the ducks' great V, the flight of the cranes and wild geese, gathered and then despatched massive groupings of swallows. . . . Annotated by the most burning blossoms that exist, by the fiery sage, the dahlias blacker than the black rose, the scarlet canna, how could I associate the idea of sleep and abdication with such developments? Add to that the prodigality which assures us the possession of such free benefits as the red crab apple, the mulberry, the *cèpe*, the triangular beechnut, the four-cornered water chestnut. . . .

This last, the *cornuelle*, is, I well realize, unknown in Paris and many other regions. Besides, it's strange and chooses its lakes. To harvest it you need a flat punt, a pair of sculls, an old pair of breeches, a willingness to flounder about in cold water. Otherwise, you can buy them as I used to do – a hundred and four *cornuelles* for four *sous* – after having awaited the arrival of Frisepoulet, a majestic wood-spirit whose head of hair and white flaxen beard subserved the dark glare of a sorcerer's gaze:

> *Chataignes piquantes!*
> *Chataignes chatouillantes!*
> *Qui chatouillent la cuisse,*
> *Mais qui piquent la poche!*

He cried his wares and sold them, but spoke no word to the common run of villagers or to the children. With him arrived the first chestnuts. After him there were only the blue sloes on the hedges, and after that the frost which laid a light glaze on the full buckets by the pump. I went to gather the shrivelled sloes, which my mother used to infuse in alcohol *de bon goût*. Can so many minor miracles be accomplished nowadays without the aid of Frisepoulet? I doubt whether the cheeses of my native country can ripen perfectly in the irremediable absence of a little man for whom I knew no other name than 'the good Lord', who repaired umbrellas under a staircase. . . .

'Go and fetch my umbrella, which must be mended by now, and ask the good Lord to bring a cheese. . . .'

What would become of our childhood memories were it not for their seasonal figures? If the man-with-the-rose, the passer-by perfumed with green shallot, spring onion, bay, was silent, it was because a rose gripped between his teeth permanently closed his lips. For the man-with-the-rose alone the Bengal rose-bush had neither pause nor beginning. . . .

The style, the nature of what we shall like in later life are fixed in the moment when the clear vision of childhood chooses and sculpts its enduring figures of fantasy. I set mine against indelible backgrounds, such as pines weighed down with snow, narcissi in circles round hidden springs, fiery geraniums, family tables and little jollifications grouped like a floral arrangement, an English teapot whose lid was a convulvulus. All round the table were Chinese cups, stemmed glasses for the Frontignan wine, and, in the middle, the cake with rum sauce. Autumn, autumn still, this burning cake, flavoured with honest alcohol. For the tastes of the summer garden, the summer, the meringues stuffed with fresh cream, the raspberries, were dissolved in an excess of light and warmth. In autumn 'Sido's' great fluttering sleeves shed a nightlight's white glow at the table. Her bare forearms were more graceful than the neck of an *aiguière* where slices of fruit swam in chilled white wine, in the midst of thick crystal chased in filigree. . . . The objects of that epoch were not entirely free of a gothic heaviness which was widespread at the middle of the nineteenth century. And so their memory remains impressed, marked by a somewhat frantic elegance, which attaches handles that are too light to bellies that are too bulging,

thin backs to massive chairs. . . . Where might I not be led by
the memory of Sido's arm, prolonged by a chocolate-pot, and a
pretentious chocolate-pot at that, the chair a Napoleon III imitation of Louis XV? Sido's arm derived from a pure design. But
I cannot and will not separate it from the agreeable errors which,
spread round a personality, aid in its preservation and perfect
commemoration.

Forty years weighed lightly on the principle personality of
my entire life, Sido, when she brought me into the world. But
after my birth she fattened up, became plump without being
ugly, had to abandon the dresses that used to emphasize her
young girl's waist. So I kept a blue dress that she told me she
regretted, a skirt of fine cloth, with a white embroidered garland,
whose waist measurement is barely nineteen inches.

Thus it was on my behalf that she entered the autumn of her
womanhood and established herself therein serenely. She even
wished to wear the insignia sported in those days by elderly
women, that is, she put on her head at one stage the ruched
bonnet, and on Sundays a *chapeau fermé*. Then her independent
children, who knew no other cohesion than an obscure and dissimulated affection, ranged themselves against her in unison.
They appeared outraged, cursed the bonnet, vituperated the
stringed hat with its funereal violets. They repelled the future –
'the future', said one of us, 'is what doesn't arrive' – an inadmissible maternal form, fixed inflexible limits to Sido's decline.
Autumn, and no more! For them she often made a point of
disguising her October as August. Where a stranger's glance
would have seen only a small elderly woman dressed like a peasant,
her slender feet in garden sabots, we, all of us, gained an impression of spontaneity, spryness, vivacity, a voice of ravishing
extended register, the gaiety of those who – having nothing more
to lose – excel in giving, and the pet names of a love which
perhaps has made us resistant to other loves: 'Minet-Chéri . . .
My bright sunshine . . . Beauty! . . .' This last name was not
for me but for the elder of my brothers, for autumn is never
single-minded in its passion. To a woman's heart which chastely
caressed its favoured product, to eyes which proudly took stock
of an accomplished son, I should not have blushed to confess the
living aid which later disguised, cheered and prolonged my own
decline. But Sido departed too soon.

As I write, there once again returns the season celebrated by a former schoolgirl because, precociously, she loved it. It returns all golden to inspire wisdom or its opposite, so that the chestnuts may flower a second time, so that the cat, who weaned her litter in June, may seek other adventures, so that the deceived swallow may recommence a nest, so that a mature woman may sun herself and sigh : 'I am sure it will never be winter again. . . .'

OUM-EL-HASSEN

14 November 38

Down below it was drizzling, the November dawn was less bright than an August midnight. Between the night train and the Air France car, between the weighing and the forms to be filled in, we hurried to swallow a white coffee and left our mother earth churlishly. . . .

But the aeroplane slipped between two clouds, like the thrush that spies a gap in the foliage above it and takes off vertically, and we progress on a kind of ploughland with small regular furrows which has neither end nor beginning and is pink. Pink under a pure pale-green sky, marred by a great brown wound and golden in the east where the sun is about to rise. Pink to the point where all other colour seems banished from the deceptive meadow which constitutes our temporary surface. Pink without vagaries or variations, with an azure fold at the reverse of each cloud. The breeze, or the wind of our propellers, delicately skims the nonexistent plain, cards it, brings away a tuft, a fluff of rose-pink, a celestial pink thistle seed. Under an insubstantial shaving, shorn from the dappled infinite, appears the flat distant land drowned in shadow. The snow of the Pyrenees brings a touch of white into the pink universe when the range rises towards us; but an ascending leap – the diver's kick – thrusts it away and the aeroplane crosses it.

Fez is not far. Nothing is far. A small girl hums, is bored, as in a bus. 'Mummy, may I buy a bar of chocolate at Barcelona?'

'You're being a nuisance, you can wait till Oran.' At Barcelona there is time to drain a cup of coffee, to steal one of the flowers blooming on a fence. 'Can you hear the guns?' said a seasoned air-traveller with an engaging air, as one might say: 'I can recommend our Palace of Justice, it dates from the fifteenth century.'

We sail on over the sea, an inverted firmament, above a flight of great white gesticulatory clouds. In a few moments they will be here, the reddish approaches to Morocco and the narrow plateaux, hoisted on their fluted walls like Savoy cakes. Then we shall take the car, and the road between the eucalyptuses and the gardens – zinnias, bougainvillaeas, red roses – a good well-signposted road blazed by Arabs seated on asses, native land-owners on horseback, women on foot. We shall make a stop at thronged Meknes, pricked by lights which anticipate the night, brilliant with military uniforms, souks, children, white teeth, fine eyes. And we shall arrive at the great grey cayman, Fez, lying in its valley beneath a zone of haze that gathers whatever rises from the overripe dates, new cedarwood, organic wastes, roast groundnut, capturing and composing the incense of an incomparable putrescence.

Fifteen years ago a Pasha from the South – the one who knew *le mieux Paris*, the one Paris knew familiarly as *le Glaoui* – lent us one of his Fezzan residences. It happened to be the oldest, a native palace not rendered ugly by a fallacious comfort. Between the walls, which had been pink, the interior arrangement needs – if I am to evoke it – only those words that paint Moroccan luxury: enclosed gardens, carpets, divans, slaves, these last beautiful and as numerous as you like.

On the ground-floor we were accorded a room so large that we could call it an apartment. Two great door-panels of odorous cedar, as heavy as the gates of a city, barred it at night; it extended into a paved court at the end of which yellow jasmine, palms, daturas and lilacs swayed behind the forged foliage of the gate. For our sleep we went for a stroll in the same room, an uninterrupted extent of twenty-five yards of divans, stuffed with wool. The native steward told us that such a bed of repose contained, sewn in its diverse silks, four thousand kilos of fine fleece. When the time came to retire there was no need of other mattresses or of European-style sheets. But the small brown hands of five, ten, twenty child slaves brought us, as in a dance, two pieces of a pink Bengali gauze, hemmed with blue scalloping, woven with butterflies and flowers, with a pile of thick coverings of a deep red. Thus we slept our first night of the Thousand and One Nights.

The room had no windows, no windowpanes. Through the joints of the cedar door-panels there entered the light of the night sky, the rustling and perfume of the gardens, a constant noise of the river and small cascades, for Fez streams with running water. At the end of the brief cold April night the pigeons cooed, a horizontal red arrow of sun entered above the door, a watery reflection leapt to the ceiling where it writhed like a salamander, a thousand swallows whistled. I slipped out of my winding-sheet of gauze and butterflies and went on all fours to glue my eye to the crack in the door; a large oval eye with dark brown iris and a double barrier of curved lashes and long lustrous eyebrow was watching me at the exact level of my own gaze. I heard a pretty cry and the tap-tap-tap of flying bare feet. They did not flee far. The paved court resounded with other bare feet, hurried little breathings, the creviced panels became as many traps to catch as many gleaming eyes: all our child-servants spied on our getting-up.

But when the doors stood open, the courtyard was empty under the pale sky of Fez and its palms. The Moroccan steward, who appeared without our having to call him, promised us that the children would come back. They did return, gravely, but only to the number of half-a-dozen. One rolled in the low-footed table for breakfast. There followed the rest of the oriental ballet : a young girl grasping a bowl covered by her conical straw hat, another damsel balancing the copper tray laden with thick, aniseed-flavoured bread, coffee, honey and fruit; in front of them all marched a choreographer some ten years of age, proud and useless, confident of stirring us with the dazzle of his solitary tyranny, not condescending to smile.

Bronzed beauty, in the climate which has formed and gilded it, is a profoundly seductive danger for the northerner, who is dazzled by it. On the other hand, there is no chronicle to tell us how many white beauties have succumbed to a conquering black. It is true that there are no – or very few – stories of harems. In the dwelling of our host a small group of flawless persons moved about. The steward laughed and displayed his regular teeth, wore like a collar a young black beard implanted in his smooth, rather fat cheeks. His children – a small girl of two especially, already glittering with bracelets, necklaces and earrings – were moulded from a light and varied clay, one white as the flesh of bananas, another tobacco-brown, another pink as baked earth. The African grace lay on all, and on the whole of each from neck to heels, from the forehead braided with ribbons and tresses to a small, naked belly. Young servant-girls on the eve of nubility did not fly my companion's presence, and smiled with their unveiled mouths which called to mind a black plum, the peach called Halleberge, the violet fig, dark fruits fissured in maturity.

The least cotton fabric, raw pink or bazaar mauve, was enhanced by being posed on their polished shoulders, next to their firm-fleshed cheek. It is true that a fair white woman also has a hundred ways of being fair and white. But certain latitudes deprive her of part of her witchery; the very contrasts of Africa cease to serve her. Here the sombre feminine amphora goes with the brutal blue of the shadows, the frenzied green of the foliage, as well as the earthy pink of the buildings, the spray of yellow jasmine which covers the shell of a dark ear.

The troop of child slaves, quietly playing and sparring, removed dessert and table with no other sound than the flac-flac of their little bare feet and we made a trial of the vaulted bath-room, a romantic retreat furnished with a kind of copper samovar tall enough to touch the ceiling, whose yellow belly, virilized by an enormous tap, kept a good cubic metre of water on the boil. When the released jet smashed on the ground the flags smoked and no hot steam bath ever proved better.

To reach the souks by the lanes, the steward made me saddle a black mule with red pompoms. The mule-driver was some seventeen years old and resembled the adolescents one sees in Persian miniatures, entering by the roof to descend to a young woman whose elderly husband sleeps in his beard. What might his smile have been like? But he did not smile. On seeing which, the Moroccan steward took his chin in one hand, pressed his other hand on his forehead, and opened the adolescent as one splits a purple fruit with white pips, to show us that he was beautiful all through, to his impregnable molars and the gullet red as a gladiolus. It is of remote origin, this gesture of the trafficker in ephebes. But it has not lost its horse-dealing sensuality, its ability to disturb the spectator.

Where now are the mule-driver, the tiny marvellous child – a red pearl in her ear – who used to bring me a few spring strawberries on a leaf each morning? Where the yellow-eyed cavalier, draped in black, on his black horse? Horse and rider were bordered, on harness and djellaba, with the same ardent bluish-green, the blue of neon and lightning. They advanced on us like a storm edged with phosphorus, seemed to lose their substance as they passed, avoiding touching us, as they avoided seeing us. . . .

I return in the autumn, moved by a deep curiosity, not so much to know Fez better – can one ever know Fez? – as to touch, smell, hear one of its bloodstained secrets which, though recent, seems to hark back to the very foundation of the city. Conceived at Meknes, it climaxes in Fez, in the new town that encircles the old city, divided into rectangular blocks, blind cubes of clay above which a distracted jasmine, a leaning cypress, a fronded palm, beckon to us.

Behind the ramparts of Meknes, in September 1936, a murder and its victims cried out so loudly as to be heard by the entire town. The alarm begins in almost banal fashion : in a bushy plot some children find a basket roughly tied up with string, from which wisps of packing escape in tufts. In every country in the world a torn basket is a worthwhile toy; besides, this one is heavy and deserves opening. The daylight reveals its content of feet, hands, a head and its hair, a torso and young breasts. . . . Around the pannier and its strewn contents gather several shrieking children, their veiled mothers wailing. It all creates little enough noise under a pure sky, between invisible gardens, their small doors bolted. . . . One of these doors, the narrowest, is the secret exit from a house which belongs to Oum-El-Hassen, known as Moulay Hassen.

If Moulay Hassen had to her account only a career as a prostitute, begun at Algiers where she was born around 1890 on the steep slopes of the Kasbah, she would merely have added to the uncertain and miserable number of the beautiful natives to whom unanticipated fate or some crime attract momentary attention or pity. But Moulay Hassen was not of the common herd. Did her unforgettable bronze-green eyes reveal a trace of western blood? It's certain that her subtle mind escaped from

the passivity which lies in wait, in those parts, for women sub-
missive to man.

Whether she dances at Colomb-Bechar or follows Lyautey's
troops to Bou-Denib, she pleases herself only with French soldiers,
French officers. The pleasures are always brief. Moulay Hassen
seems even to have forgotten cupidity. She lives happily with
our men, lavish with her song, her dance, her friendship. She
listens, talks, gathers the confidences of men who, in her company, abandon their solitary silence.

Does all this seem to point to the adventurous career of a spy?
No. A spontaneous feeling attracts and retains Moulay Hassen
among the sons of France. The house she throws open to the
French officers under the walls of Meknes has gaiety, luxury,
young dancers, fine firm Berber women, inscrutable Chleuhs,
passive daughters of the South. But none can rival Moulay
Hassen and the savage friendship of French blood and her own.

At the risk of her own life she hides in her house and rescues
a precious handful of officers menaced by the revolts of 1912
and 1925. It is her fine breast, her folded arms, which bar the
way to the rioters. She kills one assailant with her own hand, a
bullet wounds her in the hand. The collection to which the
officers she has protected contribute is not meant as recompense
but as a sign of gratitude. The real reward – the Legion of
Honour – is asked for by several on her behalf, but without
success.

Such was the woman whom her crimes offer to our astonishment, and who is to be tried at Fez. They say that the premature
old age of African women has almost undone her beauty. They
say that she finds consolation in hashish, hallucinated half-slum-
bers which she carries over into criminal realities. As if condescending, she has agreed that the cut-up body is that of one of her
lodgers. . . . Neither does she deny that, during searches of her
house, a fingernail scratched feebly behind a wall. Immediately
demolished, the wall vomits its secret: four young girls and a
boy of fifteen. They lived a little longer, very little. Wasting had
not erased all the marks of torture. Of the fourteen prostitutes,
four died within the year, three disappeared, seven are wrecks
for the rest of their lives. . . .

16 November

Well, here she is. It's on her account that a party of the Paris press has made a journey of several thousand kilometres by train, plane and car. She was heralded from afar, she was portrayed as the Morocco of the conquest saw her, dazzlingly young, on her small Arab with flowing mane and tail, gloved in bracelets, clashing with sequins and *louis d'or*, her brown skin powdered pink by the flying desert sand. . . . Here she is, and so close – the accused's bench touches the tables reserved for the journalists – that we can be unaware of nothing of the presence of Oum-El-Hassen, known as Moulay Hassen.

If I lean to the right, I almost brush the light silks, the heavy spotless muslins which make up the costume of the accused; from head to foot she is white, newly-ironed. A long jewel hangs from neck to stomach, her unveiled face shows more than forty-eight years. Here she is, fallen from the height of her legend and even of her strikingly bad reputation. From Moroccan custom, she holds a white handkerchief over the lower half of her face; and so there survives of her what is still majestic – a small nose beaked like a falcon's and a pair of very dark green-brown eyes, lavishly treated with blue kohl. But she has to remove the handkerchief to speak and the mouth spoils all, not only because some of her teeth are missing but because it is flat, ungracious, made for gossiping, invective and – perhaps – cruelty.

What words, what images can we use to make Oum-El-Hassen understand what we mean by cruelty, and how, accused of homicide and cruel maltreatment, is she to communicate to us her conviction that she is innocent? What we call cruelty was the ordinary, bloody and joyous currency of her life from infancy: the blows, the cord tying the slender limbs, the harsh male embrace, the passion she had for following, no matter where, no matter how, our first French contingents. . . . All that kills, wounds, withers was her first lot as an adventurous girl. Where could she have learned that punishment exercised on women, that is, on creatures who strictly speaking have no value, has any limits?

If I lean to the left, I touch the macabre little bazaar of

exhibits for the prosecution, set out at my feet and on a table. Inadvertently I jostle one of the two panniers which held the eleven fragments of an exsanguinated body; beside these are the chopper, the cord, a pestle for grinding scalps rather than almonds, the knife, the tin bucket. Here, throwing its bellied shadow against a pink wall, the stewpot! It had contained pieces of the corpse, and herbs – plenty of herbs – crinkled mint, fennel, thyme, which combated the odour of the boiled flesh. . . .

Above the stewpot hangs the strangler's cord. Here is a rusted revolver, with two little dry clay stoves of a primitive kind which might have been exhumed at Herculaneum. But these pink and white cotton fabrics, which shrouded limbs hacked off without skill or method, are not even stained. Oum-El-Hassen's accomplice will be responsible for telling us why there was only very, very little blood : 'The woman was too thin.'

This accomplice, the slave, the enemy of Oum-El-Hassen, Mohammed-Ben-Ali, is much the most sinister figure of the trial. With him we enter into a tale of the *Thousand and One Nights*. Sordid, foetid, he trails filthy shoes from which his narrow toes protrude. A convergent squint denies him a proper gaze. Seven rows of parallel wrinkles crease his forehead. When all his features cease to twitch nervously, he gives evidence, in his confession, of a strange freedom of spirit, handles the cord, shows how he pulled one end and Oum-El-Hassen the other. He lies down on the ground, mimes the attitudes of the victim. One by one millenary personages emerge from behind him. The washer of corpses who purified and removed the dead, suspect or not, and received his obol is a furtive *habitué* of Oum-El-Hassen's house. As for the scared choir of little, barely pubertal courtesans, they barely murmur, wail quietly, prostrated. . . . One of them makes a grand effect with her convulsive terror. At sight of Oum-El-Hassen she screams, throws herself into the arms of the Arab interpreter, tries to reach the courtroom exit. . . . What a heavy look of disdain for the distracted girl from Oum-El-Hassen! A purely worldly disdain, but also a Mussulman arrogance. Don't they teach prostitutes to keep quiet in public any longer? Let them entrust this shrieking girl to Oum-El-Hassen and they'll see how to educate them in the proper fashion – a touch of torture, starvation, some shutting away – all these indiscreet Zorahs, Aïchas, Fatmas. . . .

She rises in her turn and replies in Arabic. Isn't she familiar with the French language?

'Yes,' she says, 'but I prefer to speak Arabic today.'

She makes good use of the time taken up by the interpreter in translation, listens, ponders, as if she were alone. Her aura is that of the cat, who only faces danger glossy, bedizened, nails tended. The squinting devil, whose stench is detectable six feet away, serves as her foil; foils too, despite their youth, their large fresh lips, their blue-tattooed and polished chins, the living victims of Oum-El-Hassen; graceful cattle, but cattle whose impenetrable crushing stupidity is utterly loathsome. Imprisoned, beaten, starved, prostituted, Chella, Aïcha, Fatma and Zorah, faced with the same question: 'But didn't you even try to run away?', give the same answer: 'We didn't think of it.'

They didn't think of it. A laugh runs round those present. And as the victims have had time to recuperate their pinched flesh, with the help of couscous, the laughter swells, the native witnesses guffaw, the wives of the European officers shake their curls, the apprentice lawyers find it excellent, the testimony of Zorah-Fatma-Aïcha becomes a music-hall turn, and the obtuse victims laugh from contagion. But if Oum-El-Hassen disdains the indecency of this laughter as much as she spurns the cries, it is she, everything considered, who is right: we are behaving badly.

However, the end of the hearing will see the end of her impassivity. The sole succour she looked for was the testimony of the officers of the conquest – lovers, admirers, boon companions – and among them General X . . . who knew and loved her, and her alone, for years. . . . All desert her. Then Oum-El-Hassen buries her face in the silk handkerchief and weeps ingenuously.

Around the murders, around the legends and the conjectures – less sinister, possibly, than the truth – Fez the impenetrable murmurs serenely. The road to the Palace of Justice at Dar Jamaï is a twilight promenade which gives an illusion of spring.

The following morning the same illusion smiles on us in the sun, the blue sky, the morning warmth. As in the spring, children sell tight bunches of moist roses, sheafs of white arums. The back of the room is gay with blue soldiers, white djellabas, young women with long eyelashes, eyes enlarged with make-up. It is only nine o'clock: midnight will see us at the Palace awaiting the verdict, grouped round the murderess. Today she reveals only her eyes, whose gaze yields to no other gaze; and, to make it clear that she is embarking on a long silence, she has veiled her mouth and is dumb.

It is a hard day for her. The heroism she claims? The witnesses for the prosecution have denied it. The absent ones have not come forward. Ancient Morocco disowns her, leaves her stripped. Hardly one drop of dew in this drought: an old and correct man of the world who had seen her fawned on, heard from a hundred mouths praise of the services she rendered to our people during the uprisings, comes to say what he saw and heard: 'People kissed Oum-El-Hassen's hand in public, just like a Frenchwoman.'

Soon after him begins the procession of the ladies who run the brothels. Oum-El-Hassen does not expect any merciful manna to fall from the height of the superb edifices who advance, white and enormous, like great summer clouds. Fatma is embroidered in pink and blue, pale as butter. Myriam is black, with a squashed nose, rigged out in dove-mauve. Her heavy gold earrings sway to her denials. Gold too are the bracelets ranged on her white kid-gloves, gold her necklaces. She is a nonchalant queen, economizing her words:

'Yes, Oum-El-Hassen was what may be called a proper woman. Her house was a proper house. If she had not been proper, I shouldn't have gone to visit her.'

Majestic, floating, cradled on their spreading foundations, these ladies do not hang about in the courtroom but regain their proper spheres.

All the golden hours of this fine day – two hundred and fourteenth day of the Mussulman year – crush the accused, and especially the moment which sees the appearance at the bar of a child of thirteen, Driss, he who had been immured. Tottering, he barely understands, replies in a gasp. He is no more than a small handful of yellow friable substance. Victim? Certainly. But a victim without a memory; he has forgotten the dungeon, the lice, the itching, the hunger, the torture. . . .

They weren't strong enough, this vacant adolescent and the aboulic girls, to struggle against an easily aroused feminine will, avid to serve as much as to reign, disposing of scant but brutal and efficient means. We recall that she had sworn, on her life,

never to give herself except to the soldiers of our army. If, as she affirms, she kept her word, she has known no other existence than she received in return: domination, the *cameraderie* of the camps, a certain type of violence which she thought venial, and a personal ideal of love.

Midnight. The verdict – fifteen years of hard labour – does not distress the accused. Her spotless veils rise little by little, cover the extent of her cheeks, her eyelids. . . . Through the coverings of the cocoon she spins show the last movements of the larva, still just alive before its long hypnosis.

THE HEART OF ANIMALS

I am taking only a half-doze of a siesta, but the bitch is asleep. She sleeps as bulldogs do, that is to say, she is all quivers, dream races, slight twitching of the chops, efforts to escape, to cry out, perhaps to speak. At the most sombre thought her eyelids open. But her wide pupils, brown and spangled like shale, see nothing but the dramatic aspect of her slumbers. My cheek, next to her flank, perceives the uneven heaving of her breathing and the disorderly beating of her heart, five small blows, rapid as the toc-toc . . . toc-toc-toc . . . of the percussive insect known as the death-watch, which haunts old woodwork. Then a solitary blow suspended between two interminable silences, one only, the last? . . . No, just when I myself was about to suffocate in sympathy, three mad palpitations followed each other. Then four; then a deathly silence, then a return to life in a series of seven beats. . .

Such is the normal behaviour of the heart of a bulldog bitch. How many times can she survive her emotions? A little French bull-terrier, as I am beginning to realize, is worn out in ten years. Moreover, he needs a special hygiene. My long silences, the immobility of my work, save him from himself, from his passionate curiosity, his constant fear of feeling orphaned, and allay his morbid appetite for listening to and retaining human words. . . .

She sleeps, the so-beautiful bulldog bitch. That's what the man I bought her from called her. He displayed a dirty pedigree, torn at the folds, which must have served as identification papers for more than one bulldog bitch. For I soon noticed that she followed him, that her style of 'following', as the trainers call it, was irreproachable, that she stood when he got up, that she lay down when he sat down. But her heart – always the heart, visceral or sentimental – was not in it. And I saw that she continued, glued to his side, to await . . . whom? Her look, the nervous twitch of her left forepaw when anyone rang at the door, a sort of absent fixity, all this pointed to a strayed stolen animal; would anyone leave such a bitch in a training kennel for fourteen months?

That is how I came by Cessy von Heschtfurth – near enough, by a few consonants – who is now called Souci. She sleeps, she abandons herself to her disturbed repose. 'One, two. . . One, two . . . One, two, three, four, five . . . One . . . One. . . One . . .' counts her heart next to my cheek. She is warm, she exhales the good smell of a sleeping dog, milk and pasture relieved with a hint of iodine and rosemary, because of the sea-bathing and the hedge we skirt coming back from the beach; the friendly consoling smell by virtue of which a human being secretly deludes himself : 'It would be good to settle down here once and for all, it would be good to shed here the old serene tears, put aside all those years. . . .' No such fond hope. This bitch could not endure my tears. The most I was permitted to do, without her dying of it, was to break a leg. . . . Always her heart. The first moments over – one doesn't suffer overmuch from a broken leg – I had the leisure to become worried on my stretcher : 'Look after the bitch. . . . Look after . . .' for the bitch, incapable of speaking or groaning, became agitated as in a nightmare, sought for air and displayed a mauve chalky tongue : 'Give her some cold water. Squeeze a lemon in her mouth, can't you see she's going to faint?' And yet they poured eau-de-Cologne over my temples, me who was in no danger. . . .

Ah yes, to faint, as I saw a Persian cat do, the day she surprised her son attached to the dug of a black boor of a cat, as full of milk as a nanny-goat. . . . The angora cat foresaw the treachery from afar, demanded that all the doors be opened : 'Let me pass, let me pass!' She swirled down the stairs like a furious mass of feathers and only stopped to collapse from weakness, on her side, three paces from the child-stealer and the gorged foster-child.

'One, two, three . . . One, two . . . One . . . One . . .' beats the heart of my sleeping bitch.The heart of animals beats, swells and bursts in our shadow. In defiance of all anatomy, I evoke this heart and its heart-shaped form hallowed by pious imagery. It has a graceful tapering point below, two rounded summits like adjacent breasts; it is pierced by a blazing arrow, wreathed with roses, couched on lilies, wounded, with three little jewels of fresh blood at the edge of the wound. Or else it is a fruit, the 'pigeon's heart', a rather colourless cherry. Red-black is the heart of the greyhound, the greyhound so 'full of heart' in the race that he bursts with it. The grey mare also had 'plenty of heart', the mare of my elder brother, the country doctor. Mare and medico had a bad calling. Both lacked placidity and indifference. On winter nights, in the dog days, they went on, supported by the same faith, bound by the same friendship. The mare would press against farm doors her intelligent head, so charming and feminine with its short ears. She could hear a man's voice, mingled with children's tears and the long cries of women in labour. When the 'All right, goodbye!' sounded, the roan mare shook herself, reinstalled herself stylishly in her harness, smartened herself up despite the darkness, the hour, the fatigue, and off at a trot! . . . At the trot without a whip, without a click of the tongue; but she departed to an air from the *Roi d'Ys*, Rozenn's air: *'En silence, pourquoi souffrir?'*, for her master was a good musician and possessed of an ironic awareness of his bitter destiny. A mare among mares, who accepted neither retirement nor the green meadow. Deprived of her master, of the 'All right, goodbye!', of the *Roi d'Ys*, of the nocturnal journeys and the somnolent intervals during which she rested on three legs, one hip high and the other foundered, she languished and preferred to die. I certainly was not surprised.

They make a great to-do about us, all these frightened brethren with their eyes at the side, pricked-up ears, beak, long canines, hoofs. They are alike only in the terror and love we inspire in them. What did you want of me, little shadow in the garden, you who would not cross open spaces? Hidden, you spied me out, beautiful timid cat named Muscat. You waited for me to go

and pull off the dead flower-heads, tear up the dandelions in the
two borders thick with rows of flowers. In order not to spoil anything, I had to go bare-footed, advance step by step as in a virgin
forest. Then two melting paws and a febrile nose rubbed against
and kissed my ankles, my bare toes. At the end of the flower-bed
the caress abandoned me. But so that the timid spirit should
know that we were still linked, I used to sing him improvised
songs in which I mingled his name – floating and uncertain tunes,
supported by the rough ear of millet, interrupted by the prickly
caper, renewed by the convolvulus and the feathery plumbago.
I have never known any lover more silent, more attentive, than
this cat. . . . Haven't I already said too much, and too often,
about cats? So much the worse for my reader, for I have not
finished singing the Cat. I do not refuse to praise, in all tenderness, the dog. Or to seek those fleeting moments, when, seized and
delivered by a gust of air, the variegated wing, the faceted eye,
the nocturnal, silent wing-quill and the proboscis of the great
hawk-moths approach me.

Why should I not portray Baptiste himself, Baptiste, rabbit
of the cabbages, of the valiant heart? For years he stood guard
over his mistress, fruit-seller of the Rue de la Tour. Enormous,
with fringed ears and eyes everywhere, he lorded it on the doorstep, among the crates. Woe betide the passing dog! Woe betide
the intruder who grasped the fruiterer's arm or waist! My bitch
felt the piercing tooth of the champion, who lost all self-control
to run across the road among the taxis on the heels of terrified
dogs. . . .

For the dog is an orthodox type. A slight shove at the established order and our faithful friend loses countenance. He has,
where dogs and game are concerned, a precise if rudimentary
notion. He says to the game: 'You are the game and me, I'm
the dog.' I also recall, with a smile, a morning once when I awoke,
having spent the night in a hunting-lodge, near a pack of a
hundred and twenty-four dogs which dreamed out loud with
the voices of distant bells. . . . Beneath my window someone unleashed a Russian greyhound, which shone like spun glass, and
his friend, a small wild sow. Then a terrible angora rabbit was
released and if the sow, quite young, put a good face on it, the
borzoi cried like a fox and fled. The malicious owner of the
land and the packs had amused himself by training the rabbit like

a bloodhound and used to shout to it: 'Tally-ho! Tally-ho!', showing it the dogs. But he had in no way modified the principles of the borzoi which, faced with the rabbit's ferocity, lost face every time.

In the past I've had those big puppies which suck standing up – Romulus and Remus – under the stalactites of a bitch full of milk. I've known and loved the heady smell of phosphorus and fresh milk which is theirs so long as they take no impure nourishment. Well-licked, well-fed with milk, a kitten smells of hay. Could it be that the good smell of animals is a function of happiness? Lavender alcohol apart, my daughter before weaning exhaled an elusive odour of threshed corn. I thought, O Francis Jammes, of the smell of warm bread, the sweet smell of Lucie asleep in the arms of Jean de Noarrieu. . . .

To the little Danes who rattle around in their skin, generously tailored to clothe a dog and a half, I prefer the small red-stockings of the Beauce, a reflective race of pensive shepherds whose character is well-defined by six weeks. Identical under their black-and-tan livery, bearing the double hackle behind and the jutting ridge on the cranium, they cease to resemble each other, intellectually, much sooner than twin humans do. Of the litter of five my beautiful bitch gave me, I had to give away four. . . . Which one to keep? After the seventh week I settled on a small female who played a little less than the other four, who looked seriously around her at times, who moved her as yet not properly formed ears at every sound, suffered the bites of brothers and sisters without flinching or yapping, was already trying to make menacing grimaces. When I picked her up by the abundant skin of her neck, she would recognize my hand and dangle trust-ingly, as if dead. A little later, she would sit still to listen to a reprimand, instead of fleeing. 'You shall be my bitch, then,' I told her, 'and you shall be called Belle-Aude, after the shepherds of my own country.'

I had the pride and joy of seeing that her mother the bitch had made the same choice as myself, and that a strict, rather dissimulated love presided over Belle-Aude's education. For her, warnings without weakness, and even those little bites with sharply-nipping incisors which form the character and behaviour of a red-stocking in her youth. For her, the scrupulous care imposed by hygiene, those scuffles with tongue-cum-sponge which roughly turns back ears and eyelids, drowns the flea, polishes the puerile naked belly! But also for Belle-Aude a reflective smile charged with thought, a profound contemplative reverie, and the best place to sleep along the maternal flank. . . .

Between the mother and myself Belle-Aude grew up, passed the perils of adolescence bonily and awkwardly, escaped the distemper. She profited from all that was taught by a maternal government that was strange, haughty and attentive, which, when growth was barely over, no longer found a place for play or familiarity. But when the mother bitch died suddenly of a cardiac accident – ah, that heart . . . – she bequeathed to me her elegant double, her perfect likeness, one of those rare companions who fall silent at the right moment, respect our work and our sleep, groan with our tears, and close their eyes with a bitter discretion to whatever – a lover's kiss, a child's tender embrace – robs them of fickle human friendship.

Whenever it adds itself to my brood, I shall celebrate the free bird, in memory of the time when two tame swallows detached themselves, at my voice, from a whistling cloud of swallows and came to land on my head. And I await a further opportunity to protect a mother mouse, as big as a large hornet, which, when I gave it something to eat, rose above the four little ones it was suckling. Will our crimes lose us the trust of animals? It holds good. No, I've not finished with singing the cat, the heart of the cat. I have still to celebrate the cat who twice swam across the Doubs in flood to find its masters. And the cat who mastered his horror of noise and movement to travel with me by car. And the African panther, the departure of whose master deprived her of the will to live. He knew, where he was, that she was not eating and would perish. He returned, for her. At sight of him she recovered momentarily, then an embolism closed the most beautiful eyes in the world. . . .

It seems just and urgent that I should relate how a striped cat, which I had had to give to my mother, followed my tracks in the snow, searched for me for five days and four nights, returned exhausted and took no notice of its newborn, which it had left to die. . . . It is not, naturally, of the kitten's death that I boast. Rather I seek to understand why she left it to die and why, having accepted life without me when I was travelling far afield, she yet betrayed her race and her offspring, merely from having seen me again. . . .

Since there is no love without injury, I accept that I am, in the feline heart, the privileged one led by a straight and burning corridor right to the heart of the cat. When I return thence, I am received here as a somewhat suspect explorer. Have I not, when there, devoured my fellow-creature? Or compounded a felony? It must be high time for the strictly human race to be disturbed about it. . . . In fact, it is disturbed. On my table is a magazine article gravely entitled: 'Has Madame Colette a soul?'

THE SMALL CAT FOUND

The small cat is back again! I've retailed the news to the entire neighbourhood, concerned for three days now with the loss of the small cat. From La Piade to the Treille Muscate,* from Les Salins to Borély, from Les Cannebiers to La Belle-Isnarde, benevolent heralds proclaimed its Provençal description:

'You wouldn't have seen a cat, as small as that, not bad, not more than eight weeks, with stripes, stripes everywhere, with a white bib in front, Grignoulet he's called?'

The mother cat, fine and gentle, made less fuss than we did but when she did call, it was always with the same accent. She called her son by his name – unknown to me – and not very loudly, in order not to attract the attention of the lordly tomcats. These are a clique who need hanging. To prove it, you've only got to see the father of the lost child, a prowler who walks askew, lies in wait for chickens, beats up recalcitrant she-cats, sleeps out of doors and eats lizards.

The mother cat, then, sought her son. She waited for us to finish our grand manifestations, our shrill 'mini-minis', our long lament of 'Grignoulêêê!' She did not run hither and thither or bang her head against the walls, but stationed herself at points familiar to herself and her tribe, rendezvous of smell and sound,

* The name of Colette's house in Provence.

on walls struck by passing air-currents and echoes. She climbed a certain tree, gleaned mysterious pointers from the road surface. What warning decided her? She left and did not return for thirty hours. Should we mourn her already?

The morning of the next day but one, at about nine o'clock, on one of those narrow tracks between the vines which are the rights of way established by good neighbourliness, I saw the mother coming from far off and bringing her little cat. To make this possibly long trip she had chosen the dazzling morning which intimidates all nocturnal animals, tomcats included. A maternal cooing stimulated the little cat's fatigue, urged him to continue; she herself went with long strides, leaving her trotting and by now emaciated son to labour at her sides. Small paws in the shadow of long paws, triplets limping over crotchets, that is the way of the colt led by the mare, the baby camel beneath the tall camel, the lamb under the ewe – and thus ran the little cat.

Happily, ours hardly deserved by now the distress expressed and exclaimed about him. After having experienced the fame and the misfortune of being the little lost cat, he was now only an ordinary small cat that had been found again. He deserved only warm milk and finely cut-up fish, and that was that. All my attention was fixed on the mother-cat, whose large proud eyes, full of universal defiance, whose carriage of a hooded head with a vague wandering smile, whose husky gentle speech, all proclaimed: 'It's I who found him, I , I, and no one else. . . .'

The found one naturally incurred no punishment, once more became the conceited harum-scarum, the awkward one who breaks a vase, the imprudent one who climbs at a bound to the top of a tree and then develops vertigo, the one who ill-advisedly steps on fly-paper. A very ordinary small cat, I assure you. But his mother does not share my opinion. She loves him. She admires him. There are no child martyrs among animals.

PROVENCE

I

Very far from here, in the North, we left a springtime in Ile-de-France which loaded the blossoming cherry-trees with a burden of snow. Easter snow on the orchards and fields, snow on resigned boy-scouts, on deceived families, on hopeless hostelries. . .

Yesterday, all the peach-trees already past their flowering, the valley of the Rhône shone under the rain with a golden green that lasts a fortnight, weather that encourages and thickens the foliage of the fruit-trees.

Today it's the Mediterranean, it's the mistral which dries up the rain but strips the wisteria and the rose-bushes, flattens the tulips, closes the villas half-opened for Easter and the small independent shops which fear the heat in summer, the cold in winter, draughts at all seasons.

Up in the North there is a confusion of electoral strife, serious concern for the solidarity and the hostility of nations; up there reigns a clamour rent by individual cries, but which subsides to the full and confused sound of a deceptive unanimity. But here we are very far from the North. The deserted sea, ravaged by the mistral, booms and speaks of neither boats nor fishermen. It is almost in a contradictory spirit that I think of Paris, of work unfinished, of friends whom I resemble when I am with them. From here I envisage all at this distance with placidity, if not with indifference, as if I had crossed half the earth and the width of the oceans.

The region I have reached and its shores are forceful in their isolation of the *estrangier* who becomes enamoured of them, their cold and hot seasons, their familiar yet distant inhabitants, full of a local reserve which we should not understand if we did not ask the climate for light on the men it models. Provence does not know the deliberate spring of the North and Centre, the springtide which covers the earth in a steady advance. Here, from December to March, the very winter sparkles with vernal facets. But it may also happen that a surly swing of the compass, a subterranean drought, withholds all grace of plant-life from

48

the month of April. Along my road spring has declared itself
twenty times, retreated again twenty times, between Avignon and
Saint-Raphaël. In Avignon the planes, already in leaf, were
murmuring. Around Aix they still slumbered, quite bare. Cavalaire is blooming, but Saint-Tropez is more restrained. If the
Citadelle can see its eastern slope in a wintry sea, some coves of
the bay at any rate each have their local selfish spring, furnished
with its early rose, its small purplish artichoke, its young onion
and its nightingale.

I have only just arrived. The street, the port, are bereft of
summer's encumbering clutter. No tourist, the better to admire
them, lifts the copper knockers of the ancient gates, shaped like
delicate little hands at rest, fingers joined. What am I doing here,
in full mistral, in an empty lane, if not to enjoy the pleasure of
being here and not elsewhere? . . . A child dances with the cold,
runs off. A woman pursued by the wind runs, cries out as if she
were being attacked, takes shelter in a grocer's, whose door I
reopen behind her.

It's strange that no southerner ever gets acclimatized to the
mistral. Every time it blows, the whole region talks about it. The
grocery resounds with its exploits, shelters its victims. A beautiful
brunette, with a coiffure of unleashed serpents, enters with the
squall, places one hand on her heart and the other on her forehead:

'I want to fight! To fight against this wind!' she cries. 'It
infuriates me. It makes my head split! I must get my own back
on that wind!'

She seizes a minute chocolate fish, dating from the first of
April, and brandishes it:

'You see! You'll suffer for it!'

She crunches it dramatically, reopens the door with its bell
and disappears, having astonished no one but me.

The little shops are icy. The hands of a young girl measuring
cushions tremble. The lady who sells me a boxwood salt-cellar
clasps her fingers beneath her armpits. I assert:

'It's really cold in these parts!'

'It's only too true it's cold!'

'Why don't you go in for heating?'

She risks an indecisive glance toward the scoured port, the
pitiless mother-of-pearl of the sky:

'It's just that we aren't in the habit . . .'

She makes excuses for her shop being so slovenly in appearance. By this she means that it lacks bathing-slips, suntan oil, high-heeled sandals in imitation leather. I do not tell her how grateful I am to her for having put on display the mills for coarse salt, the flattened pear-shaped glass flasks, and the cages for crickets. It is all redolent of wrinkled olives and raw beans.

We exchange complimentary greetings. Those I receive on my prepossessing appearance are, God knows, out of pure politeness. But those I give do not lie. For by his parsimoniously nourished fireside the tradesman of this coast has hibernated, grown pale, and acquired a new *embonpoint*. Here and there I hear the gossip of a country which has me by the heart: 'What a winter! Six months under water!' In July they'll say: 'This heat, Lord, what a martyrdom!'

Just expressions, which I like. The Provençal has a hundred fashions of ornamenting and disguising his thoughts. I am well satisfied to find him true to himself, fine and reserved, ardent in local politics, a devotee of pleasure and trafficking, aware of the benefits of the adroit exploitation of the superfluous, and terribly quick to judge his mentors:

'This mayor, is he the man for us? He doesn't arrange any fête days!'

II

In this country of serene weather the full moon is a little frightening, and I always prefer nights without the nearby planet, the constellations, Venus, Charles's Wain which, seen from the earth, stands just over the bay, shaft in air. On Tuesday the huge moon lifted her brow above the horizon, impatient of the dying sun opposite her.

By the time it had detached itself from the low hills it had already passed through a dreary red, two or three shades of pink with small horizontal grey streaks. It escaped from a green zone, then a rainbowed halo, to assume the colour of near-white honey which it does not relinquish till its setting, at the time when it is once more seized by the horizon.

Beautiful as it is, and wandering over one of the most beautiful regions of the globe, I do not like it much. Wednesday, it was already a little obliterated to the right of its apex. But it still sent the bats into a frenzy with its dazzle. Because of it the dogs have had hallucinations and attack their friends. Put on a mask, or merely a somewhat strange hat, on a night of full moon and your dogs will refuse to follow you. Here the moon afflicts with insomnia and dreams all those who seek the shade. The hedgehog stops imprudently in the middle of the path. Instead of fleeing the wheel and the foot, the toad stares at the inky pool the moonlight creates under its belly. A charming barn-owl lives in the ivy on a fragment of wall, which serves no purpose except as the owl's daytime rest. It is used to us. When Pauline goes to hang up the washing, the owl, framed in the ivy, opens its eyes wide merely to frighten Pauline. But our nocturnal friend complains of the blinding nights. Only the cat seems to savour the moonlight which, like itself, is all ashen blue, silver, brief and broken glimmers. An enormous wing-case glitters and vibrates, a shooting star glides by, a seaplane trails its lights above: the musing cat, seated on its wall, accords each wandering gleam a peaceful tribute of attention and reverie.

On these magnificent nights of sad and unmysterious glare, those whom Provence calls 'tourists', '*estrangiers*', hardly bother to go to bed. They are not all young but they are all dressed up. Disguise stimulates humour, if not the wits. Can I use any other word than disguise when it concerns those short, very short, Scottish skirts, those boleros borrowed from Old Spain and printed with Tahitian designs in Manchester?

Seville and Papeete, Japan and the Ukraine, pile into cars, climb to Ramatuelle for the pleasure of dining at the edge of the great dark ravine, beyond which a pool of moonlight reveals the presence of the sea. The cars ascend, all lights extinguished; the prudent driver who does use his headlights is hissed by the true lovers of nature and night, those who drive serenely on a narrow winding road and point out, forty feet below, the pale, enticing bed of white mist. . . .

They go to Gassin. They go to Ramatuelle. The full moon demands it. They start off noisily, while it's still daylight, in roofless cabriolets. They will make a detour and take yet another dip in the sea, on the long sands of Cavalaire. Very few of them are ugly in these cars overflowing with bronzed arms and silk scarves. At the prow there often stands a small, almost black, maenad who shouts or sings. If she falls she will fall singing, but her huddled companions hold her back by hugging her beautiful firm legs. They all climb up to the ancient cliff villages, which have witnessed other assaults and imposed silence on worse clamours. For up there, miraculously, all fall silent. I do not think that any nocturnal uproar has ever withstood Gassin, haughty and red, or Ramateulle, spread out in folds like a screen, of which one face is black and the other an icy blue. Between a bottomless porch and an antique facade is no place for a spree.

Certain streets tolerate young girls who make a corsage out of a ribbon gathered in the middle and knotted at the back, and their half-naked companions. But these little stragglers suddenly realize that they risk meeting, at the dazzling corner of a dark lane, veritable magi : a tall angular phantom with a long nose, a black robe, without a head, standing on rustling folds of stiff faille, a horned cat, a sword dancing all by itself. Then the little bronzed itinerants descend again and go off to Saint-Tropez where all is movement and tumultuous reality. The yacht at the quayside touches the parked car. Twenty luxurious boats, which conceal the sea from us, are themselves hemmed in behind two hundred cars, waiting for September to undo this double barrier. . . .

What are we doing here, peaceful folk like ourselves, in this small café which has neither music nor dancing but which is assailed by the the accordion from the right, jazz from the left? At Saint-Tropez the peaceful folk are no more malicious than the others, with the difference that we drink malted milk and not gin-fizz. We have come like charmed serpents to the spectacle which seduces and disarms our unsociability. Between the water of the port and the restaurant terraces benevolent figures pass and repass in a St Vitus dance. The women this year are wearing a slip and a long dress open in front to the waist. According to the lighting they are green or red. They have diamonds in their ears and bracelets of painted wood, sometimes an arrangement of shells on their breasts. Between their legs, their skirts, their dogs, the local children run and play, brown, agile and very small, never put to bed.

Against the background of the sky the white riggings of the sailing-boats criss-cross like pathways. The beautiful redhead has passed and repassed at least ten times. Now she dances. The five young girls holding each other by the arm, the twin babies of around eighteen months, wide awake in their pram, the film-star, the camper who deliberately breaks the strap of her grass skirt all the time, the strange man who sports stockings, a boater, pince-nez and a moustache, and so many others – for how long will they pass and repass? I ask the time and no one answers. It is a night of summer and full moon.

III

It's as inevitable as the march to the West. Campers are going to be accepted in France as people of quality and desirable guests, will multiply therein and make a respected place for themselves. If, despite the benign climates of the South-West and South-East, their deeply-indented shores and great forest resources, the tent and the trailer are rare in our parts, it's because the camper is not yet either informed with a strict code or imbued with the honour of a nomad. But it's also because select company – all classes have their pick of the bunch – still hesitates and dares not take a hand in the game. I wait for snobbishness to become involved, impelling its faithful towards the clearings, the springs, the small welcoming mountains, creating and launching an elegance in vagrancy, an open-air style. It won't be long in devoting attention to such an economic pastime, for it has never been entirely devoid of a sense of parsimony.

I predict that the time will arrive for slow peregrinations, prolonged halts under tent or trailer, while deploring the fact that the French camper is inclined to cull the apples and pears of others, to confuse the green with the dry when he collects wood for his fire, and to strew in his wake greasy paper, tin cans where a spark of oil gleams, cigarette packets – and that's not all! – just as much as a family that picnics in the Bois de Boulogne.

To our Provençal shores the summer has consigned the best and the worst, who grouse alike about the scorching hotel, the flies, the slapdash expensive meals, the lumpy beds, the pallid coffee. Best and worst have had enough. Enough of everything, and especially of their own kind. Then they move off, rather at random, affecting the temper of hungry wolves, and tie up in the

pines, the cork-oaks, the rubble where the wild fig springs. Our
milky ears of maize, our plums, pay towards their experience.
More's the pity. . . . Perhaps it's inevitable. Tough cities cannot
breed only angels.

New savages will take shape, who have to re-experience sleeping beneath the stars, the fire in the open air, the dawn which
relaxes the limbs and the water which bathes them. A life which
costs so little is bound to make them optimistic; it will even teach
them decency, at least that which they can learn from animals,
that of the tidy litter and the well-hidden ordure. Two or three
large camps between La Foux, Cavalaire and Pampelonne are,
it seems, models of order and harmony.

In Provence the boorish camper runs up against the useful
example of the virtuoso camper, almost always a foreigner. Two
years ago a fine young redheaded nordic couple had as their
entire shelter during the summer months a motorcycle and two
blankets. Apart from a few kitchen utensils, everything on and
around them, including their magnificent skin, habituated to salt
and sun, everything was reddish – hair, blankets, and the sporting outfits they assumed at times to go to dine and dance in the
port. Each wrapped in their red vicuna, they slept on a small
beach, sanguine, fox-coloured. . . .

Five hundred metres from here an Englishman is camping.
In the Midi we speak of 'a rich Englishman'. In point of fact, I
believe that Mr P., if he wanted a villa, could have a villa. But
the entire year he travels and halts only in his caravan trailer,
English as he is, for I've recognized the heavy breadth of this
travelling home, its windows without exterior protection. Mr P.
comes from a country where camping is respected and doesn't
need to be defended. In the early morning nothing stirs in the
trailer, planted between sea and vines, save a marmoset no bigger
than a magpie which lifts to the still-pink sky its small face, that
of an Egyptian queen, and whistles to the birds. . . .

My nearest neighbours, last summer, were boy-scout campers
from a large town, a handful of little lads led by two adolescent
captains. On a strip of sandy meadow at the edge of the sea, the
other side of my quasi-ideal enclosure, they established a colony
run by the two young mentors, past-masters at washing and
scouring a tin vessel with sand, digging a safety trench round the
fire, cutting reeds, grilling steak and fish on woody stems. In the

evenings, around half-past nine, the little camp used to sing
before sleeping, and the chorus ended with a muezzin's chant, an
aspiration cast into the void, a pure and pagan expression of
thanks. . . . They left one morning at daybreak without my hearing them, leaving the place tidy; their ritual care even led them
to scatter the ashes of the last fire and to fix a flower to
my gate.

I found the most ingenious camping caravan on the road in
front of my door, one day when a tempestuous April had
assembled in the sky the black and the blue, a rainbow, great
pearls of rain, sun, eddying rose-petals, swallows which had just
crossed the sea. From a stationary truck two lads in blue overalls
got down and one of them held out to me a can of oil, a smile,
and, mingled with the jolly 'adieu' which means 'good-day', an
impromptu fragment from the *Naissance du jour*. Five minutes
later truck and drivers held no secrets for me. Open, the big
five-tonner revealed, constructed by an amateur hand, its two
berths, its wardrobe, its washing facilities, its kitchen, twenty
little wall-cupboard compartments, and its library.

The two boys declared themselves sellers of oil from necessity,
vagabonds by vocation, and poets by compulsion. Poets in the
local style, in which lyricism readily laughs at itself and collabor-
ates with commercial expertise; in fact, two lads made to roam
the world, to make money *en route*, to laud conquests and landscapes in the lyric mode. For three months they had no wish to
sleep under a roof or wake between four walls, and the converted
truck became their accomplice. . . .

'Last night,' confided the elder, 'we were in a forest. . . . "Ah,
Pierre," I said to my pal, "it's marvellous, let's not go any further,
that full moon there, what could be better?" It splashed silver on
the cork-oaks. . . . Tonight we'll camp at Les Salins, the setting
sun on one side, the full moon on the other, the bays all
round. . . .'

'The bottle in the middle,' said Pierre, 'full up too.'

The elder flared up.

'The bottle? Do I think about the bottle? I live by the eyes,
I live by the heart and to hell with reality! And to hell with the
oil-shop too, down there in the town!'

Pierre winked an eye at me:

'It doesn't do him any harm to talk like that. . . .'

He opens a last hiding-place in the truck, reveals a whole compartment stacked with sweets:

'Now's the time to think about summer visitors, salads and fry-ups. . . . In three camps we've got rid of sixty-eight cans of oil. Pure olive oil at your service.'

IV

In Provence there is no security till after the time of the equinox. But even that sulks sometimes, sheds the petals of its rose-trappings under the storm. One has to await the definitive assent which gives this region its benediction: summer.

Along the road, to the north of Avignon, we have trailed the residue of a sticky heat emanating from Paris, the heavy breezeless urban dawn. Burgundy was roasting in the heat under a singular mist which moistened hands and faces with lukewarm water and presaged the heat of Lyons, which we traversed silent and thirsty in a hurry to make Vienne, anxious especially to reach a certain familiar nameless place, a modest little hillock beyond which it seems, each year, that the easy road, the gradually clearing sky, the great sweeps of the landscape, hold no more ambushes. It's a point, unmarked by any village, which we can designate only by these words: 'You know, that place after Valence, that place where you hear the cicada!'

For at the top of the hillock, from the first hundred yards of a slope stretching towards the south, there strikes up a solitary cicada, minute and trusty landmark, a glowing songster herald of July and the Midi. Isolated, we discern that it has the loud voice of a kid, rather spaced-out bleatings. It is attached to a young plane-tree, unless, on the first mulberry, it is drinking in the sun through its beautiful myopic eyes, its brown cuirass and all its tympanons. It is the only one we brake for, out of gratitude: 'Listen to it!' Further on we shall hear only that sort of deafening silence, that frenetic and universal pulsation whose rhythm marches, during the siesta, with that of our blood, heated by sea-water heavy with salt, cool wine, white garlic, black pepper; henceforward we shall hear, in their millions and millions, only the cicadas. . . .

For the hearts which have chosen Provence it takes only July, August, to restore – new, annual unchanging – every astonish-

ment and every bestowal. I have experienced – I shudder still to
recall them – the cruel sonorous azure of January in Avignon, the
mistral which transfixes and blanches Aix in December. Where
have I shivered more strongly than on the shores of a small bay
in the Var, misty with angry spume in winter? Adore the heat
only in the hot countries, Provence in its summer glory! Behold
me returned, on a road above which the planes with their serpent
skins rustle a riverine murmur. Along the valley of the Rhône the
ripe apricots rained into our hands and the women picking
peaches did us really proud: 'Here, take some more! How
many? D'you think we don't know how much they sell for, ten
peaches?' Their proud good grace, their smile, heralded the pomp
of the meridional wine-harvest. . . .

Short nights, generous days which leave their reddish scar in
the place where the dawn will rise, warm moon that comes into
view and wanders, clear, naked, across the stars: Thank God, it's
still July with its thick verdure; and beneath the wave the white
sand is warmer than the water. It's good for the folk from the
North to bathe at noon, for their backs to peel and their brains
to melt! To bathe at dawn lightens the spirit and unleashes
hunger. Imprudent new arrival, you who lament your raw
shoulder, shelter wasn't really far off: nowhere is the shade so
cool and protecting as in these parts. The fig-leaf is made of
leather, the mulberry sets its double beneath it, round, a dense
blue. Relax, intruder, trust and prudence will come to you
together; even our local fauna lack venom. On the pink wall the
spider stuffs itself with mosquitoes; the large green lizard hunts
the clumsy fly; the huntress snake polices the garden and leaves
you its used skin as a bonus, laced with grey tracery. Under the
lamp which will illuminate my threshold tonight I shall show
you a group of toads waiting for night, the light, and the flying
manna of the bombyx. . . . Provençal summer, O plenitude,
delight . . .

V

'Did you expect us to leave him dying there on the road?'

A fine phrase, redolent of the seventeenth century, that nevertheless flourishes here on illiterate lips. A Provençal daily woman,
three years ago, had found on the little road, in front of my

door, a young man here, a bicycle there, both struck down. With much reinforcement of compresses and of 'Ah, the poor man! . . . Ah, not so bad! . . . Good mother of Jesus . . .' she had succoured the young man, who happened to be drunk and who, his wounds attended to, got up, straddled his bicycle and made off without a thank you.

'That'll teach you,' I said to the good woman.

She raised her gnarled arms, withered me with a glance, and answered me with the Corneillean reproach I quoted above.

After ten years I'm beginning to get used to it. But at each jewel of fine language, gathered all shining in the white Provençal dust, I admire the fact that a syntax of such style should be able to repulse the alluvium of slang, sporting patois and pretentious humour that floods in from all sides. It's true that the fine speakers who resist live between field and wine-press and frequent but little the towns and the ports. They speak as their grandfather spoke, as a grandfather taught. These fine incisive preterites, these imperfect subjunctives, will gradually die out. But my caretaker says fluently : *'Ce feu d'herbes, il faudrait que nous le fissions au lever du jour, à l'humide.'*

What does she know of Latin, she who uses words in their Latin sense? Caring for a swallow brought down by the wind, which had taken shelter under our fluted tiles, she said : *'Laissez, demain elle aura repris ses vertus.'*

Under this ancient soil sleep buried jars, uncovered by the pick. Leave the asphalt road dotted with cars, venture on to the narrow crossways : you won't cover three hundred yards before all is silence, bitter perfume, pagan rigidity, even though obvious Roman remains, the column, the arch, the aqueduct and the arena, are rare here. What was pagan here remains so and is breathed with the air. The dove is still sacrificed and its warm blood poured on the head of a sick child. A native sibyl will tell you that whether a patient recovers depends on whether a bowl of water, magically inverted, empties or does not empty. 'I've seen the water stay in the air with my own eyes, as if it were boiling!' I'm assured. More than one Friday spell survives on the altars of Venus. In these regions which worshipped him, Apollo is not always benevolent. In the year which saw my leg broken and put in plaster, I totted up a fair number of accidental injuries and someone here wrinkled their forehead : 'It's a *sun* that you've got on you, it will have to be taken off. Don't be afraid, I'll have it removed at a distance. I know a woman . . .'

'What does she do?'

'She practises an old-fashioned trick. She won't tell it to any-one.'

The human eye is never entirely inoffensive. So don't be surprised if an *aïoli* which was rising and whitening splendidly collapses suddenly in curds in its oil :

'Ah, you cast your eye on it!' exclaim the humiliated cooks.

Belief does not always mean reverence. The very thunder knows something about it. What does one do against the storm, which casts its massive shadow on the sea? 'You go to meet it, you grimace at it, grimace and grimace, it gets annoyed and comes to nothing.' Happy the elect who contemplate, between the lightning's forkings, the vexed face of the thunder. I've only seen in the clouds what you've seen yourself : a bearded Victor Hugo, a frayed horse, and the clown's tuft that crowned Henri Rochefort.

The power of sonorous language is great, it goes to the gates of death. All remedies useless, may an appeal sometimes halt the hesitant traveller who was about to leave us? A fisherman died near here. The priest and the doctor had left, and as the women approached with the shroud, the brother of the defunct leaned over the bed, put his mouth to the cold ear :

'Eugène!' he called. *'Venga pescar leïs ourseïns!* Eugène! Pescar! Pescar leïs ourseïns! Venga!'*

But the dead man did not stir.

He revived neither for the boat, nor for the violet sea-urchin which rolls under the green morning sea. . . . Then the brother straightened up and made a sign to the women :

'Carry on,' he said, 'this time he's dead.'

When the words themselves are not grand enough, the *langue d'oc* adorns them. This it does for the dishes, surrounded by garlic and lemon half-melted in the oven, stuffed with lean or fat meat, stuck with sprigs of sage and wild thyme, spitted on iron skewers in alternate titbits : a little liver, a little bacon, a sprig of laurel, a little liver, a mushroom, half a lamb's kidney, a little

---

* Patois for 'Come and fish for sea-urchins!'

bacon. . . . And there you are, on the live ember! And a necklace of garlic all round the fish, in the oven . . .

'It's marvellous, this fish! What do you call it?'

'Who knows? We give it a local name, the *sotto coffi*, that's
what we say.'

Dressed up *à la provençale*, would you have recognized the
name of the common stockfish? As for me, I've devoted some
time to it. Who was it that affirmed that one could not live on
air? A striking denial leaves the Provençal lips when they relate,
for instance, the pursuit of a vine-fed hare and the wasted cart-
ridge:

'I aim, I fire, I miss him – like that! He was as big as this.
What a feast, Madame! . . .'

Between the real and the imaginary there is always the word,
the magnificent word, greater than the object. The children take
to it when they're quite small. To his younger brother, who is
arrogantly urinating in the square, the elder, aged six, cries:

'Hey, you! Have you finished behaving like a Radical!'

One of those vivid little dark girls, thin as grasshoppers, who
become so white and beautiful around fifteen, enjoys telling me
about her future marriage, which she intends to be spectacular.
She sees it, over a gap of ten years, and describes it:

'And what a crowd, what a crowd! *Bou Di!* . . .'

'I hope there'll be a grand meal. A fine lunch?'

She screws up her narrow bowed mouth, the mouth of a scorn-
ful woman:

'You make me laugh! A banquet, that's what there'll be!'

'Isn't that the same thing?'

She shows all the bluish whites of her eyes, spreads her hands,
beats the air like a vehement politician:

'A lunch, that's just for eating. . . . But a banquet! That's
really something! Just see all those chairs, all those chairs, all
those chairs! . . .'

VI

'A snake! A snake in the kitchen!'

I come running. This time meridional bombast has reported
the truth; there is a snake in the kitchen, and even on the table
in the kitchen, a beautiful rather reddish snake with a narrow

head. Brought in a basketful of onions, the bizarre thing is that it does not want to go away. Weaponless, it menaces us – let's say, less modestly, that it menaces me. It marked my entry with a start of attention and pride. Now it follows me as far as the threshold. At the threshold it turns back, twines round a table-leg and makes its move on the draughtsboard squares of the linoleum, twists itself into numbers and letters. . . .

I extend towards it a finger dipped in milk. It licks it with a black bifid pistil, then disdains it. But, stretched in a half-circle, it stares me in the face. O crossing of looks! Bond that the animal tries to tighten and that man always undoes! Like the cat, like the horse and the dog, the snake recognizes and interrogates the window of the eye. It quests, it understands. Although it has ranked me as a person of importance, what can I do for it?

'Listen, snake, we've still got to peel the onions and mince the meat that's going to stuff them, you can see perfectly well that the cook refuses to let you rule the roost with her.'

That is human phraseology. We all succumb, more or less, to the need to play down to children and animals. Neither the one nor the other respond to it. When I wish to seize the snake by its delicate neck it escapes me, irritably scrawls five, zero or perhaps S, O, W on the linoleum, and fixes its small golden eyes on mine. In the end I extend it a stick which it probes, accepts, and turns into a caduceus; then I carry the lot into the garden. But there it is seized with nostalgia, climbs while running – if I may so express myself – the two steps and gets up on to the table again. How strange we find its speed! . . . The front half of its body rushes forward, seems to shoot out of itself, recreates itself, grows, while the other half still waits to set itself in motion to rejoin it. . . . In two moves the sociable red snake reconquers the kitchen, I have to push it, to sweep it up like a potato peeling. Still it won't decide to make off and establishes itself in a clump of violet asters, at the base of which the loosened joint of a water-tap maintains a small puddle, surrounded by wings. Butterflies, dragonflies, long clumsy hymenoptera, not to mention the guests of the lettuces, that's what the snake's interested in.

'Oh, let it stay there,' says my cook tenderly. 'I'll call it Malvina.'

It would not be wise for Malvina to count on a solicitude equal to that which coddles, for instance, the bathing bird. But the bathing bird has won respect and affection in two years. Who can tell me the name of this small brownish-red hydrophile? If Delamain reads these lines let him enlighten me. . . . The bathing bird awaits the watering, calls for it with a monotonous cry followed by a quiet rattle: 'Psi . . . Psi-crrr . . .' and sheds all restraint at the moment when the nozzle becomes emplumed with a great feather of water. It flies, splashes about in the very jet, traverses it twenty times, shakes off a ring of pearls while flying. Consulted on the identity of this bird, the neighbouring authorities were not in agreement:

'It's a *quique-quique*.'

'No, it's a *darnaga*!'

'It's *un-de-murailles*.'

But she who sheds and guides the watery shaft, the snowy dust cloud, the cascade, over the garden, she whom the bird follows, emits an unvarying opinion:

'And I tell you that it's the watering-bird. . . .'

Other wings escort it. Nine swallows eddy, settle on the telephone wire. . . .

'Those four little ones on the left,' she says, 'those are ours.'

Little ones, indeed, rather grey, and the fork in the tail still short, they are indeed ours.

Every year two couples return. One knocks at the casement of the small garage building. The window is opened, not to be shut again, for the swallows build their nest between the ceiling and the round reflector that shields the electric bulb. From April to October they successfully rear two broods. By climbing on a chair, we can admire, in the evening, the male seated askew, uncomfortably, on the edge of the clay cup, the female spread out over her clutch, both relaxed but alert. 'They're listening to the gramophone,' asserts my caretaker. The other pair has chosen the door lintel.

Last spring witnessed a drama: the mud daub of a nest, too dry, gave way, scattering a squawking and featherless nestful. A builder's labourer was working in the vicinity; he hurried up, shaped a nest out of cement and briskly inserted the network of strands of cottonwool, horsehair, down and fine grass that the fall had not broken, tucked up the fledglings again, and we committed the whole thing to fate, which was benevolent. The pair of swallows accepted this human handiwork and promptly resumed their duties. It's so difficult to disabuse an animal of its stubborn trust. . . . It discards the idea of a trap from the outset and advances to greet the slightest human attention. The glass drinking-trough, hung in a tree, excites cries of joy. Pour a libation of milk, fill a bowl with water : the hedgehog laps, the black and yellow tortoise hurries through the pines and their litter of burning needles, one and the other take up residence, approach you, recognize your voice and step. . . .

As I write a frenzied peace, a silence irritated by cicadas, covers the empty countryside. Today, two kilometres from here, the inhabitants of Saint-Tropez boil, roast, become soaked with sweat and mop themselves in honour of the fair of Saint Anne, whose charms are already faded for me since my early morning visit there. There I listened to the genius of a showman, the one who makes up 'lots' as in the heat of improvisation, seizing a cotton bedspread here, a cake of toilet-soap there, moreover six handkerchiefs, a sewing-kit 'guaranteed of English manufacture', a glassware necklace, a vegetable-masher, a pair of mauve braces. . . . He throws the lot into a tin bucket and brandishes it under the noses of the chilliest, most circumspect and contempt-uous of audiences, that of the Midi, who purse their lips, touch with their fingertips, stay silent and move away. . . .

I had some dealings with the dark corseted saleswoman who cried : 'Look around! Feel it! Profit from what's left from a great misfortune! All we could save from a fire!' I smiled at the gilded, laced, pomaded stall-keeper, a troubadour who sings the praises of his display of feminine lingerie : 'How dainty! Knick-ers, knickers, ladies! If I tell you . . . Try them. . . . Five francs off. . . . Ah! Ah! Ah! . . .' His lingerie doesn't bear talking about but what a delightful B flat!

Eventually, loaded with a patent secateur, several pieces of wooden-ware – salt-mills, rosewater ewers, round spoons for fishing olives out of the large green jars – I consider myself to have paid my tribute to local commerce and sociability and to have earned the right to sleep. The middle of the day behind the shutters is half dream, half night, floating, a light, waking torpor. Even the tuberose rests from emitting its fragrance. A solar ember falls from the sun to spread over the sea, which it tarnishes. The flower of the feathery mimosa turns away from the blaze that withers it and shows only its white under-surface.

Where is the blue convulvulus, mirror of the morning? It ceases to exist when the sun reaches the zenith.

Noon, in Provence, should illuminate only the fertile deserted earth. But strangers, struggling in the water, peopling roads and beaches, disturb an order rigidly laid down by the climate. The prostrate cat, the folded bird, the dog pale with dust, our pacific snake, the ass effaced in the shade of the cypresses, withdraw at noon from the absurd life of men.

Under the slow passage of the daystar the smallest shard of glass abandoned in the forests catches fire and darts its ray. A solitary leaf of the aspen flutters its wing. A solitary oar streaks the bay, bringing back a solitary belated fisherman who fears the heat and, in order to reach his pink house, takes the path bordered by wild figs, crosses a great patch of tender clover which the morning often sees trodden down; but at the noon-tide hour there is no couple to be surprised by the passer-by.

Truce imposed by a sensual region, the chaste crushing noonday separates the clammy lovers whom the Provençal night, chill just before the dawn, links and restores to their pleasures.

The Flight from Paris

JUNE 1940

No more the ox-carts, the hay-wains, the great dust-covered motorcars, the wheelbarrows and charabancs, the series of peaks stretching ever further, the regions shadowed by bluish vegetation, the meadows of lush grass whose every dell sheltered a sleeping tribe, a car crowned with a mattress, a sleeping child wrapped in a towelling dressing-gown, a pair of doves in a cage, a fox-terrier tied to a tree, a young girl clasping a man's overcoat around her; beyond the five hundred kilometres of road crowded by a France in disarray, a credulous forgetful fatigue brought illusion. Lassitude and fever, when they are extreme, are merciful to us since they usher in a place and time unique in happiness as in despair. We did not need a long rest to get going again, to share the common lot. Wherever the writer may halt as time passes, thinking himself done for, there gleam his favourite enigmas and his loves: the human face and its distressful secrets, the vertical pupil, the reflex of a nocturnal eye, a bird's chatter, the wiles of childhood. . . .

Our craft, however ancient and deeply embedded, deserts us when some glory, some disaster, some exodus, involving an entire nation, engulf us in their swell. . . . But it returns. I had not expected that, at the end of a long road, I would have come so far to end up at a table – a terminus, an obstacle, a reef; crane-like, devised for meals taken in bed, a rickety hotel pedestal-table – at a writing-table. Every spectacle elicits the same obligation, which is perhaps only a temptation: to write, to depict. I have witnessed none of the violence of this war in any incendiary light. To every writer falls the task dictated by his faculties, by chance, the decline or vigour of his age. I have made my halt among the peasants who witness, as war's caprice decrees, the passage of armour-shielded invaders over their labour. The peasant did not always know the name of the flood that, in one century or another, called itself Saracen, Spaniard, Revolution. . . . But he stood his ground and they merely trod down his harvest and passed on. After them he resumed his tilling. He is always there. Of peasant stock myself, I like to believe in him, to see him motionless with his brave wife, his flocks, against a background of modest steeples, the hesitant dawn.

It may seem strange that, separated since 15 June from the abode I consider mine – four rooms in the first *arrondissement* of Paris, not far from Montfort-l'Amaury – I am sometimes less concerned about them than the changes I fear the war may have inflicted on the village where I was born. I graced it with but a brief visit, and that was sixteen years ago. It is just that I want to make a precise allotment of recollection to the places that formed it. One of the gardens of the deserted château contains festoons of old rose-trees, a warmth as of hot bread on the facade they adorn: I know about that, everything's in order. Then there's the house where I was born, which ages – I declare – less rapidly than I do. As for the little town itself, I condemn certain new roofs and electric swan-neck street-lamps. The rest fits faithfully over the pattern to which I cling.

But the war? . . . A beloved *revenant*, Sido, refers it to a distant past unknown to me, since it is to do with the war of 1870 and I was born three years later. 'Your father', Sido used to tell me when I was small, 'made his way outside the village on his crutches despite the snow with a few other men. He was the only one who spoke a little German and could make himself understood. Thanks to him there was no looting and not too much alarm. *They* thought him brave.'

'And you, where were you?'

'I was looking after the house and the children. Your sister was twelve, your elder brother seven, and Leo was three.'

'What did they say?'

'Oh, nothing! How do I know? What does it matter what they said then?'

At the first discord her intolerance reappeared, was ranged against the questioner, the contradictor. She was ignorant of the first word of the stupid language one uses to children. So that even her invectives left us feeling honoured and more grown-up.

'Ask them what they were thinking of at the time. They're still alive, aren't they? And I didn't bring idiots without a memory into the world!'

She calmed down again as quickly as she had flared up.

'But you know, I think they have forgotten. Your sister was staying at Mlle Ravaire's. Leo . . . Do you expect him, at three, to have understood and remembered anything about the war?'

'But I don't expect anything, I'm just asking. . . .'

'Achille . . . yes, you can ask Achille, of course.'

She smiled, filled with infinite pride.

'He was seven. He trotted about in the streets, he was big for his age, among the Prussian soldiers. But they stopped for a moment when he went by. You see, they'd never seen such wavy chestnut hair, such dark blue eyes, especially not such a mouth. . . .'

'But you, mummy, didn't you see them?'

'Yes,' said Sido indifferently, 'but I've also forgotten them a bit. I can only remember the first time.'

'Was it awful?'

'Why awful? Lord, how stupid the child is! On the Route des Renards. . . . At nightfall it's nearly always misty on the Route des Renards because the spring smokes. Then I saw in the middle of the road a soldier with a spiked helmet. He held his rifle dangling like a hunter. I could make out that he wore a short thick beard. And for a moment I had the impression that the German army consisted entirely of grey men like that one, with grey clothes, grey faces, grey-haired, like graven images. . . .'

'What did you do?'

'I went back to the house and buried the best wine,' replied Sido, not without pride. 'The wine that went back to my first husband. Château-Larose, Château Lafite, Chambertin, Château-Yquem. . . . Wines which were already ten, twelve, fifteen years old. The fine dry sand in the cellar made them even better.'

She winked her grey eyes, tilted her chin with the air of a *gourmande* and connoisseur. In fact, though she had a fine palate, she drank hardly anything but water, distrusting the wine, half a glass of which would make her giggle and her cheeks burn.

Nothing is less like the actual truth than this picture; I admire my mother for having made it so striking in so few words. So striking that I can envisage no other when it comes to picturing, seventy years after '70, the appearance of a German occupation force: a grey soldier against a grey background of mist, and marching to meet him a plump energetic little woman who suddenly catches sight of him, turns around, and goes home to shelter behind the ramparts of her ample crinoline, behind the gallantry which decks her like a radiant plumage, her entire house, her children, her frightened servants and her best bottles of wine.

Thus the spume of a spring – that of the Route des Renards never ran dry or ceased to smoke in cold weather – acts on my imagination like breath on the magic mirror. I am not as skilled in retrospection as was, for instance, my brother, the last one, who died five months ago and did well to die, for as an invalid he would neither have been able to flee nor bear with what the invasion would have demanded of him, that is, the recognition and awareness of the present. Between today and yesterday, he had long ago made his choice.

He used to come to dinner with my husband and myself pretty regularly on Sundays. I was not distressed to see him grow old, at least, not until his feet, his legs, immensely fitted for walking lightly, for soundlessly covering long distances, began to betray him and he dreaded the stairs in the metro.

Tall, greying, thin, his garments flapping and often in disrepair – when he was sixteen, Sido used to call him the *lazzarone* – he was overjoyed to find a wood fire at my house. He would hold out his red hands to the flames until they were warm and then, if the two of us were alone, sit down at the piano. His fingers, which he pressed flat on the keyboard, seemed stiff. . . . I recall Maurice Goudeket's amazement, the first time that, coming in quietly, he heard the 'Old Sylph' interpreting Schumann, Beethoven and even *Jardins sous la pluie*. Inexplicably, the red fingers, cracked at the joints, held the secret of a rounded sparkling sonority, the intelligence of majestic phrasing.

But the 'Sylph' detected the presence of a third person and stopped timidly. He asserted that my faithful Pauline was waiting, as on every Sunday, to cut his stiff grey moustaches in the kitchen, and made his reappearance only with the soup-tureen.

The conversation of my brother, Leo Colette, belonged, like his memory, to the past. One evening in 1939 he emerged from a long silence to say, in his hollow discontented voice:

'Albert Leroux is dead.'

'Who's that?'

'Albert Leroux.'

'Who was Albert Leroux?'

'A schoolfriend of mine.'

'Did you know him well?'

'Very well.'

'Did you see him often?'

'Every day, once.'

'But when did you see him last?'

He half closed his eyes, which were rather like mine, but of a grey less blue.

'In 1879.'

The last time, I think it was, that he came to dinner I noticed his shortness of breath, the grave cough of chronic bronchitis, his extreme thinness. Certain of a detailed reply, I asked him as usual a dozen questions about 'down there', about the village where we were born. For me there was no more refreshing bath, no more powerful illusion than that in which his sure memory would plunge me, no recreations more gripping than those he could conjure up in two words. Maurice Goudeket declares that when I was chatting with Leo Colette I gave the impression of taking a lesson:

'. . . on Thursdays,' I might say, 'when I used to go gathering beechnuts in the woods, with Hélène Josset . . .'

'No,' interposed the Sylph, 'Jeanne Josset.'

'But I tell you . . .'

'No. Jeanne Josset. You're getting mixed up. Hélène Josset was the one who had a white eye because she fell on a bottle in the school yard when she was eight.'

'Ah, yes, that's right! . . . Well, once when we were looking for beechnuts in the Chemin du Thureau . . .'

The grey eyes opened wide, severe:

'In the Chemin du Thureau? First I've heard of it. You're mistaken, my good woman.'

'How's that?'

'I tell you you're mistaken.'

'Because?'

'Because either you didn't go round by the Thureau way or else you weren't looking for beechnuts but for chestnuts.'

He drew a map on the table with the tip of a dry finger.

'Over towards Thureau, chestnuts and nothing but chestnuts. Towards Vrimes, beeches, pines here, more beeches, and a stone cross here. Bibi will show you.'

He said 'Bibi', pointing to himself, as was customary thirty or forty years earlier.

The last time, Pauline had given him a weak and well-sugared hot toddy, made up a little packet of bon-bons, and Leo Colette, sixty-three years old, aglow, well mellowed, smiled over his past life. . . .

'Over the Raimbauds' door . . .' he began.

'Which Raimbaud?' I asked. 'There were at least ten Raimbauds "down there".'

'Raimbaud the carpenter.'

'Where did that one live?'

My brother gently shrugged his shoulders.

'Going towards the station, on the left. Do you see where I mean?'

'Yes. . . . No, I can't see. . . .'

'On the left as you go down. Before the Morisset house, but on the other side. Next to the Luzottes, there!'

He spoke to me as one speaks to placid lunatics or idiots, in restrained, indulgent fashion. But his left knee danced impatiently.

'No, I tell you, I don't see. . . .'

His wide eyes and big nose, made more salient in his face by recent wasting, turned severely towards me:

'Look, look! . . . In front of the Raimbauds' entrance there were always some very long planks which he used to prop on the lintel of his door. . . . They made a kind of slanting palisade that you had to go under to get inside. . . . Now d'you see?'

Humiliated but sincere, I made a sign of negation and an expression of utter contempt spread over Leo Colette's bony features.

'Extraordinary. . . . Ex-tra-or-dinary,' he chanted, and I bridled.

'Why extraordinary? Do you think that "down there" I had eyes and attention only for Raimbaud and his planks? And that I haven't had more important things to think about since then?'

He did not soften.

'Whether it's important has nothing to do with it. What it shows is that you pass by without looking at anything, it shows that you're hare-brained. After all, I'm not talking about a period that's so very long ago. . . .'

He half closed his eyes, his hand drew in the air the slanting palisade of planks supported on the lintel, in front of the Raimbauds' door :

'Why . . . it's not more than . . . no, not more than forty-eight or forty-nine years. . . .'

LA PROVIDENCE

If, instead of a village inn, she had 'held' a salon, how happy her intimates would have been! They would have had decent chairs, good fare, a delicate solicitude. To those she helps today she can give only what she has : straw seats, a long dark room whose shade benumbs the flies, and the food for which she searches everywhere, for us. We are not the only ones to live on her. How many refugees, coming down from North to South, have had the idea of leaving the easy road, to take the difficult path, the steep slope, and wind up here? I think it was chance that brought them to her whom we call 'La Providence', who makes a great deal out of nothing. For all around there is really nothing to be had. The hard peach seems to be unaware that we are in July. Not to speak of walnuts and hazelnuts yet. Apples and pears are reserved for the future. No meat except, twice a week, the 'white veal' which, between birth and death, has known only the darkness of a ditch where it was fed with milk, the veal pale as its name, the sight of which deprives us of all appetite. But La Providence watches over us and works a miracle or two every day :

'I've made a big dish of haricot beans with lard,' she says. 'And I've put a strong sausage in it. And have you heard the news? I've managed to get hold of six eggs! I can serve them up on sorrel, if you like!'

If we like! For want of butter, of milk, we yearn for greenstuff and vegetables. No sugar either. . . . Chut! La Providence has lumps in her apron-pocket, nicely wrapped in white paper, and for the six of us she inserts them between the long slices of wholemeal bread cut from a round loaf. We eat a lot of bread here.

and we smell it before eating it, so exciting is its odour, honest, far from sour, all wheat and rye. Good grey bread, hard enough to keep the teeth in order. . . .

'It's my brother makes it,' says La Providence. 'So I get a bit over my ration.'

The first small pears with their long stalks begin to quit the tree. La Providence shuts them in the oven while it's still warm. They melt in their skin, become soft and succulent. La Providence does not include them in the week's account.

'Do you think I could sell what I get for nothing?'

In the evenings, after dinner, we go for a stroll round the hamlet. Passing before the inn, where the servant is quietly washing up in the kitchen, we lower our voices, for our Providence is already asleep in the light of the long day, a ray from the setting sun across her bed. At three in the morning she is up and about, beginning her round and her worried monologue:

'It's getting low, the jar of fat. . . . And the row of tins of *pâté*, there's some teeth missing there! What are we going to eat? Shall I make rissoles out of yesterday's veal-stew? It would do better as meat-balls, but I've only a handful of flour left and a drop of oil at the bottom of the demijohn. . . . Daylight already! I can go as far as B— on the beer delivery-man's lorry, but I'll have to catch him at the bottom of the road, that ill-mannered fellow. . . . Mignonne, *ma petite*, get up, will you? Do you want to take your bicycle and get some fresh air? You can go as far as that woman by the river, she promised to sell me her chickens before they got too thin with the heat, you can bring them back. Chickens like that won't be much good to anyone. Ah, I shan't mind when this day's over. . . .'

But she keeps her troubles within her and a smile on her face. She is spotless, and does her hair neatly. Hatted, she is a real lady. When she returns from the distant village, tired from battling, from having beaten down and wheedled alternately a wholesale grocer-woman, a Sub-prefect, a dealer in rice and noodles, a rabbit-breeder, when she stands erect at the back of the lorry, haloed in her straw hat, we address her using a name which she does not realize is borrowed from the vocabulary of hagiography, we call her 'our Patroness'.

THE POET

He is a very pleasant lad, rising thirteen. His eyes have the velvety blue of the ageratum flower. They are burdened with lashes, which must be a nuisance, since he often rubs them as if he were waking up. He is gentle, polite, says 'good morning', pulling at his forelock, and is called Tonin like his father. When the radio is bellowing at the post-office, Tonin joins the folk who flock along, for the hamlet lacked for a long time this voice that churns everything out. The children lift their heads to snatch the news, catch it in their eye, a wide open mouth, an ear. But Tonin does not stay long under this cascade of sound. He sits three paces away, on a low garden wall. A moment later he is to be seen astride the bench placed by a generous donor at the entry to the hamlet, so that the inhabitants might sit down 'to see the view'. The bench is always empty since the inhabitants of C— have been familiar with the view for quite a while.

The hillside declines towards the river, invisible between alders and poplars, and if the opposite slope did not rise so steeply, the whole scene would assume the gentle mildness typical of the less mountainous parts of Switzerland. But a hillside like that which encircles C— limits the horizon; we must be content with the great shadows cast by the twilight and the hues of the woods, blue as the verdure of ancient tapestries.

Suddenly, Tonin is no longer on the look-out bench. Not anywhere. But no one's worried; he'll be back on the stroke of noon and, Lord knows, it certainly strikes noon here! The angelus comes first, descending from its deep-toned bell. Then, in its turn, a liturgical clock strikes noon, and noon again five minutes later.

'Is that the first or second noon?' asks a housewife from her doorstep.

'The second, but I'm not sure,' replies Tonin's mother.

'You don't know where you are nowadays!'

She adds, as she regains the shade of her low house:

'Everything's topsy-turvy!'

Sibylline utterance, heavy with resentment. Everything's topsy-turvy; it's not just the war, dragging its fag-end of an armistice and all its paraphernalia, but there's her husband, Tonin senior, carpenter, with nothing to do. Hardly anyone bothers to die here. What's the good of a small coffin every now and then, I ask you? Everyone makes do and saws away on his own to make a beam out of three planks. And how is anyone to tell that it'll soon be midday when the premonitory fragrance of oil, singing the praises of eggs and escalopes, potatoes and bacon, on every stove has deserted the village. Those are lucky who have a reserve of goose-fat to break into! Everyone conceals, everyone dissembles. . . . Only the 'sealer-up' sees everything, since he's the one who seals the tins of conserves. He used to sell petrol and blow up tyres by the roadside. Now his tanks are dry and his garage trade reduced to sealing. A pretty skill takes from your hands the open tin, full of vegetables or *pâté*, closes it for you without soldering but with a neat hermetic seal, and restores it ready for cooking in the double saucepan.

'How shall we be off for conserves? A few miserable tins of peas and string-beans. . . . *Pâté*? You must be joking. Made of what? We'll have to live on air this winter, practically.'

The sealer-up is discreet. From among the scattered parts of unusable bicycles, dejected automobiles and drained petrol-cans there is a constant procession of tins now full which he sold empty, tins of a gleaming, flashing white, only he knows how many. The sealer-up seals and is silent.

Where I was born they only knew how to melt butter and pack quarters of pig in their own fat in the bottom of earthenware jars. Here, haricot beans, *pâté* and *confit* and mushrooms are sheathed in white metal. Here the cellars and larders resemble a grocer's store-room and induce nostalgia for our own romantic cellars, where the sight of the tall jars, narrow at foot and neck and wide at the hip, made me think of headless women.

Twelve o'clock, and again twelve. Tonin senior, smelling of new wood, sits down at table and places his right hand – from which two fingers are missing – on the tartan oil-cloth. He smiles at this hand, which has kept him out of the war, and always keeps it in sight, like a reference. . . .

'Where's the boy, then?'

'Don't worry, he's not far away, he'll follow his stomach.'

And in fact, a little flat leveret's stomach and meagre hindquarters slip into the straw seat opposite Tonin senior.

'Where have you been just now?'

'I was out, over there. . . .'

Over there . . . there, in the no-man's land indicated by a movement of the chin. Daphnis without Chloë, Tonin presents to all enquiries the sleepy blue of his eyes. Tonin senior does not insist. He rarely looks at his son opposite. So much blue, and all those eyelashes, it's not decent. Nor this way of coming and going like a wisp of smoke. But so what? The child is on holiday, and a carpenter has no animals to be taken to the fields.

'Do you want some tomatoes?'

'Yes, mummy.'

'Do you want some veal?'

'Yes, mummy.'

He also wants bread, and more bread, and some of the big hard cheese, and three plums which he slips into his pocket with what's left of the bread. To finish, Madame Tonin spoons some pale coffee into his mouth with a melting lump of sugar. Tonin junior folds his lashes on his cheek as he purses his lips. It is always just at this moment that Tonin senior frowns:

'Well, is that the end of this behaviour?'

But he never waits for a reply and himself changes the subject:

'Have you heard the news this morning, wife? No more petrol except for the doctor. No more bread, only two hundred grammes a head. Jam-making forbidden. Selling flour to private persons for making cakes forbidden. . . .'

There is a long litany of: 'Prohibition . . . forbidden . . . ban on . . .' When he finally falls silent Madame Tonin, engaged in covering the round loaf with a napkin, merely says in a funereal tone:

'Cheerful, isn't it? Did you hear that, boy?'

She throws the blame on young Tonin, who awakes with a start:

'What? What's that you said?'

His father, who is about to return to the temple pillared with satiny beech, fresh pine whose eye-shaped knots still weep resin, blocks of oak smelling of vinegar, turns back:

'Where d'you come from, the moon? You were there when the radio was on. You're not a savage. You're not deaf.'

Young Tonin flutters his eyelashes, they tangle:

'But he talks so badly, the man on the radio . . . it's difficult to understand him. . . .'

Tonin senior gives his son what he considers to be a penetrating look and goes out. Madame Tonin washes three plates, three forks, three knives and two cups. Tonin junior has imperceptibly gained the threshold. . . .

'Where are you off to, Tonin?'

'Out, mummy.'

'You won't go far?'

'No, mummy.'

'You'll be back early?'

'Yes, mummy.'

He departs, he descends the hillside. As he goes, he chants the last words with which he took his leave of the outside world: 'Yes mummy, no mummy, no mummy, yes mummy . . .' Words which lack conviction and commitment but which ensure temporary liberty and peace.

I do not undertake to follow this deer in espadrilles. But curiosity, even benign, is an ever-yawning trap. Curious about this child because he is like a flower, some mild furry game, because he is beautiful, because his eyes remind one of the mauve aster under the dew, because, devoid of sin or malice, he has the mystery of all that is unfilled, I often cross his path, I who used to notice him only from time to time by the niggardly fountain or under the vain deluge of the radio. He wanders along the river bank, but with arms dangling: he does not catch frogs or fish with string and a bent pin. He does not make bouquets or disturb the birds or suck at the goats. . . .

Once, when I was lying under the alders, the reflection of whose cold leaves in the river is so sombre, I caught sight of Tonin who was swinging on a half-submerged root thirty paces away. As he swayed he babbled, recited, stretched out his arms. 'A child-poet,' I opined. 'A sensitivity and lyricism discouraged by environment. . . .'

I could hear nothing of what he was murmuring. The river at its bend runs up against a rustic culvert which thrusts it aside; it runs disconsolately into the islet of pebbles it has itself transported. The double obstacle draws from a small river a great grumbling sob, a vehement protest in which the child-poet may have sought and found his earliest rhythms. At one point Tonin very nearly fell into the water. He saved himself by clutching at some strands of willow and his seraphic mouth opened to utter a rude word, which I guessed.

That same evening, seated on the paternal doorstep, he was helping his mother to braid garlic. It is an easy task to interweave their dry leaves. With a little skill one can construct festoons in which the heads of garlic hang regularly spaced like the crystal balls on a chandelier. But a glance showed me that Tonin did not have the knack. I felt all the more benevolent towards the inspired one, whose sombre and celestial eyes saw further than his fingers, further than the humble task. . . .

I promised myself not to spy on young Tonin's solitary excursions. He continued to dodge adroitly the daily flood of radiophonic 'news', disdained the supplementary information proffered as a contribution by the purveyor of ducklings and lemonade. He tolerated the paternal scolding, which went in one ear and out of the other:

'Don't you understand we've an armistice? Don't you realize how terrible that is?'

I strained to hear Tonin's contrite replies:

'Yes, I do understand.'

'And doesn't it mean anything to you at all?"

'Yes, it does.'

He had to defend himself, one morning, against a mob of children who jokingly attacked him, aping Madame Tonin his mother, crying: 'He doesn't know there's an armistice! He doesn't know it's terrible!' I noted that if Tonin lacked verbal arguments, he reacted vigorously, as much by some brief words rich in meaning and sonority as by blows with his fists and espadrilles. His attackers were promptly dispersed and young Tonin, having reshod his bare foot, took the path which descends to the alders, to the coolness that hovers a little feverishly in high summer over the meadows drenched with secret streams.

I wished neither to follow nor to hinder him. But just as only the one road leads from the hamlet to its modest height, so only one road winds between the hamlet and the bottom of the valley for lazy ones like me to saunter down its pleasant slope. After which they have to climb up again. It's well worth paying for the pleasure of a prolonged rest, forgetting the night's worries in a short and sudden sleep, listening to the water, spying two furious ants, a hornet heavy with its golden weight. . . .

That afternoon I was woken by the hollow murmur of the radio announcer and I paid due attention, for ever since a certain uproar of artillery which fissured the sides of a small suburban house, I've taken to dreaming of precarious shelters which crack like a clay pot in the firing.

A light afternoon nap does not prevent one from discerning that something is beyond the bounds of probability, and before lucidity sets in there comes a sort of scandalized awareness of what is proper and what is not. How could the radiophonic voice mingle with that of the river and the 'puic-puic' of the finches? I sat up, I listened harder. The voice originated from the other side of the dense hedge, a dividing wall which opened only to let the river through. . . .

'This is Radio-Corrèze,' said the voice. 'By a decree dated . . . we bring to the notice of our listeners that the armistice is not true, and that on the contrary everything is going very well. Neither is it true that the Arnoux boy has been killed. Our savage adversaries have sought to sow disorder in our ranks by announcing his glorious but untrue death. Now here are the announcements. The sale of chocolate, which has been restricted, is entirely free by decree dated . . . in the form of bars, croquettes and chocolate creams, also the sugar ration is increased from a hundred and fifty grammes to three kilos. Relayed from Radio-Toulouse, we learn from a reliable source that requisitioned cattle and horses will be restored to their owners. In compensation for the disturbance, the horses will return with a new carriage at their . . . Ladies and gentlemen, dear listeners, the programme is over. The *Marseillaise* will be played for you by the *Amicale* of Seyrac. And three cheers for the courageous orator. One, two, three, four, five – one, two, three, four, five – one, two, three, four, five – One! Two Three!'

Lying on his back, gazing at the sky through his lashes, Tonin, with the aid of his two hands like a conch, altered the sound of his voice, imitating as best he could the ample organ of the announcers, which so often seems enclosed in an empty watering-can. So I had not been mistaken. Solitary, exalted, Tonin devoted himself wholly to the poet's mission : to forget reality, to promise the world wonders, to celebrate victories and deny death.

SWALLOWS

All the apertures of the two dilapidated châteaux absorb the grey swifts and restore them a hundredfold. There are swallows too, steel-blue with white bellies. These are smaller, more graceful, their flight less swooping. Circuits, descents to ground-level, threading the ox-eye windows, glissades, vertical leaps in the air, whiplash turns, these games begin with the morning twilight at four o'clock to end with the night. The ferocious cries that accompany them are also unceasing. Listening to them, for it is ear-splitting, one clenches one's teeth, screws up one's eyes. But why listen to this rather than the wind, a downpour, an aeroplane? If these are hunting cries, the utterance of birds provoked by the conquest of flies and maybugs, how can they snap them up and scream at the same time, sup the insect and give forth with this almost endless unrepetitive cry, this prolonged exhalation of a powerful winged creature?

We are no bother to them. They are more tolerant than friends. If we lie down on the grass, their tracery, momentarily disturbed by our passage, soon covers us anew and ignores us. A great wing swoops down on us, a high-pitched whistling fills our ears, it rains little white droppings which don't spread and dry quickly.

I try to discover some meaning in their frenzy. The nests are empty; every hole, every gap, was once a nest and will be one again. Under the machicolations the swallows have built uninterrupted rows of little clay baskets, but the young have all left by July. Let us try to follow them at their exit from the uppermost crevice, whence they delight to shoot forth in swarming spearheads, hurling themselves into space, head down, whistling madly. Then they encircle the round tower, gain the square tower. It seems that the rule of the game is to 'touch base' against the vertical wall, claws scrabbling at the granite, wings spread. For a moment one sees the arrogant profile, the short neck, thick beak, a solitary, beautiful black eye. One after another they cling, let go, fall into a now shutterless embrasure, glide along a stairway that no longer has any steps, spiralling around its still standing, contorted, coxalgic, stony axis, flee as if the ruin were on fire, with a clamour that startles the goldfinches on the thistles, the chaffinches on the elders. . . . Where are they now? Nowhere.

The sky is empty, and we are deafened by the harshly enunciated silence. Have we seen the last of the blue swallows, the grey martins? . . . Take cover! It was only a feint. Mind your head! They pass like a whirlwind between the leaves of the lime-trees and our heads. They could put your eye out, scalp you with one snip of their great scissors, don't you see the steel gleaming in the sunlight?

They just wanted to frighten us. Miraculous flight, which brushes against us but is only writ on water! Once more they attack every breach in the tower. The speediest fixes its sights on a small oval hole and proceeds to ram its head into it. . . . But at the very moment of arrival it plies its two blades to take advantage of the air and turns into a shuttle, pulling all the others at the end of its thread.

DANGER

DANGER. It's painted on a wooden placard, nailed to the trunk of an old acacia. But the placard seems much older than the acacia and three of its six letters are obliterated. The danger itself does not age, and conducts its own monologue. Because of it we are able to evict the *amateurs* of ruins. These are recruited from the Belgian and French refugees, the evacuees from Tours, the fugitives from Limoges, the panic-stricken of Brives, halted in their flight to the South by the signature of the armistice. It is forbidden to visit the ruins, forbidden to let the children play at the foot of the ruins. But we, who dwell in the heart of the chaos, are free to pick the ox-eye daisy and the mallow in the guard-room, put up a line in an apartment of honour to dry our linen if it's not raining. All the beams of the flooring have fallen in; they constitute our stock of firewood, which will last longer than the peace itself. Under the canopy of a small vaulted room where traces of fine painting still remain, the boiler boils for one and all, provided that each replaces, in pitchers of cold water, what they withdraw in buckets of hot water for toilet or laundry purposes. The old wood, even when damp, burns well in the open air. From time to time a woodworm, a tick, a large wood-louse, a centipede all hairy with legs, explodes in the fire and the two dogs sheer off; they've been taught to hurl themselves on any suspicious individual who might, one night, try the panels of the gate that has no lock, but they have received no instructions on the subject of explosive millipedes, earwigs and ants' eggs. At every wood-louse that bursts the boxer bitch quivers, gathers the skin between its perplexed eyebrows; the omniscient and braggart dachshund regains his seat, asserting that if he moved away from the fire it was because it was too hot.

What motives led the *seigneurs* of Plas and those of Saint-Hilaire, around the fifteenth century, to construct, so close to each other, in a narrow confine above the village, two châteaux only six or seven yards apart?

Saint-Hilaire began, Plas followed suit. One preferred the cylindrical, the other the cube. We know nothing about them and have plenty of other things to think about, for the radio is dumb and the telegraph deaf and we've had no butter these three weeks, nor newspapers or petrol. The butcher comes when he comes and only has veal. Come autumn, all this greenery around us will disburse pears and apples, walnuts and chestnuts. Until then, no fruit. One's mouth waters for the July peaches, the light-heartedness, the idle friendships of past summers. . . . Chut! It is our rule not to evoke delights beyond our reach.

Who would have believed that all that was necessary to cut us off from the world was for the red puppets standing over the petrol tanks to lose their pachyderm trunks? The road belongs to a solitary ox-cart, a single little ass pulling the framework of a light cart. The verges of the lanes are all campanulas and knap-weed, daisies and pink hemp; a shower has washed from the flowers the dust raised by the lorry-loads of soldiers. There will be no more transport of soldiers to the North. They will return as scattered individuals, marching towards the South. The child-ren can walk arm-in-arm, barring the road as they go mushroom-ing. With the help of the rain the seasonal mushrooms spring up in half a night. They grow so rapidly as to bring with them, over their caps, a roof of dead leaves. The *chanterelle* is a little turned-up umbrella which embellishes the sauce for the veal. But the *cèpe* needs oil and we are forced to refuse it. We give it a grilling on the embers, a drop of oil when it is grilled, a little salt and some chopped garlic. It is satisfied, and so are we.

D A N G E R . . . Whenever we go out, whenever we return, the worm-eaten placard warns us, in vain. Yet this enormous relic of twinned châteaux never stops falling to pieces. In the great silence of the night hours the ruins stir. At six o'clock one morning a great stone falls, lands in the centre of a tower, passes through the yawning gateway, rolls to meet me like a welcoming animal. Its path is marked by a little powdery train of mortar, restored to sand. After a heavy rain the ruin murmurs, stretches itself, spits out some rubble, blooms with new poppies and sedums. A lizard makes its zig-zag lightning path from the base of a tower to a fine fireplace which hovers in mid-air like a piece of Daliesque furniture, or the materialization of the dreams that visit the Comte de Beistegui. Every storm strikes at the highest tower, and stuns us. Danger, that's for sure. The young girl who wears the colours of the night – intensely black hair, intensely white skin – and who scrambles over the ruins to forage among them with a sleepwalker's serenity tells us: 'I've found a new dungeon. . . . The cornice isn't where it used to be. . . . One tread of the staircase has fallen all by itself. . . .' Certainly there's danger. The anticipation of impending danger kept us alert and anxious under the inscrutable veiled sky of Paris in June. Can it be only a month ago? Here the very days lose their names. . . . The old woman who minds two cows and a goat stands at ease at the gap in the hedge, on the unmade road. We stopped to watch her knit, without needles, the rye stalks from which she fashions a kind of fan which is placed like a veil over the animals' muzzles and protects them from the flies.

'It isn't Sunday yet, is it?' the old woman asks us.

Very aged, faded, absent, she is one of those old women who, for three-quarters of a century, have never failed to sit at their doorstep every day at the same time, to peel a few potatoes, call the scurrying hens, shell the peas, cut the grey bread. What can she know about invasion, about defeat? She watches the flowers of the chestnut grove whiten, orders the goat and the two cows about in a cracked voice. She may have asked us what day it is, but she knows the time without a watch. It may be that, men dying earlier than women, she has passed the age of having

living sons, a husband. In these high regions, husbandry makes
no great call on human hands. The cattle have the meadow,
man the chestnuts and also the little milk, the thin white cheeses,
which we were given in the early days and which are now not
to be found. . . .

The old peasant woman is entrenched under a straw hat which
was black once, for in this high country old women don't go
about bareheaded. Bent as a sickle, she has already forgotten us.
Thus she makes us aware of a danger against which the acacia
warns us in vain : the danger of forgetting, of being out of the
world, the danger of ceasing to suffer, to love, of being preserved
from whatever is harmful despite ourselves. We who have seen
Paris and its suburbs change and age with expectation since
September would never have believed that in the heart of an
unmolested village, dreaming remote from the century and its
dramas, the very depths of sadness were in store for us.

D A N G E R . . . Let's not forget the danger that comes from
solitude, from lack of work. Why get up early? Why eat when
it strikes noon? Why wash on getting up, bestir oneself to clean
the rooms we occupy? There's no hurry. None, only the persist-
ence of an obtuse dignity, the need for a routine, however simple.
'Come along, come along, let's get a move on!' I say to the
young women and clap my hands to chase them towards the
boiler, the unmade beds, the breakfast table. 'Everything must
be tidy before noon!' If they were not kindness itself they might
ask me : 'And why *must* it be? Are we catching a train? Shall we
be late for Mass?'

It's rather ridiculous to be busy for no reason, as I am daily,
as if one had invited 'people to lunch'. 'Are you expecting
visitors?' sighs my daughter, who wakes up and falls asleep in
two stages, first the left eye, then the right. . . . She does not
realize how right she is. When I feed the plank fire, when I slip
the bouquet of wild mint under my counterpane and hear the
chimes from the little church at the end of the garden, it is my
own visit I expect, my own strictness that I dread; a scrap of
paper is as ugly in a heap of ruins as in an avenue of pink sand,
and throughout these long mortifying days when one sinks deeper
into oneself at every moment, I would wish to find myself in
something more than mere vacancy. 'Get a move on, get a move
on!' It is not, perhaps, too absurd, the memory that returns just

now : a child was dying and during his last day he occupied himself only in pointing out about him – so that they should be taken
away – the tufts of cottonwool, the moist compresses, an empty
ampoule, the crumpled envelope of some medicament. . . . The
room tidy and the sheet spread to his liking, he closed his eyes
and yielded to his exhaustion.

He was only an immaculate child, yet already he wanted all
tangible ephemera to exist in his own image. For a long time
now we have lived with what was unworthy of satisfying us and
were satisfied with it. That time is far away, the irremediable
has interposed between it and us, just as at the bottom of the un-
cultivated garden a street has interposed between the ruins and
two small watch-towers, exactly the same as those remaining on
our side, erect but tottering at the angles of the boundary wall.
These here, those over there, no longer have anything in common;
the torrent-like little street keeps them apart and channels the
communal life, the straying poultry, the heavy lumbering cows on
its furrowed surface, the foamy water after showers, the children
in clogs and the women carrying on their heads the basketfuls
of dough that weigh twelve pounds.

We are a handful of fine folk but, save for three young women
and girls, we no longer have enough ingenuity to ignore what
physical work can and cannot do for our good. There's no doubt
it helps us. Its efficacy rivals that of a cup of herbal tea for a
bad influenza : warmth, litheness, transient stimulation, pride in
overcoming a humiliating evil. But if we neglect it for a single
day we know what is in store for us – worse still, if we cease for
a single day to give the impression of belief in its urgency, all
is lost.

D A N G E R . . . Look, it's written above the acacia, on the
board which hangs aslant, clinging by a single nail. The danger
of recognizing our true situation here, furnished with little linen,
little money, having all made the same accursed journey. The
danger of perceiving that we are elderly intelligent, unhappy,
strangers to the serenity that surrounds us. So we behave, in
consequence, according to the honourable convention of those
who take care not to expose their sufferings.

Risen early, we allow ourselves only a few moments of lucidity,
vertigo and fear, of unbounded astonishment, of 'Is it possible?'
The rest of the day belongs to decent behaviour, the lie, of some

scout's exercise. We pretend to exhume a kitchen garden from the ruins and general subsidence, to retrace the avenues; my daughter's 'green fingers' tend and cultivate the flowers. The 'green fingers' are those which make the sap flow in the channels of a cutting, which preserve the graft, maintain it in life and in slumber. With loud exclamations we boast of our least activity : 'Look at my pile of weeds!' 'I'm on my eighth barrow-load of pebbles!' '*I* drew the bucket of fresh water from the well!' 'I've found a spade in the ruins!'

Yes, that's how one has to act. And so we clamour and compete in efficiency! Oh no, little one, you're quite wrong. My dear chap, hand over the axe before you lose all your fingers. And just look at her using a secateur, does she think she's cutting her nails! The handle would stay on your pickaxe, my friend, if you had left it to soak in the cistern overnight.

So we chaff each other and prattle. And scamper from task to task. And at night, *belote* and more *belote*. We must defend ourselves! And all rather than give way, break down and confess, sit down on these ruins, our ruins, and take our head in both hands to call on the absent, cry the names of scattered friends and abandoned cities. . . .

RUINS

When it rains, the moisture soaks into and revives the colours of a small circular room some four or five yards above our heads, in the ruins. The dry weather makes its paintings – which seem to date from the Renaissance – faded and powdery. We contemplate them from below, because it's not possible to prop a ladder against a firm wall. These inexpugnable frescoes, all in decorative patterns which converge at the apex of the vault, closely cover a base of dark stone. They enlivened with their yellow, blue and olive green the solitude of a Lady who kept warm without a fire, her feet tucked inside her great fur-hemmed skirt.

It is her alcove that we burn, in carved wood with coloured designs; beneath the paint it crumbles and oozes like a sponge.

From her small square window the Lady watched the ascent of invader, ally, merchant; she witnessed the arrival of what we lack – her freshly-beaten butter, her honeycombs, her rentals of chickens hung by the feet and of pure wheaten flour. . . . Whether she was a Plas or a Saint-Hilaire, the Lady of this place at least had the advantages of her immobile existence. The curfew was not, for her, the hour we dread above all, the hour from which each of us has to depend wholly on herself until the pure dawn, chill as in the mountains, proclaimed by a hundred goldfinches standing on the tips of the pea-sticks.

The large frames of dangling windows, bereft of all their small square panes, witness that under Louis XV the masters of the double château were in the fashion. Beneath one of them a balcony, gently splayed, spreads its cockleshell-inspired lip. From the first ten days of July, the last ray of sunshine is no longer impeded by the fallen western facade, touches this window and reddens the lip of the balcony, as one come from a nocturnal fête. 'Ah!' says my daughter, who is a poet, 'the phantoms' ball. . . .'

A cold July, storms which succeed each other at the same time in the afternoon, a week at a stretch, and shed the water from the lowering sky. Then, punctually, two concentric rainbows painted on the screen of the receding rain . . . So many omens which will be explained later, they say in the village. What point in reading the clouds? We are invaded by a little of the serenity of those who have lost everything. And for us there are no longer any omens, good or bad. The rainbow is only an incomparable piece of architecture, one foot planted in a meadow, the other solidly inserted, with its seven insubstantial metals, in the middle of the small river. The rest of the bow is missing, a rift of blue allows the passage of birds and clouds. Then the septicoloured miracle reasserts itself; facing the setting sun, it straddles peaks and valleys. The rain, which created it, obliterates it.

Soldiers have been seen for several days now. Embarrassed by their empty hands and unburdened backs, they had all cut walking-sticks, peeled and white, from the hedgerows. They entered the shops and the sombre inns, spoke loudly, threw off military pleasantries, used the stock behaviour of the ranks; but they did not persist in this for long. For the most part they were lads of some education and the peasants' silence was felt as an admonition. They have abandoned their white sticks, their regimental expertise, their nervous fluency. They walk silently, arms dangling, now they haven't their tools on their shoulders. Now they watch and listen instead of talking. They know at a distance the name of a man sharpening his scythe far off, of another controlling a pair of oxen with his voice, the name of the bird whose short song mimics the sound of a fistful of glass marbles chinked in the hand. And when they encounter a strange woman, instead of taking stock of her they say a thoughtful good-day.

'When I've nothing to read, I scratch.'

'I have to stop myself gnawing my nails when I've nothing to read.'

'It's because I've nothing to read that I've taken up sewing.'

'If only there were a library here I wouldn't smoke so much. . . . They say that a couple of miles from here a retired teacher has a collection of two or three hundred volumes. . . . If the rain stops I'll go there for a look round.'

'. . . and you'll find two books from a prizegiving,' grates the most deprived among us. 'Perhaps *La Maison rustique des Dames* and a *Manuel du Parfait bricoleur* if the teacher is under sixty-six, and some Alexandre Dumas if he's over seventy.'

All of us have come here driven by the terrible floodtide; what is strange is that our different paths should have intersected here. None of those who pass under the ruined arch has anything more or better than a valise and its contents. We thought we should be stopping here for a few days. . . . The grocer-cum-innkeeper has sold us her remaining blue overalls, which make it possible to husband the precious tailor-made costume, the blouse, and even the vest. But we would gladly exchange our vest for five kilos of printed nourishment. The real dearth is the absence of books. Twenty or so volumes make the rounds from room to room, complete the circle and start over again. Five or six Prousts, three Balzacs, are much in demand. We learn to read, we draw lots for the nuggets as for the dross. For the first time in a long while, reading sheds its egoism: 'Did you see that? There, at the bottom of the page, read it, it's delightful.' We are also learning to share.

But pleasure engenders pain. What is the minor pain of soaking bare bread in coffee untempered with milk compared to the

certainty that we shan't have – not tonight, nor tomorrow, nor
after the meal or during the night – a fresh newspaper, a virgin
novel? Ah, the books behind the window and the prodigal display
accessible to the passerby at Stock's, the goods spread like a multi-
coloured harvest! As for the de luxe editions, the pearly 'Japanese', the bluish 'Chinese', the creamy Holland, I feel coldly
towards these well-dressed ones. Like all those who re-read a good
deal, I prefer a broken specimen, its stitching hanging out at the
back, which spreads flat whatever page you open it at.

Companions of insomnia and fitful sleep, the twenty or so
volumes here deserve our attention, including the Montaigne in
green cloth. 'It's two o'clock . . . it's three o'clock in the morning. . . .' chimes the minute church. The smell of the garden
enters through the half-open window, the dawn is about to break.
A fine rain patters on the leaves, we relight the lamp. A volume
under my elbow provides for the short slumbers, the frequent
awakenings. I am almost capable of reciting it like a familiar
score, which one follows by eye though one sings it by heart.

As everywhere where he is not decimated, the bird rules the roost
here. On the stake supporting each haricot plant a goldfinch
blossoms. Yesterday two wheatears, quarrelling on a branch,
put foot to ground to fight more conveniently. A red wheel of
furious wings and beaks lashed the dust. Neither of the combatants took any more notice of my presence than if I had been a
wall or a cloud. On nights of full moon owls of various kinds
inveigh freely against the great incongruous clarity, and the
splashes of white dung betray the presence of the brown owls on
the highest steps of the staircase, which is broken off in mid-air,
exactly right for the flight of a bird or an angel.

In the presence, the constancy, of a 'water feature' dwells a
charm due to surprise. The more subterranean and secret the
water, the more homage we pay to it. The ruins do not conceal
any water, the forked twig barely moves, listless between my
fingers. A square well supplies the water for sprinkling and
ablutions. But it's best not to look too closely at the film, like
collodion as it sets, that forms on the buckets and jugs. But
twenty feet lower down, from the rock itself, springs the water
which refreshes the hamlet and ourselves. A seigneurial spring,
which means that for centuries everyone has been entitled to

benefit from it. It is communal, as was the bakehouse. The old folk here and their grandfathers have seen no change or decrease in it. At six we go down with the buckets. A neighbour woman, opposite the spring, holds the cord, always damp and glistening like a snake, looped at one end for passage of the hand and wrist, furnished at the other end with a stout iron hook.

The water, contained within the base of one of the thick walls of the ruin, levels out at three yards underground to blow its pure breath on your face. It has produced an ornamentation of toadflax and maidenhair fern which wreath your reflection if you lean over. When the bucket is hauled up there is a gleam of pale blue limpidity, the liveliness of dancing cold sweet water. It is a wholly good fairy. The wicked fairy is not far off. She slumbers, lazy, yellow when it rains, at the bottom of her cave. 'But,' I say to the woman with the rope, 'what if the bad water should get mixed up with what we drink? It hasn't far to go.' The woman with the rope regards me with a scandalized air: 'It's one of those things that never happen.' And she re-knots the damp hempen snake at the balustrade of the little flight of steps.

The human hand, powerful, delicate, awkward, perfect-ible . . . Here it tries to relearn what it has forgotten. The women's hands succeed better than the men's. Women discover that, beneath all the great panoply of manual labour, what really matters is skill. Two women, handling the large cross-cut saw, rapidly cut up the beams. To the astonished man they say: 'There's nothing to it; you, you push the saw and pull it, so you get tired. All you need do is pull, each in the opposite direction.' When it's hot, a man chases flies, waving his handker-chief and losing his temper. A young woman unfastens a piece of metal sheeting from an old window, cuts out a rectangle which she attaches to a rod of iron wire; in two minutes she has con-trived an efficient fly-killer inspired by the American fly-swatters. Even the axe and hatchet yield to delicate fingers. But their epidermis betrays them. It cracks like tissue paper, bleeds, comes up in blisters, and one of our pioneers who, the moment before, had surrounded herself with a whirling cutting edge, oblique and blue, lets the blade drop, sucks her palm, whimpers over a splinter, turns pale over a cut.

The man transplanted here admits his awkwardness and applies himself. Humble in the face of necessity, he exhibits patience and surprise. 'What!' he exclaims. 'Am I only capable of knotting a tie, filling a fountain-pen, emptying it penful by penful on to paper? What a comedown!' And he accords the expert handyman an unbounded admiration. He sets himself to study. He learns how to make a fishing-line, how to arrange the blazing wood under the boiler in a star; he shells the peas and whistles like a small boy on holiday. Why does this gentle mutual aid of castaways turn sour on occasion? Nothing prepares us for the pain of suddenly feeling enemies. But this is the inevitable tax on sociability. A malevolent glance, a sneer, the terrible desire to wound, to triumph in a few words, the horror of being one of the group, the cruelty of the incarcerated, all come to the top. They are going to stop, to condemn one of us. . . . No, there'll be no outburst. There's more to it, it's better to suffer. With a vehement toss of her head, a woman sewing throws over her shoulder a tear suspended from her lashes without interrupting her work. Wild youth, on the point of abusing us, pulls itself together and comes to lay its head on our shoulder. . . . Once again we gaze on its inoffensiveness. Alas, how beautiful it is! Alas, that it should be armed in vain, in this place which is like a verdant overthrown tomb! . . . Alas, how it would prefer to be cast into the heart of the flames, torn by love, stuck with arrows! . . . Once again it is given to us to love its sunburned forehead, the hair it ruthlessly crops, the mouth which refuses to complain, and to make it the secret promise it desires: 'Yes, yes, you shall burn, I promise you.'

FEVER

A precipitate but regular beating of the heart, which seems to have deserted its source, the great propulsor muscle, to settle at the base of the neck, in the thumbs, the shoulder burdened by the weight of the recumbent body . . . These are the first drum-taps of fever. Behind them sounds an organ-swell of waters – not flowing but poured out in masses, the faint sound of heavy, distant waters. . . .

Fever, when it does not mean for me the flare-up of an old pleuritic focus and cough, is a sort of fate; and I am far from greeting it with frightened mien or having recourse to aspirin. Does such an enchantment deserve only crude antidotes? It is wrong to reply to its warnings by stupefying it with brutal analgesics when it touches us with its so subtle finger there, between the ribs, just where I feel it today, just where the ribs begin to quiver. A barely sensible tremor, an initial warning that mounts to the jaws . . .

It was nothing, the finger withdraws leaving me unscathed, normal, more or less. A little stiffness, perhaps, in the play of the eyelids and an imaginary band drawn tight around the forehead . . . An aversion, also, for bright light – nothing, less than nothing, in fact, except that the smell of tobacco is revolting and the taste of wine. . . . How could I ever have liked this wine which leaves an aftertaste of ink? And this coffee, how bitter! Or else my palate is perverted and all my senses, since the material of my skirt, a curtain, are harsh, so harsh, to my fingertips. . . . Harsh: there's a good, well-modelled word, shaped like a rasp. It creates thirst. Harsh – I could do with an iced drink. But our ruins secrete no ice and are unacquainted with refrigerators. In December stalactites of ice will hang from the ruined balconies, the machicolations. And if the sun touches them they will fall murderously, like swords, points downward. December is a long way off. A long way off, like Paris. Am I then so soft-hearted today that, at the memory of an abandoned Paris, of the small apartment where the dust thickens, I feel a catch of the throat?

No ice, then. Perhaps a hot drink. A pity that at the mere idea of the fumes of a *tilleul* or insipid violet *tisane* I screw up my mouth in apprehension. Anyway, it's no time for drinking, or eating. It's time to try to work, to collect the scattered blue sheets and . . . And here I am, felled, seated on the tiled floor, by order of the fever which sent me, its subtle finger not having sufficed, one of its most winged vertigos. A major vertigo which pounced at the same time as myself on the strewn pages but which, to arrive before me, gave me a gentle blow on the head with its feathered shoulder. I almost glimpsed it in passing. It occupied half the room but had no shape that I can describe. Patience it will have, for its touch has just brought about an

exceptional state and it is this that fixes my temperature at around
38.5°. Everything is illuminated with a superb fatuity. I feel
capable of waiting indefinitely for the monocotyledonous newspaper that is printed in the region, its prefectorial decisions, its
news of the Colorado beetle, and its notices to the demobilized.

Fever is a matter of consent. I could insist on postponing the
proffered appointment until . . . yes, until around ten o'clock
tonight, and between now and then to weed, add a few pebbles
to the tumulus of transplanted stones, lift the vast leaves of the
cucumber plant which, from one day to the next, one hour to
the next almost, surprises us with its great squat ovoid fruit :
'The cucumber has laid again!' announces my daughter. All the
ritual of our days at the foot of the ruins is still at my disposal,
if I wish. To what end? An abdication, of whatever nature,
brings its moment of inadmissible pleasure which is consum-
mated, arms dragging, head thrown back, as in the moment of
sex. Who knows the feelings of a mistress convicted of unfaithful-
ness, a leader who has just surrendered his arms, a deposed
monarch who hears the imagined sound of his crown rolling on
its edge like the hoop of a barrel? This king, for instance, this tall
young man, self-conscious of his awkward fair body, shall we ever
know what he felt when, conventionally immobile, apparently
prostrated, he was swept by the furious wind, the paroxysm of
surrender?

If I am thinking of the King of the Belgians, what more notorious transients may not my fever evoke, night fallen? Heightened
after its fashion, it alone can yield me creatures and landscapes,
all other hope of excursion failing for lack of petrol, the steep-
ness of the hillside, an arthritic disorder of the leg. The fever will
convoy hither the unnamed, who yet are not unknown. Among
them a certain number escape the human pattern and have
become subject to the law of evolution and of growth. In a novel,
La Chatte, I postulated that the favourite dreams of Alain
Amparat were endowed with chins and moons, great round eyes,
living convex entities which dazzle by virtue of their convexity.
If we may believe Huysmans, this sort of explosion, which dis-
solves the visiting dream, is characteristic of demoniacal
attacks. . . . But I don't believe Huysmans. Poor demons like
mine are confined for the most part in their convexity like a
flower within a glass paperweight. I have accorded my heroes

my most faithful phantoms. All else of these febrile accessions is tenuous, is born and dies with each attack, leaves but a dusty souvenir, an ash of petals; images fringed with a pale fire swirl on a black background tinged with another black, two or three other blacks. . . .

It isn't easy to talk about the colours fever paints. That great poet, Hélène Picard, used to tell me that a violet splendour always lightened her nights of sickness. 'I call it violet,' she would add, 'but it really deserves another epithet. I call it violet from impotence, from ignorance of a word as yet unborn, which the dreams have not confided to me. . . .'

Night falls. It begins in the house, which darkens, then passes outside, flows over two steps and the north facade. Where the warm dryness and golden aerial grains of the mayflies reigned, now stretches a long pool of shadow. But the height of the ruins shines in the privilege of light. Up there all is still sun, swallows and yellow sedums. The planet rotates rapidly. Its small breasts of hills catch and quit the sun, knead and thicken the twilight. I shiver openly, now that I can unashamedly move towards bed and hot-water bottle, make my submission.

A writer taken with the fever remains a writer. He is even, for a few hours, a better writer. What scruples! This is not the hour I would choose to lie, improvise, bedeck myself, scratch the inventive faculty until a little ink flows. I would not dare to be satisfied with some provisional word and say to it: 'Wait there for me, I'll be back soon to dress you in your Sunday best.' With the fever it is always Sunday, and finery. Shouldn't one write only at its dictate, to the sound of its drumming? Burning aegis! If only I could rely on its being my guardian angel. . . . To be permitted to scribble lying down I have had to accept that those who look after me should envelop me in my husband's large pyjamas. On top of that a winter-sports sweater which belongs to my daughter. Then a knitted jacket of uncertain origin, whose chemically green colour provokes, if I look at it, an insurrection of the salivary glands.

Shivering very strongly changes one's handwriting. I'm very fond of these little strokes, more numerous than were ever necessary to write pothooks. Unaffected by the blankets, the rubber bag full of boiling water, the attack is so chill that I drag my long woollen sleeve down to the end of my right hand. The fever takes its course, which is certainly not boring. It breathes great *vvvou*'s around me, with a profusion of v's; it seems to have appropriated all the v's belonging to such aerial words as *vent, vortex, vol.* . . . It is a musician and brings me a fragment of melody, lost these many years. God knows how I've searched for it ! 'Put it down on the bed-table,' I tell it, 'between the alarm-clock and the glass of lemonade; I'll take it with me when I get up.' A milkman used to pass whistling that tune (a *bourrée* probably) at five in the morning in the Rue de Saint-Senoch.

Sometimes he would rattle with his hand the leaves of my iron shutters, which resounded like the notes of a xylophone. A sound does not die, then, since I hear so clearly the mouth-organ of the metal slats and the skilful voluble flautist who had imbibed, through the Paris mist, the acidity of bilberries. My bed gently shakes and whimpers; these cursed English mattresses, in metal filigree, which creak like a new saddle, are meant more for hygiene than for indiscreet abandonment. My fever, though I think it nears its climax, barely disturbs it. I have written only a few lines, I haven't felt the time pass, suspended as it is between the real and the less real, the shiver and the siliceous warmth. . . . Siliceous. I have well weighed, turned and returned the word in the insubstantial basket where I stow my words. One was too puffed-up, another too deflated. Let's settle for siliceous, since the burning back of my hand smells of flint.

38°, 38.5° are temperatures without interest that teach you nothing. Variety begins at 39°. Or stubbornness, which is much the same thing, since in satisfying myself with a repeated word, some musical passages, a game with my toes, I can multiply the visual and auditory effects.

The grand Vertigo has just recrossed the room because I bent down, as quickly as a well person, to pick up my pen. The grand Vertigo descended as usual from the ceiling and assumed the familiar shape of a rock of hazy variable outline. Weightless. It just descends. Its descent constitutes its entire menace. When I was ten and had the smallpox it inflicted itself on me, I watched it develop like a bottle-imp in the turbid water of my child's room, rise and descend, always descend. For a long while I've known that it will only crush me once, the last time, and that time is not today.

Writing. Rest. Writing. Why should the fever fetter the hand when it accelerates the blood? To be frank, it is not conducive to great work. But it's only a small wager I proposed to myself, to write to the end of the attack.

A charming face leaned over me. It exhaled the fragrance of night and evening dew. The robust attachment of its bare neck was marked by a mobile dimple which attracted and ravished attention.

'You promise me', said the charming face, 'to call if you feel worse or if you want anything. Or else to knock, on the partition, it's so thin.'

And the charming face knitted its brows with an inquisitorial air.

'Good Lord, daughter!' I replied. 'You look exactly like your father!'

She lowered her eyes as if I had gone beyond the bounds of propriety. And, in fact, had I not just made a remark, for her, in rather bad taste?

Three cooked pears, a jug full of blue water, exactly what I wanted. If, instead of this scribbling, which progresses as drunkards do, haphazard and zigzag, I were writing my last wishes, I should write nothing else than: 'Give me some crystallized fruit and some very clear water.' I've been ordered to drink a lot, 'to flush the kidneys'. Very well, I'll drink! They're preparing for bed on the other side of the partition, doing their best not to disturb me. But I hear everything, and more. Between the barking of the boxer bitch and the admonition, fit to waken the dead, which suppresses it, I hear the high-pitched *i-i-i-i* and the great *vvou* characteristic of the fever. I can even see through the partition my careful companions marching about like bears, backs crouched, a crock of hot water in the hand. Each has just drawn his ration of water from the boiler squatting in the ruin. These are moonlit nights. They do not suspect, since they haven't the fever, that they return all gilded with nightshine. . . . The three little ones, as I refer to them, all have cheeks pasty with fatigue, eyes drowning in sleep. Henri de C—, a hybrid variety of demobilized lieutenant, comfortably wears khaki breeches brought back from campaigning, the remains of a military hospital nightshirt from which he has cut off the sleeves, and a small pink pullover with crystal buttons, which constitute the whole of his present wardrobe. Maurice Goudeket* brings up the rear, dark-jowled at this late hour. He would like to come in to say good-night to me, but mature and feverish ladies have, thank God, the sound conjugal sense to bar their door. He goes by on tiptoe. . . . Why is it that delicate intentions so rarely meet their reward? He stumbles on a loose tile and catches at my door-handle to steady himself. What was the din of Ethelred's shield in *The Fall of the House of Usher* compared with that created by an enamelled jug allowed to fall on a tiled floor? I hear the little ones laughing quietly and I laugh out loud. Why not laugh? Fever isn't a gloomy thing. After which a chorus of voices wish me a good rest and the house at the foot of the ruins admits, through its open windows, the night, its eddies of air, its river murmur, its marauding cats, its bombyxes, its little tree-frogs with their slender thighs.

No, it's not gloomy, the fever which is based on no organic disease. It's much less gloomy than the waiting, the lucidity, the aimless liberty which reigns over this spared region. Neither is my own room gloomy. The ingenious arrangement of a rustic cloister has respected the low worn pillars and the roof of ancient tiles, partitioned off the long gallery. As at the Palais-Royal, the dwellings go by arcades. To each guest his low archway. A bed, a stool, a press for clothes – involuntarily I use outmoded words – and my room is furnished.

I had at one moment put out my lamp; I have just prudently relit it. Not that the untended garden had entered my room through the drawn curtain; on the contrary, it was I and the gondola of my bed which were heading for a promenade in the moonlight. Inundated with white phosphorescence, pierced by rays, I felt the incongruity of such an excursion. So I returned in the gondola and once again the yellow lamplight combats and warms the light of the moon. It is incredible how bulky the shadow of the ruin can be at certain hours. It is one o'clock in the morning. The shadow is, in a real sense, blinding, of a sharp blue, and covers the house so densely that it would be worth-while removing our dwelling from it, or shifting the ruin. I'll mention it tomorrow. The weight of the edifice to be trans-ported? Pooh . . . tell me of any other weight as crushing as that of a shadow.

* Colette's third husband.

This one, now my lamp is out, touches my bed and prevents a child, who is barely visible, from joining me. The little girl occupies in my room the corner opposite my bed. I am well aware – my head isn't turned by a febrile attack – that this is a little girl of the fever and not of the present time, also that she has long flat hair, a dress of faded blue zephyr, and yellow button-boots. She has no disclosures to make to me and I am without curiosity. If I were weaker, more nervous, I should be frightened by her return, since I did not know her in her earthly life. But she is simply a child of the fever, and harmless. It is very naïve to mistake a ghost for a hobgoblin. One has the apparitions one deserves. My little girl, as well-behaved as myself, approaches as far as a permitted limit, looks over the barrier. I make her no sign, nor do I advance to meet her. Note that it was Little Red Riding Hood who was the first to speak to the Wolf. If, seeing a Wolf in place of Grandmother, she had gone on her way, the Wolf would never have existed. One knows that unusual beings exist, just as there are animals reputedly dangerous: don't make a move, don't raise the voice, or everything may be spoiled to who knows what extent. Look, an example: every time I stretch out my wool-swathed arm to reach a quivering sheet of paper, a timorous spoon that rattles against the saucer, a ridiculous handkerchief that flaps its wings in my hands as if I wanted to wring its neck; each time I move, within the jug of thick glass there is a sort of silver-fish with pink fingers. (Why shouldn't a fish have fingers? The gurnards, at the bottom of the water, dream and watch, supported on their barbels like bassets on their fore-paws.) You would swear, to look at this prisoner of the carafe, that it is the deformed reflection of my hand and fore-arm in the belly of the pitcher? You should not miss such a good opportunity to trust appearances. That is what happened to Red Riding Hood when she cried 'Wolf! Wolf!' because a fold in the ruched bonnet on the head of an old woman, asleep or dead, and Grandmother's great muzzle gave a wolf-like appearance. Then the apparition rose up and devoured the little girl. It is commonsense. My silver-fish will not leave the interior of the jug despite his seductive swerves and his pink fingers. He demands nourishment. Ingenuous larva! You will stay captive and unfed. You are dealing with a Red Riding Hood capable of frying and eating you. Follow the example of the little girl, there in the corner. As far as she is concerned, I don't have to put up with extravagance or grimaces. No doubt someone has told her : 'You can look, but not touch.' Hands held behind her back, she gazes at me as if I were a garden. Recurrently, some obstacle, some flame, some thought, interposes between her and myself. While I was growing up, growing old, she has had the luck to remain a small girl. She hails from some remote time. In hours of fever Sido, my mother, would bend over me : 'Do you want a drink, Minet-Chéri?' I was particularly anxious that she should not perceive my suspect twin, the little girl with the flat hair, whom she might have loved.

I must have dozed off. . . . Yes, a good quarter of an hour. Such halts are familiar and never disturb my work. I keep the pen between my fingers, the horses sleep in harness. During my lapse the pen has slipped on the paper and drawn a diagram. It's this diagram I'd like to interpret. It must surely have some hidden meaning. This unfamiliar handwriting can bode no good. Steeple-like angles, wormlike spirals . . . The room is empty. Tired of waiting and staring, the Little Girl has left. When I refill my glass the silver-fish disappears. A sad thirst . . . I feel that I am going to relearn what a sick person has the right blissfully to forget. I anticipate that in a moment the war will be over, that the lees of the war have yet to be be drunk. . . . Help me, grand Vertigo! Descend and crush me!

But nothing prevails against the crow of the cock. I'm going to win, I have won, the wager to write during the attack of fever and the cock crows as at the end of all temptations. I've defended myself only too well. The shivering inside me is no longer this icicle robed in hot ashes, the fever, it's the poor victorious body, worn out with victory. The cock crows, a tough glittering little cock with the voice of a weathercock. What illusion could defy this little cock, village boss who chases and defeats the big dogs?

Delirium is a difficult matter. Let's erase the illegible diagram. Let nothing marvellous remain on this manuscript. Now return the day, the hamlet, anxiety concealed and shared, goodwill spread out like a housewife's apron, loved faces, those daily tasks which safeguard the heart's dignity. . . . O, dignity of the heart, let no one see how much this hour of dawn affronts you, probes all your weaknesses, insists on tears. . . . Now it's mastered, that sob of weakness. A gulp of water has got the better of it, stale water which, after passing the night next to me, has lost the glacial virtues of the obscure well. . . . Water soon to be restored to vapour along the temples, as moisture under the chin, on the neck, the back . . . I was more rejuvenated by the fever, in the depths of the night. . . .

The Angelus bell assigns a precise limit to obscurity. It makes a poor sound, vexed by an old crack. But this illuminating moment and the dazzling arrival of the day need no other heralds than raucous cries, the cock, the bell, a stable chain, a pump, the axle of an ox-cart. . . . I have the right to open this hand, which grasped the pen firmly enough to write during a night of fever, and to extend it, hollow-palmed, humbly, to the supreme donor, to sleep.

GONE . . .

'He's gone. . . . They've gone. . . .'

'How d'you mean, gone? Where to?'

'We don't know. They've gone. They managed to get a lift in a car which promised they'd cross the frontier at ***. And from there it seems that a boat should be able to take a few passengers to South America, or at any rate to the *** Islands.'

'But how . . . but their life, over there . . . but when they come back. . . .'

'They weren't thinking of coming back.'

These words put an end to our interrogation. We can only add exclamations: 'Fantastic. . . . What an extraordinary story. . . . It beats everything!' Especially it surpasses the idea we've had of him, of her, these twenty or thirty years. They've gone. Fear or pride has taken them from us, extracting from them an admission which they would never have uttered if it had not been for the war, this war, and the peace, this peace.

We learned the strange news by the slow and capricious route that rumours from the inhabited regions follow to arrive here. A sub-prefecture is involved where, it seems, soldiers with fixed bayonets guard grocers' shops which still sell acid drops and eau-de-Cologne weak in alcohol. Then they make a detour, reach a county town to be picked up by the young lad on his bicycle. But it may happen that they mistake the county. Then they have patiently to return to the county town, not without sometimes diverging *en route* like a badly-hooped barrel. They leave the county town again, finish by climbing on foot a steep green slope, since there are neither cars nor petrol, at the top of which we await them hungrily.

Apart, we question each other, we continue to protest:

'But after all, it's not likely! How could they have had such an idea? You know very well what he was like, so meticulous, so stay-at-home. Do you remember when we used to tease them about the summer holidays?'

'And she too. . . . You recall, at the beginning of June, she said: "My dear children, I won't stop you doing what you think is right, provided you leave me in peace in my corner. . . ." '

We remember. Of the figures slowly evolved by twenty or thirty years of civilized, narrow-minded, decently hardworking life, we are now left only the memories contradicted by an unimaginable reality: the husband, his wife, are on a boat – what boat? – they have hardly any luggage since they've been picked up by a car. . . . Perhaps they've not much money either. She has taken her light summer coat and perhaps the yellow veil she used to tie under her chin, Russian style, whenever it was windy; she always disliked the wind. And he? Has he got his heavy overcoat and that frightful cap on his head? . . .

'That cap which he'd never get rid of, which he fished out of the water, discovered when we hid it from him, *you* know. . . .'

No. We don't know anything any more. We draw from memory what is obscure to us; but we lack the force and audacity to invent the truth: a mature thin woman, without powder, without rouge on her hard mouth, already indifferent to the wind she used to detest, clutching to herself a coat stained by sea-water. We know how instinctive it is, when navigating, to keep one's eyes turned forwards. So the little man with the round back looks forward, blinks under the spray and the smoke. I'd like to know if they are ill, if they miss us, or if, on the contrary . . .

Others have 'gone'. It's new, this definitive word, which lacks a complement. Those two brothers, for instance, uncouth in their pleasures, uncouth at work, whom we all knew . . . 'The packs of cards they must have taken for *belote*, those two!' said some-one awkwardly. For it suits us better to imagine that those who've 'gone' went away with their usual habits, their daily toys, the badges of complaisance. I believe the truth is otherwise. A terrible blow between the shoulders has made them spit up a bloodstained truth which made them short of breath and, relieved, they departed.

At Notre-Dame-du-Laghet I once met a man who, having escaped from a fire, had hastened to hang his personal ex-voto on the figured walls of Laghet. You can imagine that this showed a victim in night attire, standing at the edge of a window and enveloped in flames. 'I had one of those fears!' he would say. 'Think of it, three floors! And then I took advantage of being so frightened and jumped.'

Occupation

A pink roof of fluted tiles, so-called Roman tiles. A spindle-shaped cypress, black beneath the splendid light, and some top-heavy willows with great crowns whose tresses are a tender foliage that the wind combs, divides and reunites. Behind the cypress a small patch of rye sparkles with a dazzling spring green: a great pale April sky covers this peaceful corner of the universe.

'How do we know that we are in France?' says my companion. He explains:

'I'm not speaking of geographic certainty. I mean the thrilling conviction that tells us: this is a French beauty, a balance and composition which seem to be the result of art. . . . The solitary cypress, the old willows with their new foliage, a pink roof, these may nestle in any corner of Italy as well as in our own Midi. The dry rubble of the hillside might belong to Spain and this great hazy sky has the bland discolouration we have seen over Morocco. But transport me here in my sleep, put me down here, and I shall wake and cry: "This is France!" Why?'

I made no reply to my companion, who is a poet. A poet accepts silence as a reply, even a flattering one. In lyricism some truth dwells. A poet perceives, and generously expresses, what our own sensibility retains no less acutely but less musically. So that when he exclaims: 'How beautiful this is!', moved, we fall silent. . . . But when it concerns France and the beauties of France? Then we all become poets after our own fashion and sing her, ravaged and diminished, we pity her shackled, with the great wound that divides her down the middle, her borders consumed by fire. Could we not have acquired such tenderness sooner? In French hearts love dwells hidden and incurable like that of an over-faithful woman exploited by a lover assured of perpetual forgiveness. We were the spoiled children of a country worth all the others put together and now her portraits of yesteryear break our hearts.

I date from a time when the French, more or less ignorant of their own country, had not yet taken to travel. When they did take a fancy to gadding about, they crossed the frontiers and left France behind them. They returned and, to paint an Italian

*lake, a Kabyle forest or icebergs swimming like swans, they sat
down beside one of those French landscapes created by a careful
chance, climate, a rich soil and its subsoil, whose delicate nuances,
moderation of line and pleasing nobility would attract foreigners
and make a resident of the passer-by.*

*Before the war French young people used to travel; let's say
rather that they covered distances and knew by heart the stopping-places on many an itinerary and, unerringly, the numbers
of the trunk roads. Granted, in this number of hurrying young
persons, some there were devoted to the beauty of their country.
They were easily recognizable in that they slackened their pace,
abandoned the preconceived itinerary, sometimes deposited their
car in a town and loaded a rucksack on their backs. Or maybe
they forgot themselves between a mountain, a blue-black river
and some reddening heath, and you would find them there a
month later. . . . Your true lover of travel delights to stop.*

*I recur quite often to the pages of Taine's 'Voyage aux
Pyrénées'. Does the author, in his three hundred pages, cover the
daily ration of five hundred kilometres that a pre-war motorist
would swallow? I doubt it. But he did discover the country between Arcachon and Bagnères-de-Bigorre. Better, he describes it
in such a fashion that we discover with him this French mountain range, its legends, its flora and its dangers. The true traveller
is he who wanders yet often sits awhile.*

*I am happy to be one of those home-birds who can't poke
their noses out of doors without exclaiming with admiration.
Lazy but shrewd, obsessed by pigeon-girdled steeples, riverside
wash-places, lime-shaded avenues, I have in all seen rather few
countries. A strip of Burgundy, some cantons of Switzerland,
Savoy and Franche-Comté, Provence, leagues of coastline in
both Picardy and Brittany, fjords, Morocco superficially, Algeria
hurriedly . . . I am not forgetful of them, but I hardly yearn for
more, for I have still at my disposal some much-restricted French
excursions. I know that in France there is no need to plan a visit
to a site or a view. The one comes to me when I'm not thinking
of it, the other falls into my lap. For me the flowers and trickling
fountains, for me the ancient steps of a ruin covered with children and birds. It has also happened that certain desired scenes
have been denied to me; for example, the Tours de Merle, the
caves of Padirac, Albi, have interposed between themselves and*

*me certain malicious accidents, a screen, a mishap. What matter?
If chance took them away, it can restore them to me. Or maybe
it will offer compensations.*

*It has already given them: I live in the Palais-Royal. Like
many other, rather timorous, grumbling French people who yet
continue to admire that which pleases them, I cherish a dormant
worship of my country at the bottom of my heart. We were
spoiled by the succulence and grace of French earth, warm from
having sheltered a human being in its every fold. At the bend of
the road, the corner of the street, on the beaches, above the coast,
we received inestimable gifts paid in phosphorescent waves, in
blossoming apple-trees, in pastures, historic palaces, fruits from
the Rhône valley. We did not know that the wounds inflicted on
such a beautiful country would strike a blow at us all. Now we
do know. It is as true for this as for the other love: joy teaches
us very little about it; we are sure of its existence and its strength
only in grief.*

I

Like flies on honey they hasten, cluster, feed. . . . The comparison
is not new but is inevitable. Everything suggests it : the noonday
hour, the splendour of these autumn days, the haste and assiduity
of these open-air readers.

Their meeting-place is old, beautiful and respected. The rarity
of passers-by exposes to view and aerates this square, which gives
access to a famous theatre, a garden, a palace, which were royal
once.

The Louvre and its flowerbeds, Rivoli and its arcades, the
Bourse and the Bank release at noon a small wave, a crowd of
toilers who take their repast and their recreation in less than
two hours. It seems plain to me that they are concerned more
nowadays than formerly with the one, to the detriment of the
other. In the avenue de l'Opéra a second bookshop receives the
same devotions and I am assured that the treacherous draughts
beneath the Odéon discourage none of those absorbed in reading.

But here, in my neighbourhood, which is also that of the Théâtre-Français, the honey-trap, the book, bursts its bounds and spills over, offers itself to eager hands and eyes. The ancient atlas, with its copper-plate engravings where Aeolus puffs the islands and dolphins sport between two continents, oppresses Giraudoux and Victor Cherbuliez with its due weight. The 'bargain book', old before its time, hot and peeling, its stitching hanging out at the back, belongs to you, to me, to everyone. But leave it, as I do, to those who will not buy it, who read fifty pages today, as many tomorrow, the end of the volume the day after. . . .

They are recognizable. Young for the most part, they read standing up and, standing, they rest with one leg over the other. Bare-headed, boys and girls, they haven't yet any overcoat or three-quarter jacket; perhaps they'll be without one right through the winter. . . . For the moment they're not in need since, with the autumn, the sun gradually moves south and touches their shoulder and, above all, they hold an open book. The handy outdoor display serving as a desk, they turn the pages and keep one hand free because they lunch while reading. I should much rather – so great is our cowardice, our desire to avoid what wounds us – I should much rather not know what it is they lunch on, so hastily, so meagrely. They too, proud as they are, prefer us not to know that, for instance, the large cream-horn they put to their mouths is a loaf which may or may not be stuffed with meat, disguised in a bundle of papers. There is also the meal hidden in a pocket, in a handbag, from which one detaches little mouthfuls between two fingers, as if absentmindedly. . . .

Standing, absorbed in its dream, part of Parisian youth reads passionately. It has always read at the bookstalls and along the *quais*, imprisoned under the stall-roofs like a sparrow in a trap. But I believe that it did so in former times with less ardour and application. I'm the more sure of this from an attentive reading of the letters I get from strangers.

'Madame Colette, I would like some books, how can one exchange books? We have a varied enough little collection – travel, novels, natural science – read and reread, and it's hardly possible to buy new books just now.* . . . Madame, why aren't there more reading-rooms? . . .'

* This was in 1942.

I shall be told that the young people of both sexes, eager to read – that is to say, roused by a painful aspiration, a need to fly in spirit towards a mental illumination, to forsake their daily tasks – are engaged in reading, precisely, 'no matter what'. Agreed. I tell myself as much. Where is the harm? They read and contemplate entomological works, odd instalments of books on art, a fine old novel by Alphonse Daudet, incomplete runs of medical journals, manuals of practical science, a stout legal tome, the diary of an eighteenth-century traveller, a miracle of slow-ness, naïvety and fond curiosity. They leaf through a marvellous *Paris ancien*, raise their eyes and, astonished, recognize it all around them. They make contact with a past which they renoun-ced from ignorance, a capital where they were born but which they do not even look at; they are moved by the thought that it might have perished without their having ever truly loved it. . . .

So let them read no matter what. That's what I did in my youth, given the run of a library where everything was grist to my mill and where nothing would have been considered suitable for me at six, at ten, at fourteen. . . . Forbidden books, over-serious books and too frivolous books as well, boring books, dazzling books which shine out at random and close their temple doors behind the entranced child . . . The very randomness of reading is noble. Every book, initially ill-absorbed, is a conquest. Its jungle of ideas and words will open out, one day, on to a calm and friendly landscape.

Twenty-six years ago, a long and murderous war called women to fill the place of the men who were fighting or sacrificed. They held it by the physical and moral effort which is well-known and of which they did not believe themselves capable. Since then woman has not thought, has refused to think, that a day might come when she might be asked to seek her full stature in home and hearth. Gallant, often ambitious, having lost the habit of idleness and modesty, women have no longer been tempted by obscure goals and have turned away from their ancient mission: to organize and distribute a homely happiness.

The great change for women a quarter of a century ago was to adopt a mode of existence where, initially, everything was injurious to her. Later she had need of no motto save that of Fouquet. But she had to adapt herself to every hasty apprentice-

ship, accept the atmosphere of the factory, get used to cloak-
rooms, refectories, the hubbub of communal labour, the hostility
of fellow-workers, the unfeelingness of administration. But just
admire what she made of herself in so few years! Seasoned she
certainly is. But she no longer has any acquaintance with labor-
ious solitude and silence. To work in a shift, if not in a crowd,
is a compelling habit and the female worker may complain of
it but does not dream of escaping it. Edgar Allen Poe never
wrote a sequel to *The Man of the Crowds*. The communal work
imposed by the epoch has guided woman to communal leisure
and pleasure and she has demanded them. The factory overall
leads to two identical plus-fours, two twin pullovers, and two
seats on a tandem.

Rivals in work, conniving in pleasure: it must be admitted
that this is a destructive life for a woman. The hum of a factory,
the echoing of gangways, the harpsichord of typewriters – it is
certain that to the sound of this ungrateful music an active
woman overdoes it. But she would not think of exhausting herself
were it not for the devouring passion for necessary gain and
emulation. And therein she acquires and augments her worth to
the detriment of her personality.

In which women, which young girls, do we find the charm
that tells of reserve, a pleasant past, modesty, if not in those
whom their profession compels to a busy solitude, untroubled
silence, an interior monologue? I've no need to search very far
for my examples, provided I take them elsewhere than from the
centripetal temples which swallow and standardize feminine
energies. A humble singularity has its attractions, the solitary
worker intrigues us. What! She hasn't got a hair-do like the Roi
Soleil, she uses her room as a workshop, she has little to say?
Why! She's bringing up a child without fuss, prepares the family
meals herself at the cost of what difficulties and diplomacy! We
are amazed, and with good reason.

Such women are obstinate survivors of a quasi-millenary
female species on which pride, city fever, the ambition to succeed
and the problems of living, bend their energies without succeed-
ing in making it disappear. It persists, preserved on French soil
by the admirable women who work in the fields. In the village
it is personified by 'that queer woman who must have been
very good-looking and who does such fine lace-work', by the

schoolmistress who teaches the piano; it also clings to the stones of Paris, like a yellow wallflower at the foot of an old wall; it appears as the daily woman who only comes in the afternoons because she does not want to neglect her own household; the ironer who does her ironing at home, the young woman who does piecework, patching quilts, and who does not wish to leave her husband to lunch alone. . . .

Guardians of these undeserted hearths, I end these lines by saluting you, you for whom your companion's morning departure and evening return constitute the flux and reflux, the vital rhythm, of each day. It was you, young woman of the quilts, who said to me one day, raising your eyes from your beautiful sky-blue work: 'One of the best things about love is just recognizing a man's step when he climbs the stairs. . . .'

It's here already, and too soon, striking fear into women. Never have they been more ill-protected against it, more deprived of all that ensures and regularizes the flow of blood in the veins and keeps the lightly-shod feet warm. They have a proper fear of cold; they list the great winters of the past. I hear the less young speak of a prolonged and terrible wartime winter (1917) which saw them queuing up. They carried away the coal in lots of five or ten kilos in work-bags, small suitcases, straw baskets. . . .

Those who are young and vigorous defy the cold out-of-doors. A girl-messenger, a delivery-boy, the many workers who forsake the metro for the bicycle, catch fewer colds than the sedentary seamstress, typist, clerk, the more so in that the prize for stupidity had been earned, twenty times in twenty years, by the architects of buildings who suppress fire-places.

'I'd very much like to know what you'd put in your fire-place,' grates one of these hare-brained individuals.

To be frank, I know nothing about it. I only know, as do my readers, that, rather than endure hours of physical and mental chill, we should act like Bernard Palissy. An old armchair is sure to burn slowly and steadily. I used to know a Breton set of shelves which would go up very well in smoke. . . . The skeletons of crates, the handles of broken brooms, the empty case that once held a dozen bottles of champagne – let's make faggots of them all. Let's screw up rolls of newspaper with an iron wire, which will burn almost without flaring up. This last tip comes to me from that fine composer, Albert Chantrier, who had it from his hard childhood years. . . .

What would one not throw on to feed the flames, to make a dark hearth yield light, heat and reverie so that, around it, children and animals pressed against our knees may contemplate, in silence, the fire shaking its glowing tresses?

Such a marvel illuminated my village childhood. But abundance did not rule out economy. A virtually peasant existence makes the best use of what does not have to be bought. I cannot hope to be useful to my readers in telling them that balls of corn or oats, moistened just sufficiently, piled in even layers on a wood fire, keep it controlled and prolong its duration. But, having lit and managed all sorts of fires with my own hands, I do advise that, at the moment when a full bucket of these balls flares up in the grate, a dusting with ashes is indicated. And there's a right way of doing that. A judiciously tempered grate restrains its gluttony, sleeps without ever going out, night or day. For four consecutive winters I have had no other form of heating. Gently – and not with great shoves of the poker, which empty and chill the grate – gently you make the ash fall by scratching its belly from underneath, as do the ticklers of fish who poach by hand beneath the unwary trout. . . .

In my part of the world, when it's time to shell and press walnuts, do you think that we throw away the broken shells? They too went on the fire, poured by the basketful on the wood embers and sprinkled with water with the aid of a moistened broom. They were converted into an igneous crust whose warmth lasted from dinner – at half-past six – until the family curfew which struck at nine o'clock. There was nothing, not even the winter prunings of the laurels and the variegated aucubas, which did not contribute to our heating. Cut in autumn, still full of sap, the large-leaved branches crowned a too lively fire which suddenly subsided and crouched down. How clearly I recall the strong, rather hydrocyanic, smell of the laurel crackling in the flames! . . . Suddenly dried, its foliage showered a burst of sparks all over us, me, the dog who loved the fire, the cat in its winter coat.

One of the sparks would always travel through the room further and longer than the others, like a minuscule streak of lightning seeking its goal and its victim. . . . After which I would replace the laurel with branches of pine and thuja so that a premature aroma of Christmas reigned around us. . . .

There is a certain cruelty in evoking here the memories of sumptuous fires, the combustible that one gathered gratuitously for amusement – crackling pine-cone! – at the same time as the last mushrooms and the first chestnuts. My lady readers will not be slow to point out that they have neither corn-balls, nutshells nor logs, nor that beautiful anthracite which gleams when it fractures. If it consoles you, dear ladies, you may be sure that in reviving those moments of security, abundance, youth, those winters when the present tragedy of cold was no more than a nipping diversion, you may be sure that I am causing myself as much distress as you.

Someone reads out aloud, wishing to make us laugh, a gastronomic recipe of other days, I mean of 1939: 'Take eight or ten eggs. . . .' 'From whom?' asks a young girl who does not laugh.

She is a young girl of our times, approaching adolescence, slight, sarcastic, with an eye for everything. She sees our life, and hers. Equipped with her small camp-stool, her basket, a piece of knitting and a schoolbook, her bobby-socks rolled over her ankles, she goes to queue, outside school hours. Whatever she thinks or covets while she marks time or picks up a stitch outside a big grocer's, she takes care not to inform us. But with a single word she has just shown us that she has her own ideas about the property of others, on what is permitted or prohibited: 'You *take* eight eggs. . . .'

She knows that eight eggs are not to be bought anywhere. Her nostrils, her sharp look, are those of an alert fox-cub. She seems to aim at some dream hen-roost, and at the hen as well as the egg. But like many children she has admirable self-control. She buckles the belt of her waterproof, pockets her sheets of coupons, leaves her mother to whine, and goes forth to win a slice of cheese, a kilo of chestnuts and some Brussels sprouts. After all, all these, properly cooked, make an excellent dish.

France is full of reasonable children, precociously mature, patient and reserved enough to bring the tears to your eyes. Some control their growing appetites, organize each weekend as a regular food spree, in an economic and *gourmand* spirit. I know a keen fifteen-year-old scout who educates his mother in this wise :

'What have you got before you?' he declaims. 'You've got papa, Marguerite and me : holes. During the first few days of the week, don't bother about the holes. Stuff them with vegetables, with the thick soup that stands up by itself, with *portugaises*, baked potatoes, a piece of fish if you like. Let us complain, papa and me. But then, at the end of the week, let's feel it go down, your roast or your boiled beef! None of your lacework beefsteak, none of that ham you can see through, no sausage cut as thin as honesty flowers! And what's left of the meat as balls with sharp sauce, or hashed up with onion sauce, for Sunday morning! And a tart from the baker, that's the idea! Starting on Sunday evening, transformation scene : a cup of cocoa with water to go to bed with, after the cinema. And I say, keep a bit of the onion sauce, if you can, to improve Monday's potatoes.'

The mother of this victualler protests on grounds of hygiene and regular, if insubstantial, meals. She is wrong. Her glowing-eyed scout, already responsible for the commissariat of a band of little boys, understands that rhythm and contrast satisfy both the idea of mortification and that of reward.

A village childhood and youth have preserved me from one of the town-dweller's requirements, that for meat, revered and ineluctable meat, monotonous centre of every Parisian gathering. A plateful of white cheese, well-peppered, is lunch enough for me, as is a pumpkin pie or leeks *au gratin*. The hollowed tomato, the stout onion, the marrow stuffed with fat or lean, rival the minute steak. But in the Midi I've often been astonished to see holidaying Parisians reject the magnificent Provençal vegetables : peppers, tomatoes, the glossy aubergine, sweet onions. So, it seems, the Hindus deprived of their rice reject wheat. My 'furriners' yearned after their traditional beefsteak and fried potatoes.

French families take a great stand on principle when confronted with something new, and therefore suspect : 'My mother couldn't stand game. . . . My sisters are like me, you'd have to make it really worth our while to swallow the skin on boiled milk. . . . My son takes after his father, he'd sooner die than eat a stewed rabbit!' Sated nibblers, incurious gourmands who pick at your food as long as you can choose, are you now prepared to eat what's going, including the green vegetables despised by the stronger sex? I wish you joy.

Does this mean that the manual labourer can compensate for his muscular exertions during this hard passage, this long intermission, with the help of a plateful of noodles or a *gratinée*? I'm not so stupid as to think so, nor to belittle your absence, coffee, black and bitter tonic which stimulates the cerebral activities of the paper scribblers, nor to remain unmoved by the grill where a red slice of beef splutters. . . .

While I'm waiting, I shall continue to fill the little pot with water to boil chestnuts. Admirable white flesh of the brown chestnut, providential complement of diminished meals! You are the delicate bread brought by this cold season, sparse in lentils and dried haricot beans; you abound when all else becomes scarce, when the earth closes. I take leave to mention that the boiled chestnut – the water for boiling must be salted – peeled, cleaned of its second skin and all its little septa, crushed into a smooth paste with caster sugar, and finally compressed into little cakes in a clean napkin, is a healthy and simple treat, a complete dessert if you serve it with some red jam. A bit filling? Not a bit! For you will have taken the trouble to open hard by a bottle of sparkling cider or some good, rather sweet, white wine.

2

In the morning men and women rush off, some to work, others towards the difficulties of victualling. It is still so much night, so little morning, when the six official strokes of four o'clock strike at the Bibliothèque nationale, that every now and again the small beacon of a pocket torch flashes in the dark. 'But as you make up in the afternoon what you lose in the morning . . .' That's all very well, but it's colder at four in the morning than at six. The early working hours are dark. And anyone with any tendency to hibernation shakes off his pre-dawn sluggishness with difficulty.

Man endures the night like a plant. Not every bird is an early riser. One knows that there are flowers which bloom nocturnally. The white sand-lily, between midnight and three in the morning, becomes barely recognizable as it opens wide, stretches its stamens like claws, and casts its nets of perfume all around. The human species is also prolific in night-birds persuaded by pleasure to delay their retiring, but no instinct incites them to leave their beds in the middle of the night. The strain imposed daily by double summer-time on workers of both sexes is considerable. Let us hope that it will not last the whole winter.

Even children refuse to make up in the evening for the two hours they have been cheated of in the morning. Sleep, that tutelary syncope, functions outwith the bounds of human decisions and takes hold of children again when they are already up, dressed and washed. Heads bowed, they return to the unfinished dream, curl up after their fashion which is also, toward the end of the night, that of the cat rolled up like a turban, the strutting pigeon, the fern's crozier, the quivering petals of the anemone.

As I am past the age of long slumber and regular waking hours, I am well placed to see the pricking of the little pocket torches between six and seven in the morning. They move rapidly, without stopping, grow bigger; some, having reached the Bourse, opt for the Rue du Quatre-Septembre; others turn off into the Rue des Petits-Champs. The remainder dive beneath the arcades of the Palais-Royal. Their clear roundness, directed down towards the pavement, encircles the feet of the torch-bearer with a halo. So many transparent stockings, so many openwork slippers ! . . . The tulle stocking and thin shoe demonstrate female determination to persist with an expensive fashion which is neither reasonable nor seasonable.

I am old enough to have known, in my childhood, well-to-do old *bourgeoises* and provincial chatelaines settled firmly in their chimney-corners by age, like an armchair or a pair of fire-dogs. They used to show my mother the relics of their youth : a flowered dress, a Malines veil, an over-shawl pierced and repierced with openings, encrusted with lace; a nuptial night-dress, the stockings for ancient balls : 'Weigh them !' they would say proudly. They laid in Sido's hand two silk stockings, heavy and cold as a pair of little snakes.

Natural silk or not, a pair of stockings today uses eight to ten grammes of textile material. A frail protection, ten grammes, against frost, against rain and storm, against the staircases of the metro and thin soles. The remarkable thing is that women suffer without yielding, and that only the comfortable and sensible wear woollen stockings. And even then they pay dearly for this privilege, which does not extend to the possession of footwear suitable for such voluminous stockings.

'Since I've had really warm thick stockings,' confides one of these irresponsibles, 'I've got chilblains! Can you understand such a thing?'

And she shows me chilblains brought about by pressure, the chilblain like a cushion above the heel – the worst – the chaplet of chilblains on the poor humped toes.

Some women, unmarried workers or widows without children, have asked me to suggest to them a way of employing their leisure hours.

'Get us', writes one, 'away from our "spick and span" houses and from the cinema! Is it really credible that our minute dwelling needs so much looking after, or that we neglect it during the week? To go out is just another burden. . . .'

I rather fear that my tired young working women may make a face at the advice I am going to give them. But in the cold season, with the animal regulation of life slowed down, economy and hygiene are presently in accord with me in saying: sleep. The countryside is far away, the day short. You have the luck – or the bitterness – to live alone? Sleep. Saturdays or Sundays – meal over and the household jobs done, sleep. A hot water bottle at your feet, the window half-open to the dry cold or the sharp shower, let yourself go. . . .

The worst that can happen to you is not to wake up until the following morning at the usual time (so much the better for the ration coupons!), relaxed, somewhat dazed, body lightened, fit to crack your joints and exclaim, like a small girl I know:

'It's incredible how much I've grown last night!'

I am writing in a thick obscure dawn. It is seven o'clock in the morning if I can trust my clock – but I don't trust it. In the street the little pocket-lamps follow their general post. An umbrella of light approaches, the handle of which divides into two slender legs, terminates in two open pointed shoes. When did those two graceful legs get up? When will they take their rest?

Lightly they cross the steps of the Passage du Perron. Be of good heart! The hour is so ambiguous that I hesitate from the height of my window, between saying 'Good morning' or 'Good night. . . .'

Silence . . . It is not mere circumspection that keeps mouths closed. One doesn't stop out of doors to gossip in December. The shops allow hardly any coupon-fiddling, now, since there aren't any more coupons. The metro, which goes so fast, is not a place for confidences. There's certainly the 'tea-room' where they serve you with chocolate made with water which is nevertheless excellent, relaxes the nerves and loosens tongues. Lukewarm, a tinkling of spoons and cups, a thread of vapour at the spout of each teapot, poeticized by the aroma of chocolate and coffee, it's thus that, having avoided it for half a century, I bring myself to discover that the 'tea-room' is a charming place. Even the sound of voices improves it. The fact is that we have hardly any occasion now to hear the human voice brought to the pitch of frivolous sound. The children play an octave lower down. Noisy imprudent youth, berated, is on its guard, the men have said 'Ssh!' to their wives and the women have taken the men to task: 'You try to hold your tongue to begin with!'

At the restaurant we lunch in an undertone, we dine mouth to ear. It took neither more nor less to make us realize, astonished, that the sound of the human voice is a tonic for us, that conversation forms part of our moral hygiene, and that the presence of a fellow-creature, however unwonted, however tiresome, often deserves that we should treat her with the consideration she merits.

'I want to say something to someone!' exclaims, in *Pelléas et Mélisande*, the trembling child who struggles in a silence darkened by forbidden love. Nowadays we all have something to say to someone and something to keep quiet about. How to resist what, out of false shame, we deny, how to resist the need to be effusive? What, if not effusive, is my neighbour's reply when I seek some information: 'Come in, then, you can't tell me that on the doorstep!' Night fallen, and the thick old door shut, that is when our narrow building – fronted with three windows – comes soundlessly to life.

From her room on the fourth floor a solitary woman descends

for a rendezvous in another room where another woman knits. Sometimes the first floor visits the mezzanine, the fourth comes down to the first. . . . I imagine that much the same goes on in many other houses and it seems quite natural that economy in heating, lighting and housing should impose customs in themselves courteous and pleasant.

Economy, maybe. But you may be sure that sociability is imperative, even though it disguises itself and shelters timidly behind some banal pretext which deceives no one. Outside, the pitch-dark night and its dangers press on the portals of a dwelling that has survived wars and revolutions. But the very thickness of the outer shadow creates in the hearts of its denizens an idea of security, of poetic liberty. My personal lyricism is not so dulled as not to respond to the 'Good evening' of whoever climbs or descends the glacial staircase. I have known, not merely imagined, the spirit of the old *veillées* of other days.* It borrowed the aspects of some midnight child, some old woman with curled silvery hair, blinded by her large spectacles; it swung a lantern shaped like a pepper-pot tower. Just as here, a cat followed it, pursuing a ball of wool which bounded down the steps.

In Puisaye, in Forterre – oh, give us back those regional names! – the spirit of the *veillées* used to sit in the middle of a vast kitchen studded with copper implements, and reel off hanks of yarn. In Franche-Comté, it shelled walnuts and hazels, it tied the tart crab-apples into bunches and it sang. In Limousin, it stuffed itself eating balls of firm forcemeat and cleared its gullet with a good drop of wine. On the Millevaches plateau, a desert cloaked with red heather, it brought a good woolly sheep, feet tied, in whose fleece the company would keep its feet warm. . . .

Here the spirit of the *veillées* is a poor one. It hasn't even a footwarmer, for where would it find the embers? It's not gossipy, to begin with. It is banal, from lack of boldness. It skims the ground, recounts the small events of our time, issues figures and names of commodities, gives the recipe for a dish that can be made 'with three times nothing'. . . .

'I tried it,' replies one woman slyly, 'but I wasn't successful because I'd only put in one times nothing!'

The women laugh. If any men are there they don't make much

---

* *veillée*: a neighbourly country evening gathering, particularly in winter.

noise, so they may be forgotten a little, the better to enjoy an hour which resembles no other. The spirit, encouraged, raises its voice, flutters hither and thither above the ground. It depicts what it has seen : a forest, a family, the war, a journey; it waits, it fishes for replies, it evokes memories. One insignificant-looking little woman has been to the other side of the earth. Another has hardly ever left Paris and proves richer in anecdotes than the pilgrim; a third is amused at our astonishment when she relates how, before managing a grocery, she used to train saddle-horses. . . .

All the fine, imaginary, small coin of human life dances, changes, gleams, clinks. . . . The spirit of the *veillées* restores that which had been dying, for years, beneath the coarse dirty speech, the drunken laughter, the slack slang, the bastard neologism, general listlessness. Let us but accord it the support of curiosity and disinterestedness, and we shall see it well on the way to reviving conversation.

The front-door bell is working again. 'Now I'm going to fix your telephone.'

The professor from the Conservatoire never makes a promise that he does not keep. Seated on the ground tailor-wise, he extracts from his pockets a simplified set of tools, sets to work, dismantles, reassembles, screws and unscrews. There in front of me is the complete type of conscientious virtuoso handyman.

'They're pretty, those little tools with black handles. Hand me one. Where did you get them from, Wague?'

'These? They're treasures! It's a little set of tools that the workers at Bréguet's used to make themselves, for doing their job. Look at that hexagonal handle, in real ebony. And the little copper sleeve which connects the handle to the steel gouge. It's love for the job which produced all that.'

A handyman is rarely not given to poetry. The whole of France is addicted to handiwork. Only an inventiveness and a private skill could have created the small cold chisel I found one day, with a handle of fluted copper, easy in the hand, engraved with arabesques, honoured with decorations like a Chinese curio. Its owner, who must also have been its maker, must have missed it.

Skilful, jack-of-all-trades, indiscreet, artistic, industrious, modest at heart, boastful on the surface . . . when I paint the portrait of the typical handyman, I paint that of the Frenchman. In France we are impelled by the desire to meddle with what is not our affair; my greatest pleasures are of this type. A small cyclist delivery-boy mended the useless clock in my kitchen. If, in the street, a strap of my sandal – for hard times go with soft leather – should happen to break, a passer-by, two passers-by, seek to help me: 'Wait,' says one, 'I just happen to have . . .' In fact, he just happens to have, in a small folded paper, five or six shoe-nails.

Another has in his wallet a piece of webbing and knows how to make a nail-wrench out of a key-handle. What are they doing in these town-dwellers' pockets – the shoe-nails, the strap, a razor-blade nicely fitted like a shoemaker's knife into the end of a clothes-peg? Mystery, odd-jobbery, and an element of childishness to crown all. Luc-Albert Moreau is a dream of a handyman, does carpentry, plans and plants his garden, solders, nails, sweep chimneys, for his leisure from painting and his innate inclinations have for long been set in the best school, which is that of the peasant.

My handyman-friend works at my feet, better and no noisier than myself. Thanks to him the porcelain horse of 1830 regains its limbs. Not a single drop of glue sullies the low table that serves as a work-bench. In fact, deprived of a workshop and having to make do with a table-end, a handyman acquires a dexterity and modesty of execution which contrast with the emphasis of the professional. He operates without debris, planes without shavings, paints without stains, to avoid being told off by his wife or admonished by his offspring. . . .

'Can you sew, Wague?'

'Like an angel.'

'Look at my divan-cover, it's all worn there. . . . It's a pretty enough old material, but faded. You wouldn't care to mend it for me?'

I meant it as a joke; but my artisan examines the damage very seriously. It was marvellous afterwards to see him cut out a square of black adhesive material – scissors and fabric from his own store – heat the material over the light bulb, separate the threads of the tissue, and slip the dressing under the flowered material. . . .

'A makeshift repair,' he says offhandedly.

All handymen! Henceforth the pursuit has its proper place in our conduct and its letters patent in the language. It seems that the *bricole** was a military machine, before we so designated an activity which is used to remedy the calamities of peace, to make something out of almost nothing.

The lake in the Palais-Royal has been empty for months. Max, who is twelve this year, is forced to go as far as the Tuileries – so he told me with annoyance this morning – to try out his 'boat that goes'. It's a curious object, consisting entirely of two sardine-tins, two wooden reels, a driving-shaft and a brake of iron wire; two rubber bands twisted under the keel act as propellors when they unwind. I ask for an explanation of how the toy works.

'It's not a toy, it's a model,' says Max with irritation.

'A model made by whom?'

'Me, of course. I knocked it up out of odds and ends.'

My naval constructor is called Max at present. Max who? Just wait. Let's all wait. Maybe he'll be called something like Max Niepce or Max Lumière. . . . Those are names of handymen of genius.

Midnight mass at five in the afternoon . . . Children, you won't have had your young vigil in the expectation of a luminous midnight. You won't have had the departure and return with lanterns. You will have been satisfied with the night in the church, burning bushes, flowers dedicated to Jesus, evergreens which mingle with the incense the aromas of box, laurel and fir. It sufficed to enchant your sensibility, which is responsive to every stimulus. What you have had will ensure that your memories, later on, will tell you of a Parisian midnight that sounded five strokes.

Paris is too dark for you to be allowed to stumble about in it, you children who, for one night in the year, haunt the streets and go to bed late. I loved meeting you during this past year under the lights – already dimmed – at the moment when you were returning from a mass, a fête held under the branches of a tree. You were the luminous signposts on my journey for, in passing, you threw me the glitter of some spangled toy – a

* *bricoleur*: handyman.

walnut, a bunch of grapes, an apple of spun and gilded glass, a tinfoil crown – children, our future, our last treasure. . . .

Christmas nights in the country were no more opaque; half a century ago no one bothered to light the streets of my village other than by the aid of large lanterns suspended from the fist by a ring, reinforced by bars. The divergent shadow of these bars still sways in my memory, still progresses at my side, stripes the walls, the dresses of the peasant women, wavers over the dog's back.

For the dog – whether its name was Domino, Patasson, Finaud or Lisette – the dog used to accompany us to Midnight Mass in memory of a night when the ox and the ass received the gift of speech. He sat in our pew of notables, between Sido my mother and her daughter, without evincing any surprise, listening to the hyms and the harmonium. In the church of my childhood no one has repaired the steeple that was struck by lightning some two centuries ago. But the village prefers it as it is – and so do I.

Returning from Midnight Mass . . . Here I shall stop short if my lady readers were expecting me to record the annals of a day and a night unparalleled in the year. Sido, my mother, my never sufficiently nor sufficiently well loved, already saw with terror the growing emptiness of her maternal hands, her barns. So we took care not to ask for what she would not have been able to give us. It is to our credit as children and adolescents that no progeny less grasping than ourselves could have been found. The two boys were happy enough if they had the wherewithal to buy a butterfly-net, two display cases and some long brass pins, nets to fish for crayfish. I was the youngest, yet Sido put a strange trust in me. Will you laugh at me, reader, if I confess that for my seventh Christmas I asked for the complete plays of Labiche . . . and got them?

The following year I was more difficult. I wanted crystal balls and great scintillating tear-drops like those that hung beneath the chandeliers of a nearby château. I gave those up.

But, recollecting this dry-eyed renunciation, you may well believe that on the day when my daughter, at the age of seven, asked at Christmas for corduroy trousers 'like the men who work on the railway-line', she got not only the corduroy breeches but also the red cummerbund, the woollen belt with fringes at each end which goes thrice round the loins.

Parents cannot be too conscious of the fact that, in children, the avowal of a ritual covetous desire is the flower of a long dream, the single phrase which sums up a novel. When a little boy plied with questions resolves to say: 'For New Year I'd like a ruler, some green oil-cloth, and a wire to cut butter . . .', I could wish, parents, that you did not crush with humiliating raillery a dream with its special privacy and romanticism. Give the oil-cloth, the ruler and the wire to cut butter – your dairy-man hardly uses it now, anyway – and on top of that, try when you give them to adopt a shrewd knowledgeable air. It will do a lot for you.

You may find it strange that my childhood Christmases – down there they say '*Nouël*' – lacked the fresh-cut fir tree, the sugared fruits and little lights. But don't feel too sorry for me, our evening of the twenty-fourth was none the less a night of celebration in our quiet way. It was very rare for Sido not to to have found in the garden – surviving full-blown beneath the snow – the flowers of the hellebore which we call Christmas rose. In a bouquet at the centre of the table, their oval closed buds, assailed by the heat of the splendid fire, opened in mechanical fits and starts which alarmed the cats and for which I was as much on the *qui vive* as they were. We had neither black pudding nor white pudding nor turkey with chestnuts, but only the chestnuts, boiled and roasted, and Sido's *chef d'oeuvre*, a blancmange studded with three kinds of raisins – Smyrna, Malaga, Corinth – and stuffed with preserved melon, slivers of citron and small dices of orange.

Then, as we were permitted to stay up, the feast continued as a calm watch-night to the accompaniment of whisperings of rustled newspapers, of turned pages, of the fire on which we'd throw some green prunings and a handful of coarse salt which crackled and flamed green on the embers. . . .

What, no more than that? No, nothing. None of us desired anything further, or complained of having too little. The howling winter assailed the shutters. The great copper kettle, seated in the ashes, and the clay hot water bottles it was going to fill, promised warm beds in cold rooms. . . .

'Mummy, I don't want to go to bed! I want to watch all night, every night! . . .'

'As you wish, Minet-Chéri. . . . There's the dawn. You see, the snow's turning blue between the slats of the shutters. Can't you hear the cocks crowing?'

I imagined I was still watching. . . . But in fact, surprised by the late hour, I was already asleep, head on my folded arms, my plaits alongside my cheeks like two guardian snakes. . . .

3

It's cold. You can read those two f's* in the double puff of breath leaving the mouths. They are two words that can be seen at a distance. If a lucky minority is able to keep warm it obeys the rule, it cannot disown the thought of the cold, of its reality, of concern for those who suffer from the cold.

The presence of the dry cold penetrates everywhere. It has soiled the snow, pure these several hours. When dawn lightens the sky a little at nine o'clock, the curtains are drawn at the windows and faces ask: 'Has the wind changed at last? Shall we at last see the onrush of those impetuous children of the West – blue skies, rain, a breath bearing the scent of rain-soaked earth, changing light, the laughing peal of thunder which heralds February?'

But the north and east winds are still masters of the sky, miserly of their humidity. When, then, shall I see the children playing without coats under my window, in the garden that was once royal? For many days now the pigeons have not trodden the loose earth or opened wide their wings to the benediction of the shower. Water fascinates birds, frost deadens them. In this ancient quadrangular edifice we depend somewhat on each other, in co-operative fashion. It's cold here – it's colder than last year because the building on the right and the building on the left, identical twins joined to the one I occupy, are also empty of coal and warmth. The attics of the Palais-Royal get their light through their slightly sloping roofs, through the square eye of the *tabatières*.** Under the slates live modest employees, solitary

* *Fait froid.*
** Literally 'snuffboxes' = hinged skylights.

women workers. No fireplaces in these attics, where gas is not municipal, where electricity retreats before the shade of Richelieu. The petrol or alcohol stove, the paraffin lamp, were till now the modest flames of many a silent small existence. But petrol, alcohol and paraffin are far removed from us.

It's cold. . . . It's this sovereign cold which has obtained from women what ordinary commonsense had demanded in vain. They haven't yet got as far as the most effectively protective gaiters : newspapers fixed round the legs by string gartering. I think they will come to it, to judge by an elderly streetwalker whose majestic shadow I have watched for years, promenading beneath the arcades of our secular cloister. In winter she would lean against the closed gates to do up the strings of her printed gaiters. The soldiers of the Great War did much the same, shod with pieces of carpeting, packing paper and corrugated card-board. . . .

While awaiting these paper leggings, the women stuff thick woollen stockings into their small shoes. I've already mentioned the damage inflicted by this confused hygiene; one has never seen so many chilblains and the men, provided by their wives with good knitted socks, are no more spared than their spouses. A young secretary I know goes to work every morning at nine o'clock. Like the little Siren of Hans Andersen's story, every step costs her acute pain for she has a chilblain on each toe. While she types, telephones, conscientiously takes shorthand, does she sing a song of Frehel's from the time when Frehel resembled a slender and ravishing wild animal, and the chilblain, that torment, was classed as a comic diversion :

> *J'adorais sa figure,*
> *Son p'tit nez, vrai bijou,*
> *Avec une engelure*
> *Au bout.*

From the comic we turn to the dramatic, and from leather to cork. Dr Jaworski makes his rounds on the icy roads from patient to patient without being able to buy a pair of snow-boots. Jean Marais, creator of *Les Parents terribles*, anxiously notes the gaping of his snow-boots. . . . Both, dumb with envy, have wit-nessed the entrance of another of my friends, just returned from

his Normandy province in boots soled with wood, feet turned
up, wide and fur-lined. But as this last prides himself on his
elegance as much as he cares for his comfort, he has varnished his
sabots.

These lines I write – and I am very sorry for this – will bring
no relief to the women who write to me, demanding action
against the cold, confiding that it reduces them to tears. My only
resort against it, and it has been my enemy too, has been to go
barefooted in all seasons since the age of twelve.

Going further back – much further – I recall that my mother
used to prepare in summer, and keep in reserve in case any of
her children should develop those open chilblains we used to
call 'chaps', a bottle of rose vinegar – petals of red roses infused
for a month in strong vinegar, all clarified through filter-paper.
The pungent subtle odour of this remedy I have still not forgotten, though I have never suffered from chilblains. But I knew
how to deceive, to extend an index finger, proffer a bare toe, beg
for the fragrant compress which I would suck in secret for its
double taste of vinegar and roses. . . .

It's cold. A happy memory is a poor protection against the
cold. However, some shift took place in the atmosphere during
last night. The blue needle of the barometer has glided two
degrees towards the left, attracted by the promising word 'variable'. Tomorrow morning we shall peep out again through the
curtains, will once more study the course of the clouds and the
direction of the rare smoke-puffs which plume the roofs, and
we'll talk among ourselves in a hopeful and anxious tone, we'll
discuss the temperature once again: 'It's going to change.
Tomorrow, with the moon, or after the moon. It will change
because inevitably, mercifully, it must change. . . .'

To bed! To bed! Let those whose age or health or enforced
inactivity forbid them to seek a remedy for the cold in running
or energetic gesticulation have recourse to bed! To bed, children
of an unheated house!

Even if the icy spell recedes today it may return between now
and March and we are well aware, in the absence of fuel, that
there is no question of improving the state of affairs and the
temperature. Our aim must be to reach the end of the winter by
adopting the tactics of the poor. The tactics of the poor are

often at odds with the hygiene of the rich, the rich who – more or less – we used to be; for we had freely at our disposal taps and handles which supplied heat as gas, as liquid, heat as expanded air. We also possessed heat in dancing flames, in light wool, in pink fat, in lard, in a juicy side of ham, in butter of various kinds: 'I've a weakness for Charentais butter! – Ah! The Isigny is pretty good too. . . .'

All this was the same vital felicity – warmth. Easily kept at a distance, the cold stopped at our threshold, our windowpanes. Today it is our greatest danger, a punishment for the reckless fools we are. What! No double glazing in our windows? No solid shutters? No. Does this icy blast penetrate into the kitchen via the outside larder? Yes. 'It's always been like that,' answer our negligence, our routine, our false progress. The Eskimo's snow-house, that has no draughts. What! None of our doors close? The light of your lamp filters the length of your door if you read at night, friend. The concierge slips a folded newspaper under the landing door without opening it.

And the style of these so-called winter clothes! These little skirts for us, those little child's underpants beneath men's trousers! Don't forget your knitted gloves if you go out, madame! But don't be surprised, if you come back with a frost-bitten ear if you go bareheaded, risking erysipelas. Was it not you, madame, who used to take skiing lessons on the mountainside, hair blowing in the wind, ears insensible, beside a native instructor wisely bundled into a rabbit-skin bonnet from the nape of the neck to the eyebrows? It was you who entered a drugstore, the hem of your skirt brushing your knee, to ask for 'something for chapped skin'. . . .

'Is it for your hands?' asked the white-coated dispenser.

Somewhat embarrassed, but frankly, you replied:

'No, it's for my thighs. . . .'

So we are all mortified, justly or otherwise, dismayed before the images, themselves glacial, of what we used to call 'gracious living'. Under-floor heating, the air-conditioned apartment, the garbage-disposer, the water at 80°, the lift, the vacuum-cleaner, so many toys for lazy and exigent adults! And now here we are at a crossing crowded by queuing women, petrified and dumb with cold. Cold and war have given their message: it is that, destitute of the appliances which human wizardry has deserted, we may well envy our fellow who, in periods of cataclysmal cold, bent down, gathered the dead wood, and made a flame spurt forth.

But in practice, what is to be done? How to safeguard the children? If they seem less sensitive to the biting cold it's because they think of it less, they cease to realize it as soon as there's no more snowballing or skating. Thank God, they do not, before adolescence, relate suffering to its causes. One could wish, at this time, that a gesture – no matter whence its origin – might offer to every child a kingdom for ever safe from harm.

'Run around the flat, stir yourselves, play about!' says the fireless mother to her children. Another counsels: 'Rub that furniture for me and see that it shines!' Lessons in eurhythmics and dancing are also palliatives. But a child, several children, cannot dance all day and I have still in my mind a woman's remark: 'I teach them quiet games; when they run they get too hungry.' Too hungry . . . not warm enough. Between horrid excess and hateful lack, is there no place for the children in the midst of a temperate climate?

I should very much like to offer my readers something other than recriminations. But I am at a loss for domestic recipes and wizardries. To whoever works sitting down, to whoever writes, to whoever makes the short movements of the needle, hammers at the typewriter, handles a fountain-pen or the engraver's needle, I say: 'See that you're accompanied by a hot water bottle, emptied and refilled as required. Sometimes it can be under the rug that covers your feet, sometimes against your stomach like a good dog, sometimes under your hands or behind your loins. It's not as good as a radiator, but it comes to the aid of many regions where life flows unevenly. And if you have two rubber bottles available, then it's a holiday for the heart and all the senses.

To all those who currently possess a bathroom without a bath, a mean-spirited geyser, to women whose work expels them from the house before broad daylight, I venture to advise something that's successful for early rising at any season: however tired you may be, shake it off at night to make a scrupulous toilet. You will profit thereby in being warm when you go to bed, sleep more deeply, feel well, snuggle into your blankets, and sleep longer in the morning. What goes for the grown-ups is true for the little ones, too.

And now I stand by what I say : to bed, to bed, those whose work or whose age – whether three years or seventy – exempts them from duties out-of-doors, from any work save sedentary tasks. To bed with your picture-book or your sewing or writing. To bed, while the pioneers – your sons or your parents – brave the risks of an expedition through the generally unvictualled shops.

Twilight and the thermometer descend; slip between the flimsy bedcover and the counterpane a spread-out newspaper or some packing paper; leave room for the cat, if there is a cat, and its powerful electricity against your flank, for the hot water bottle *near* your feet and not stuck to your soles.

It will soon be six in the evening : to bed !

'For when it's raining,' said a small girl, 'I'd like to make something that I could hold over my head, like a piece of paper or some material or a small board. . . . I'd fix it at the end of two little sticks, or one stick even . . . it would be so convenient. . . .'

Thus, in all ingenuousness, she reinvented the umbrella. If I may believe some of my correspondents, our epoch is about to reinvent, from its need to read, the book-renting business.

Given to haste and the ease of superficial living, happy epochs betray the written word. A flabby felicity always excels at burning the hours, hurrying them on to demonstrate how void, vain and flying they are. A tardy clear-sightedness restores their importance and their essence to poignant memories, reduces the pleasures we derive from sounds and fleeting images to their real worth. Whatever is installed in us by the eye, whatever stimulates our thought, the spirit of comprehension and contradiction, by means of the printed word, is worth its weight in gold; is it not the best possible augury that the lost generations, searching for their way, should rediscover that reading is a vital necessity?

It's not just a matter of the appetite, as normal and as renascent as the need to eat, which devours new books in the order of their appearance and succession. 'Never,' say my neighbour, a large bookseller, 'never have we sold many classics.' So should our country despise romantic fiction, the so-called detective story which, its riddle read, no one can reread or enjoy? That would be too much to hope for, would be premature.

But we may believe that a very sure instinct inclines a sorely chastened people, ignorant of its future condition, to interrogate its past, to desire an acquaintance with the foundations which assured its greatness and may yet be accountable for its future. Three thousand copies of Montaigne are sold each month. Dare we assert that the French reader gives his most solid support to facile authors?

Love of reading leads to love of books. If our curiosity and our poverty come together to revive reading-rooms, they must also restore the respect due to books. The 'reading-room' was a sort of tobacconist's shop, 'a business suitable for a single lady'. Such a woman, unlucky but pleasant withal, used to make friends of her subscribers. Balzac gave the beautiful Antonia Chocardelle a reading-room. Solitary in fact, at a loose end, how many lonely women used to exploit, without genuine liking, a business traditionally looked down upon.

To read is, according to the book and the reader, rapture, an honour, the service rendered to a cult, a patient pilgrimage through the writer and ourselves. It will not be an easy matter to inculcate respect for the perishable book, for short-lived paper. It will only come if it is cultivated, that reader's conscience which consists of not scratching one's head over the pages, of refraining from eating while reading, from turning down the pages. . . . The human species never has sufficient shame when it comes to concealing the traces of its stopping-places. A horrid little toothless pocket-comb fell out of one book that I bought on the *quais*. Similarly, I nearly gave up eating chocolate-bars from having once caught my teeth on a trouser-button enveloped in the goo. . . .

A sincere affection being characterized by tact, I note that the young people who read in the metro apply a loose dust-cover to a newly-bought book and deal with its uncut pages. A fair number of these careful readers would be on the way to becoming bibliophiles, were it not for their inadequate means. To possess in his aristocratic form the author of one's choice, clothed in a contemporary binding, to cherish, while reading, the era evoked by its typography and format, these are pleasures which chance and ingenuity may render accessible. Beside the period 'originals', impregnable within their signed binding, the re-bound bargain book does not – yet – cost more than a new book and withstands time better.

The amateur's pleasure is not obsessional. I don't, for my part, know the first thing about the delights of some 'faulty edition' which is worth a fortune, of some 'Jansenist' binding, severe and sleek as lacquer, of some multi-coloured 'marbling', which their owner half opens with the tips of his fingers and keeps jealously behind glass. Does it follow that I profess disdain for signed bindings? I am not so boorish to ignore, to speak only of the past, the names of Padeloup, Derome and Simier.

To scorn the wisdom which dissuades us from contemplating what we cannot have, I advise the young friends of a renascent cult to bring a curious eye to bear on every book, to become informed, albeit platonically, in the art of adorning and preserving the written work. Their vocabulary will thereby become enriched with typical, ancient, exclusive words such as *pontuseaux, coiffe, tranchefile. . . .**

Do you expect me to explain these in ordinary language? No. You can look them up. You'll find them. By following with a finger, on some worn but solid binding, *le dos à nerfs, la roulette, la dentelle, les filets, le décor à froid,*** you will spell out every avenue, every effort of an art which enables the fragile sheets, the obliterable impressions to reach, readers, your grateful hands.

They are queuing up, too. . . .

Who? Why, the animals. I am not afraid, in speaking of them, of appearing to abandon myself to an inopportune sensibility. I can rely on the pity that Paris feels towards the creatures which the exodus, our disarray, and our changed conditions of existence have reduced to a miserable fate. I know Paris when happy too well to mistrust Paris when unhappy, and the friendship it devotes to that which enlivens and excites it in all seasons: its birds, its stray animals. It is these who are queuing up, expecting from us the licence to live, and expecting it only from us.

There is no unseasonable pity, pity is never exclusive. The interest we display towards the suffering may vacillate but is never narrow. The elderly woman who puts down some scraps for the benefit of the cats sheltering within the walls of the Bibliothèque Nationale wears on her face the expression of a pure and universal gentleness, reduced to means bordering on indigence. One of

---

*
** Technical expressions in book binding,

my neighbours, who must often find her sign, *Alimentation générale*, particularly ironic, has collected some four-footed friends; but she is no unkinder to the clients who walk on two legs and live on very little.

She is no exception, and our *arrondissement* is no different from other *arrondissements*. May the future reward her, this deserving Paris! It has just gone through a period of severe cold, without light or cars, after which – I should like to think – the rest of the winter will consist only of crumbling icicles and ephemeral snow. A clenched-teeth courage guided its population towards goals it will not and cannot abandon : to acquire the means of subsistence and to give to each the share that will prevent him from dying.

Such an allocation is no mean task. But why should it perish, the city-dwelling bird which has got into the habit of relying on us. Why should the end of our prosperity entail that of the familiar pigeon, which writes its passing shadow, that of the Holy Ghost, on the asphalt? Why should that cooing die which issues from our ungrateful walls like a spring escaping from a rock? *We* have not so wished it. There has always been a brave pair of hands to seize the broom and sweep a place for crumbs in the snow where the feet of birds might alight. Whenever I have opened a window beset by sparrows, another window, other windows have opened and scattered bread-crumbs.

From living in a great city and depending entirely on its inhabitants, animals become terribly knowing. They interpret our gestures, note our habits. Our punctuality shapes theirs. A fine free communal cat answers to the whimsical name of Mickey Vefour simply because the Restaurant Vefour often feeds him. In hard times he climbs my floor and a half, asking for no more than warmth, a few hours of profound slumber, and a rest which improves the beauty of his striped coat and relaxes his curved claws. After which he seeks adventure, the empty street, other encounters. . . .

A dog, given shelter by a bookseller, did not consent to relinquish the fortunes and habits of a stray animal. He gave his host to understand that he would have preferred the door to remain open. Then the dog applied himself to a more studied observation of our manners and realized that one gesture of the customers led unfailingly to the opening of the door. He watched the goings and comings and acquired the certainty that every person who deposited money on the till followed this by opening the shop-door.

For every animal soon manages to learn much about ourselves, who are still ignorant of the rudiments of their everyday language, the meaning of its complaints and its songs. They offer us the fruits of their untiring observation, of their tender exploitation. Thank God, it is an offering which succeeds in opening the hard human heart. The bird stands at our door; the dog succoured the previous day returns next day to keep a watch on us. Studied, dreaded, implored, we live under the bird's glittering eye, the vertical pupil of the cat; the dog's warm gaze is fixed on us, interprets us unerringly. . . .

When, thirty years ago, I took on the literary editorship of a daily paper, I used to go to my office five afternoons out of seven. For my little Brabançon terrier bitch a single problem existed: would I or would I not take her? Just before I had pushed back my armchair, closed my notebook, announced my departure, I would notice as I turned round that the terrier was wide awake, on her feet, ready to go out, alerted by a signal other than the coat, the hat, the pair of gloves or shoes. My thought was of telepathy, until the moment when I perceived that, eliminating one by one all the movements which could have put her on the track, the bitch had judiciously given the entire credit to the least obvious and most significant movement, that of putting on and screwing up the cap of my fountain-pen.

4

Magnificent long evening-dress in black faille, decorated with pale blue ornamentation. . . . Dinner-dress in blue-green satin. . . . Evening-dress in white jersey, metal belt and jewellery. . . .

Do you think that I'm reading, out of nostalgia, a fashion magazine over a year old? No. Magazine, models and captions are those of today. And even if I covet neither the white jersey nor the blue-green satin nor the ornamentation, I leaf through

these pages dated February 1941 pleasurably and attentively. I
tell myself I must save this journal to be reopened at a later date
when it will bear witness that in February 1941, together with
queues for milk, swedes, oil-less and eggless mayonnaise, Candle-
mas without pancakes and shoes without leather, Paris brought
forth her most typical *tours de force: Figured velvet dress.* . . .
Well-cut blouse in pink lamé. . . .

'I've just been out looking for slippers,' interrupts my daily
woman. 'They still had plenty left.'

'Did you bring some back?'

'Oh no! You had to show the old ones. Do you think I'd have
dared show them in the state they were in! I'd have been
ashamed.'

And rivalling, in a word, some inspired *couturier*:

'I'll rig up something,' she added.

For Paris lives not just by restrictions but by inventions and
paradoxes. Apparent paradoxes in the sense of that enunciated
by a farmer's wife from the rich Perigord country:

'As meat's too dear this week we shall have to eat *foie gras.*'

And she broached the tins that a year of plenty and easy living
had filled. Does this mean that, in the threatened absence of the
tailored costume, we should do our shopping in a 'magnificent
long dinner-dress'? We haven't reached that point. We shall
resort to the combined efforts, the ingenious ideas, of the costume
photographed over sixty years ago by a traveller in the Marquesas
Islands: a little silk furbelow like a bustle round the bare loins,
a shawl *à la* Charlotte Corday crossed over the breasts like a
calabash, and . . . the wig known as *à la frégate*, beloved of
Marie-Antoinette. Even more threatened than ourselves in their
need to be correct enough to pass unnoticed, the men are becoming anxious.

'I'd be glad if you could make me (he said *fissiez*, if you please)
a dozen detachable collars,' said one of my friends to his faithful
shirtmaker.

'What with?' asked the shirtmaker, deadpan for the first time
in his life.

'Soon,' say our mates, 'we shall have to go out with a scarf
round our necks, without socks, and wearing sandals. . . .' With
a sigh of male pride. Almost in the same tone as their refrain
when it used to be time to abandon the city for the countryside

in August : 'Soon, soon the bare neck, hurry on, the sandal !'
But we don't care for being made happy in spite of ourselves.

I pick up my fashion magazine again : *Exquisite ensemble
in figured velvet forming a trefoil pattern in relief . . . shoes
encrusted with material similar to that of the costume. . . .
Unusual new bracelet, figuring interlacing strips studded with
diamonds. . . .* Why should I not enjoy these pages which, on
glossy paper, speak of luxury, assemble portraits of slender,
winged young women? A pleasure and a consolation. In this
frivolous compilation there is not a photographic smile, a fluttering gesture, a graceful fold, an ornamentation, which is not the
fragile realization of a long and stubborn effort, marked by grace.
To the very details of metal, tooled leather, clasps and feathers,
even to the refinements of make-up and perfumery, everything
expresses a smiling willingness, the determination of ten valiant
corporations to bear flowers and fruit.

The client of today, fearful, impoverished, does not frequent
the salons of couture and fashion to choose this pink lamé,
mother-of-pearl faille, cut velvet or lozenged silk. She is not so
naïve or so spendthrift. She knows how to interpret the fashion
and transpose it; in any case, these dazzling creations are only
there to be seen, to be fancied, then discarded. They are stand-
ards. The 'long encrusted dress' becomes a black outfit, the mink
descends to rabbit, and all would be for the best if it were not
for what *Le Médecin malgré lui* calls the matter of the hats.

The hat has been incorrigible for a long span of time. Its
absurdity defies everything, even national disasters. One hasn't
seen its like for irrelevance and pettiness since before and after the
war of 1870 – I draw the parallel without pleasure.

It's curious that the hat which is too small creates an impression
of lunacy much more than does the one that is too large. A lunatic
hardly ever puts on his head a hat which is too big. He readily
covers himself with a bottle-top, an empty matchbox, a child's
small boat turned upside-down, a jampot. Before the crisis of
contraction affected our hats, I recall that at a Saint-Tropez ball
it was by means of a batch of minuscule hats that Jeanne Duc,
then an innkeeper, obtained the effects of greatest extravagance.
She would not have obtained them by reviving the immense
castles, the superimposed strata of feathers under which shone
the languishing eyes of Lantelme.

Today there is no woman of taste who, behind closed doors, does not condemn in judicious words the strange productions, impossible to balance, with which fashion would crown her. But her lucidity deserts her once she arrives at the milliner. Initially hesitant, the woman of taste is caught in the trap the more easily as it departs from normal dimensions. I don't know how otherwise to explain such a phenomenon of befuddlement as when, having arrived full of circumspection and critical intention, the woman of taste returns home with a clump of violets on her nose, a cascade of printed ribbon on the nape of her neck, a tambourine full of balls of silk across her right eye, one of those veils which leave vivid souvenirs in the metro, a suspended turtle-dove, a turban capsized under a cluster of hyacinths – all of this, of course, about fit for one of those wretched little flounced monkeys which used to jingle on barrel-organs. . . .

'I'd like to see you in my place!' wrote a reader encumbered with her two young children, aged seven and nine, confined to the house by the bad weather, unable to play freely.

Madame and dear reader, I too should like to be in your place, if only because I should be barely thirty years of age. For another reason too . . . There is some sadness in admitting that – short of being a grandmother – one has passed the season and the possibility of being a close and passionate observer of childhood. It was a sort of 'hide' I used to much enjoy.

Well, there you are, and not the first, burdened with your two little ones who buzz at the windows like captive hornets demanding liberty. I imagine you to be a young, tender, gay mother, a rather weak mother who often allows herself to be ruled by her nerves. If I dare expound to you my own ideas on how to bring up children, you may consider me a torturer. I have not yet discarded them. I persist in believing that it is possible to ensure the happiness of some without causing unhappiness to others, and that besides the rights of children there exist the rights of parents: the right to rest, the right to silence at certain hours, the right to untroubled work.

I persist in believing that a child can grow and flourish without shouting, that tears – so long as it is well – are no more than a bad habit and a bad education. I maintain that it is not inhuman to deprive the urban child of such toys as drums, rattles, trumpets and whistles; that savage vociferation is not an essential employment of the respiratory passages; and that the suppression of toys without rubber-shod wheels does not conduce to rickets or depression in children. You see, Madame, the kind of ruthless mother you have to deal with.

My principal victim was bursting with health, and even beauty, despite my maltreatment. Alerted at an early age to my callousness, she soon accepted the deal we are in the habit of making with animals in the apartment: be wild outside and well-behaved in the house. If it is not very difficult to establish maternal authority, it is less easy to consolidate it, for we are spied on incessantly by the keen and subtle instinct, the varied wiles, of childhood. It is for us – for must I not speak of them as so many adversaries? – to thwart them. If dancing on a parquet floor is an amusement, walking on tiptoe can be another, suggested by us and just as diverting.

Have you the habit, Madame, of smiling when you say 'No' to your sons, and sticking to this firm yet amiable 'No'? Yes? So much the better. That means plenty of time gained and painful words spared. An elderly nanny from whom I learned a great deal used to say, in her Anglo-French jargon: 'It's all the same whether I have to undertake the training of a dog or a small child. The first two days and the first two nights are bound to be hell, but you mustn't give in. After that all goes well, because the baby and the puppy have drawn their conclusions about you.'

You confide to me that your boys are 'intelligent and difficult'. These two adjectives seem almost irreconcilable to me; of all children, the intelligent one is most easily won over. Are you sure that you are appealing often enough to their powers of comprehension? You don't belong, I sincerely hope, to that blameworthy species of parent which prefers prohibition to explanation, scolding to forewarning? You're surely not of the 'Don't touch that!' school? You don't include an innocent clumsiness in the list of childhood sins? I'm glad to hear it, for I was raised from an early age in the contrary school of which the great principle was 'Touch that'. This constitutes an unforgettable training which I have endeavoured to transmit to my beloved 'victim', less authoritatively, no doubt, than I myself received it. . . .

'Touch that' means to say 'Become involved with everything around you. Feel, under the cat's fur, the convulsive movements of its little ones who want to be born. Hold the yellow chick in your hands, don't hurt it. Do you want to drink from the beautiful Chinese cup? Drink. But if you break it, you can't ever expect to enjoy drinking from it again. Look out, the wasp has a sting. But in the end it's your own fault if you get stung. Knives cut, pincers pinch. One more reason for learning how to use one and the other. . . . You see, you're bleeding. Next time you'll be more careful; I advise you to try again, to touch again. . . .'

I have never been afraid, Madame dear reader, of not being understood because a child was too young. For from his earliest age he is capable of finding us puerile. I once encountered, on a Provençal beach, a young mother overwhelmed and ruled by two small boys of eight and seven who were so handsome, so strong, already marked with such masculine authority, that I called them 'the supermen'. Like so many children, they had carved out in the bosom of their family an entrenched, peaceful, impregnable existence like two explorers on a desert island. In their conversation they often made allusion to a certain person whom they designated merely by the name of 'the little one'.

'Let's go to Pampelonne on Sunday,' said the elder.

'With the little one?' said the younger.

'I'd prefer it without the little one. She'd want to bring a whole heap of things like she usually does.'

'And she's bound to be late. . . .'

'Let's go without the little one. We needn't tell her.'

And their mother sought among the children on the beach for the small girl for whom this pair of supermen voiced such tender if somewhat severe sentiments. She sought, and fell from her high estate, as they say, when she discovered that 'the little one' was no other than herself. . . .

My postbag this week resembles the season itself, the sky which mingles eddies of rain, flakes of snow, bonbons of hail, twists of straw and sparrows. The sort of post I like, in fact. Women, especially unknown women, use it to admonish me. Those who do not admonish me ask, strange as it may seem, for advice concerning the education of their children or for 'stories about children'. Not that I'm short of them. I'm all right for stories but I suppress the *bons mots* of children, even when they are genuine. Anything that smacks of the child prodigy and precocious humour on puerile lips is not to my taste.

A sort of combative maternal love was always native to me. I love, whether with child or animal, to have the last word and also to make an onslaught on certain educational and training methods. Readers for whom motherhood is a long assent, an unlimited abnegation, what will you think of me if I say that a child should learn to read before three years? What an outcry I arouse! . . . Before three years, I maintain. My mother, Sido, did as much for me, I did as much for my daughter. Since, my young mother, you don't hesitate to teach your eager baby the name of the table, the flower and the dog, tangible or shown in pictures, why do you delay teaching it the names of the letters? At twenty-five months my daughter showed her appetite for the unknown by preferring to all others the letter X which stood, legs apart, on a lawn and which she called 'that beautiful X'. It never occurred to her, any more than to me, that learning letters or notes of music might be an effort. The great thing is to start early, very early, before the age when a lesson assumes – to art-less, agile and prejudiced eyes – the dry, rebarbative and dis-heartening aspect of a lesson.

What do you think of that, tender parents who respect the ignorance of the one you call your pretty little savage, your pretty wild creature, blooming and fresh? I agree with you if you intend the said pretty little savage for a Pacific island; even then, he would have to find an entirely virgin Polynesian island, which is not so easy nowadays. 'Let him thrive till he's five . . . six . . . or seven.' He thrives, and studies you. He deciphers, if not the alphabet, the human heart, your heart.*

A certain Pierrot of my acquaintance, armed with a charming smile and his six rosy years, sees the approach of lessons, delays them, eludes them with virtuosity. His manner is the gay manner of seductiveness. He dances a nautch dance, if I may so put it, buries the letters of the alphabet under flowers, destroys maternal gravity. 'Ah, you laughed!' he cries. 'You've lost!' And he fills the air with songs of victory, laughs and kisses. . . . The lesson will be for tomorrow. . . .

You must realize that his series of observations goes very far back. As far, perhaps, as one little girl began hers. When seven months old she would become bored in her cradle when placed there at the prescribed hour for sleep and heralded her slumbers with wall-piercing shrieks. However, she kept her ears open for every sound, chiefly those of steps. Did she hear her mother's light hurried step? She cried *rinforzando*, assured of a respite, of a consoling little excursion in the warm basket of enfolding arms. . . . But if her father's tread should make the floorboards creak, a marvellous silence interrupted the howlings. For this seven-month-old diplomat knew that the paternal tread heralded first some strong words and then a good series of six little smacks on the behind. . . .

In one house where I lived, a three-year-old Jacques enjoyed the numerous prerogatives associated with his rank as the 'concierge's child'. For him the tenants' gifts: little pullovers, woollen stockings, smart finery, sweets especially. . . . He learned precociously to surmount the barriers of his bed, to get out and climb in again. But he never publicized his agility, which remained unsuspected for a space of time until certain nocturnal upsets, coinciding with the disappearance of the sweets, made even his trusting mother suspicious. Yet the child was never alone. However, put early to bed, he used to sleep deeply from the moment his mother left him to light 'his' gas-lamp on the landing. She would leave, hasten to light three landings one after the other, return and find all in order.

One evening she bent over the little bed and her big boy and murmured:

'Are you asleep, Jacques?'

The sleeper answered very softly:

'Of course I'm asleep.'

Then he went a bit too far and added:

'Talk to me very quietly or you'll wake me up.'

You haven't any more cakes, we haven't any more cakes. They haven't any more cakes either, the children who, without much discrimination, throw themselves on pastries, influenced by their shape and appearance rather than their taste. . . .

Well, well, don't take on about it so. Admit that for some time now, and despite the honest efforts and honourable endeavours of French pastrycooks, cakes are not as good as all that! But you don't wish to be consoled, at least not immediately. When all was milk and honey, you kept away from the cream-cake, unctuous and yellow, the tart powdered with vanilla sugar, the *kugelhopf* and the éclair, like so many satanic lures, and swore only by the holy biscuit. Today your perverse spirit yearns above all for the cake as a symbol which, despite the week's restrictions, used to give us two Sundays in place of one, prolific from Saturday on with white packets tied with blue ribbons. One well-known pastry-shop in my neighbourhood is going to lose its noonday bustle, its faithful masculine customers who consume more than the others, but who dissimulate – why? – their greediness beneath an austere and preoccupied air. In Basse-Bourgogne such mock-modesty is called 'denying one's stomach'. But the renegade consumes no less.

I once saw in a pastry-shop a well-behaved child eating his apple-tart in small mouthfuls; he was admiring, with a slightly scandalized air, his intemperate father who was eating standing on one side.

'And hop! a baba!' said the child to himself. 'And wow! a tart! And boum! a walnut cake.'

Such gluttonies are on the way out. The pastry-shop used to dole out to us that little necessary sugar, that indispensable flour, the savour of almonds, of orange-flower and vanilla. The tradition, investigated, is lacking almost as much as the cakes themselves. Having eaten famous cakes, we are now capable of enjoying a not very good éclair. In the depths of the mediocre *puits d'amour* dwells the illusion, the recollection of *puits d'amour* all cream, caramel, butter and vanilla. Is it out of gratitude towards the *savarin* of yesteryear that women wreath themselves with babas?

All is not lost because your Monday titbit stuffed with mushrooms, your little Tuesday walnut-roll, and the other weekly dainties are removed from your mouth. The pastry-cooks of Paris are a resourceful lot. Eight days ago the good pastry-shop in my neighbourhood, surprised by a ban on . . . on everything, sold by the portion a panful of little soles swimming in a mushroom sauce. Great success! I suggest to the ingenious *patronne* that she might produce a thick layer of haricot beans cooked in red wine as *tartines* on square biscuits. It's the favourite snack of the children in my part of the world.

If the name 'swede' was not detested by so many of the finicky, I would inform you that a swede-tart can be made very cheaply. . . . You don't want any? All right, I'll keep quiet. But there's the *flognarde* that Pauline makes me when I've been working hard; reward your children with it too, you'll find it neither difficult nor expensive and it's the most expeditious of sugared dishes, this thick pancake which swells so in the oven that it bursts.

Two eggs only, a glass of flour, one of cold water or of skimmed milk, a good pinch of salt, three spoonfuls of sugar. Sprinkle the flour and sugar together in the basin, and gradually incorporate the liquid and the whole eggs. Then beat the mixture like a pancake mix; pour it out on a previously greased baking tin and leave to warm on a corner of the stove or hot-plate for a quarter of an hour, so that the oven should not 'surprise' your mixture. After which, with twenty minutes' cooking, the *flognarde* becomes an enormous puffiness which fills the oven, becomes golden, then brown, bursts here, swells there. . . . At the finest of its eruptions remove it, sugar it lightly with caster sugar, and divide it still boiling. It prefers a sparkling drink – cider, sparkling wine, or a not too bitter beer.

I don't claim that the home-made *flognarde* replaces all the forbidden delicacies. It will not make up for the loss of eating in town to those who have that habit. For, abundant or not, the snack in a tea-room or bar is a pleasure of sociability rather than gluttony. It takes the place of an assignation of love or friendship. Of friendship especially, young lovers considering – the idiots! – that an hour given to appetite is an hour lost to love.

For many solitary women tea-time is the most cheerful hour of the day. There are certainly some sad women in a tea-room, there are none who look sad. The place is generally warm, the toast smells good, the chocolate smells of chocolate. The poetic, deceptive odour of coffee floats. The women have the faces of travellers installing themselves in a train for a long journey. Many of them have contrived this moment of relaxation at the end of a busy day. Not one would suffer you to apply to her circumstances Forain's remark: '*On croit qu'elle goutte . . . elle déjeune.*' The false *gourmande*, even when given nothing at all with her cup of hot liquid, will come all the same to sit down, to smoke a cigarette with a satisfied air. For her real appetite is for the sound of voices, the light of glances, gossip and affection, rest, the brave falsehood; and she carries back to the confines of her solitude all the benefits she has received, in the space of an hour, from the human presence.

5

Great complaints and recriminations arise from the female camp. . . . One observer – which is what those call themselves who base their errors on precise data – affirms that women complain until the moment when they really suffer; after which they fall silent, concentrate their forces, and restrain their utterance. Women, then, complain, not being able to buy materials or shoes or balls of wool. The civil war over coupons knows a truce of uncertain duration. The elegant purchasers, who concealed their elegance beneath dingy makeshifts to go and argue, at the top of the Butte, for silk at the price of cotton, cotton at the price of packing-paper, will stay at home. . . . So they protest – in a restrained manner – and commence a regime of fresh queues, a fresh pursuit. A rather fruitless pursuit, a sport, tips whispered from mouth to ear, hopes deceived yet renascent :

'Quite a small shop, my dear . . .'

'Crêpe-de-chine? Wool?'

'No, floor-cloths!'

'Floor-cloths? That's fantastic! I'm on my way!'

So much for black-market floor-cloths. . . . Is lipstick going to disappear from the public eye, and beauty cream? Last week the women besieged the perfumers and the perfumery warehouses. Depending on whether or not they had acquired the make-up, the cream to be banned the following day, they left restored to serenity or anxious.

Your thoroughbred farsighted woman who has her store of tailormade suits and blouses is not interesting. Let us condemn her for her stocks of elegance and turn our attention to the industrious woman who, in a short space of time, devotes herself to her favourite miracle, that is, making something out of nothing.

From a bed-sheet worn in the middle she will make three summer blouses of pure linen, then a lot of little tea-towels, hand-towels, all kinds of towels. Whereas another virtuoso, who kept a collection of three dozen thread dusters, puts them together to make a bedspread.

Madame, you own two tight skirts condemned by fashion and faded with use? One is beige, the other fawn? You stuff one inside the other, head to tail, and you will manage things so well that the length of one, cut tapering to a point, supplies the width the other lacks. Rather like the triangles of the game of backgammon; do you follow?

A flea-market, deprived alas of its garlands of sausages and its gingerbread, opens in April. 'Rummage around! Rummage around!' That's the traditional cry of its merchants. Let us rummage around, then, next Easter along the Boulevard Richard-Lenoir. For instance, we can look for buttons, which are becoming rare. I've just discovered, at a nearby antiquary's, buttons similar to those which, around 1890, adorned a coat of my adolescence. They represent, against a steel-blue background, a young girl standing on a Japanese bridge shaded by a pine-tree.

One of my friends has just bought, taken from a jumble of colonial objects, a pair of Indochinese sabots in hard wood, which she is taking to her farm for the bad weather and for heavy work. You can well believe that a pair of galoshes, presently unobtainable, would have cost her over thirty francs. Rummage, rummage around in Paris, rummage in your imagination, your cupboards, sharpen your eye, your nose! Is there not, in some obscure shop in the Ile-de-France or in Brittany, one of those sleeved waistcoats finely striped in black and yellow, black and pink, yellow and green, which used to form part of the morning outfit required for manservants? Their material is serviceable and you will find them charming remade to your size, their black sleeves amputated. . . .

There was once – I am speaking of 1938 – a green cloth material, green as young barley, green as the cabbage caterpillar, and reserved for cobblers' aprons. . . . There was a sort of squared cambric of a delicate mauve, allotted to butchers' boys. . . . There was the charming blue which would be so suitable for the coming summer, the blue – more appealing at every wash – used for workmen's overalls. Useful or useless, my suggestions show my goodwill.

But my goodwill goes no lower than the ankle. I've nothing to suggest on the matter of stockings. For I've never really understood why the most desirable of stockings must be those called 'invisible' and why one has to pay so much for something that tries not to exist. I also decline to express an opinion on footwear, which I have virtually repudiated these fifteen years. Are you already in such straits that your last resort is the gilded buskin, studded with paste ornamentation, solitary star of the bare shop-windows? How many children's feet are going to suffer? . . . A child with uncomfortable feet will find a remedy : he takes off his shoes. I've often got myself laughed at in the street through wearing nothing but sandals, summer and winter. But disfavour counts for little, weighed against well-being. Every martyr has his hour; and now, in place of irony, I excite interest.

And just note how much the Frenchman is given to doubting his own merits! This week a woman passer-by with hammer-toes asked me : 'I'd very much like some sandals. . . . But yours must come from Italy, only the Italian shoemakers make good sandals. . . .' A tired man accosted me : 'Excuse me . . . your sandals are Swedish, aren't they? It's only Swedish sandal-makers who understand about feet!'

Neither the lady with the bunions nor the Swede-enamoured passerby showed signs of believing me when I confessed to them that I got my shoes, or rather managed without them, from a simple French craftsman.

A bee has come into my house, the first of the season. It found its plunder – having scented them from afar – on the willow catkins brought in from the suburbs, whose odour is exactly that of honey. Where did the bee come from? The heart of Paris, the Tuileries and the Palais-Royal, have buds without flowers. A few forsythias decorate the squares with yellow, but the forsythia is so poor in nectar! The urban bee loaded its back legs with yellow taken from the catkins and, thus clad in voluminous plus-fours, it left me without even taking the time to lap a little sugar-water prepared for it in a spoon with a broken handle which I insert like a small bathtub in the earth of a flowerpot. It came from afar, it has left for afar. . . .

On the Avenue des Champs-Elysées, thousands and thousands of bees work, captive, on the cinema screen. I'm not done with going to see them. All we already know of bees makes me pensive and full of deference. We hasten to learn everything, seized by the animated image which is novel to us. There is no story more fantastic than that of the bee. The animated enlargement of the film describes it in close-up and magnifies the minuscule worker to the size of a hunting dog. We can see that it is glossy, sharply defined, that a plantation of hairs along its more powerful legs is destined to retain the pollen. And those eyes, those vast eyes formed of thousands of eyes, which receive the images of the universe a thousand times over! And the ornamentation of the head, the rapid action of the antennae and the mandibles!

I confess that, rather unmoved by romantic films, I have difficulty in restraining my Oh's and Ah's when it comes to micro-photography, slowing-down and speeding-up. An uprush of helmeted mushrooms, the lily-bud opening its long throat, the underground groping path of seeds, the war of microbes, the life of bees. . . . I have to stop myself from calling the attention of the unknown spectators, my neighbours: 'Look! Look at the stamen and the insect! Look at the action of the bee's feet and mouth! See that great queen with her long belly, how she is set apart as a unique creature among the crowd of workers; consider her fatal and glorious task!'

We do not look, we never look enough, never attentively enough, never excitedly enough. The insipid sentimentality to which the film-romance has descended, the current difficulties in production – will these restore documentaries to favour? Is it just the laziness and frivolity of the French public that have kept them away from the screen? Where do they accumulate, reeled up in slumber and neglect, all those recorded fantasies, the mirrors of the world, the secrets of the invisible, the refracted lights, the animalcules, the feverish speeding-up, the lethargic nobility of the slowed-down? Where slake our thirst, tormented by the marvels of reality? It's not enough that, in the Champs-Elysées, the bees make honey under our eyes.

We desire other miracles, though they be less beautiful than this one, contain less information; not all, for example, can equal the massacre of the drones, the mob of bees who kill, who use their forelegs in human fashion to expel, to strangle. . . . Nor equal this slow portrayal, the maternal entombing task the queen, condemned to lay, pursues over each cell : an egg, a white sealed mummy, another egg, another, always an egg. Nor the poignant effort of the hatching : the last restraints broken by the completed larva, luminous eyes appearing, feet clinging to the edge of the cell to hoist the feeble new bee, exhausted from being born, into life, the difficulty of beginning as great as that of ending.

The inevitable tumult of the swarm is succeeded on the screen by a drama of solitude. Crazily, obstinately, a handful of men have attempted, yet again, the ascent of Karakoram. Yet again it has failed. Tomorrow it will begin all over again, for to climb is the temptation of man. The scientific spirit has its part, not so large perhaps as it itself believes. But man cannot stay still at the foot of a peak. He has to climb, to find above a dazzling desolation of snow and sun, bare rock, the blue patch of the unstained ether, the insubstantial result of his efforts; his unsullied pride receives, initially, no other rewards. For the horizon he takes in, erect on a conquered ridge, does not differ sensibly from that which he discerned at lower levels. The lesser mountains, which he disdained, seem to have grown up around him and above his head another peak, transfixing the very clouds, defies him. . . .

But the world is small. Soon there will be no more inaccessible ranges. At the top of the last slope will be found the last little bones of the man dedicated to the mountain, dead on it and victorious. Those who follow him will be mere disciples : he will have been the first.

Exhausted, frozen on one side and burnt on the other, the unfortunate devotees of the Karakoram are down again. The film sequence shows them to us as they were, sad here, gay later. Their undertaking was a great one only because of its object. It's evident that they were modest in their means, provided with porters and little ragged horses, strictly essential material. But they move us, minuscule on the spine of the monstrous Himalaya, a chain of slow ants in the hollow of a defile almost as long as France. Their beards sprout, the snow grips them, cloaks them, but they climb. Close to their goal the weather betrays them, precipitates and thaws the snows, mobilizes avalanches so vast that they seem to change the shape of the mountains. . . .

Emerging from such a film we were in no need of the songs provided to put us back in good heart, as they say. Our heart was in its proper place, moved in concert and contented by the spectacle of an almost prehistoric human courage, the human face without roof or armour, without weapons and engines. Fine, too, are the implacable portraits of the Asiatic peak, which has no desire to be trodden underfoot and thrusts the aggressor back into the plains, whither he descends chastened but not down-hearted.

It's by the height of the sun that we calculate the duration of our internment, we city-dwellers who are detained in Paris by our work, our health, the scarcity of means of transport or by prefer-ence. Our calculations are also furthered by the increasing mild-ness of the temperature. How many months is it since we last stirred from here? In prosperous times I would have heard anguished cries. What! Spend All Saints' Day at home! Christ-mas holidays without treading on clean snow or going to Nice? Easter's coming and one hasn't drawn up one's list of plans?

That's how it is. I go so far as to say that it's better this way. Haven't we reached the point where, among other economies, we should counsel and practise economy of movement? In torrid climes this is an essential part of wisdom. There is no sport in the tropics, no travelling. To endure there, the human being reduces his physical activity to a minimum, spares the precious sweat from his ever-open pores. The equator and malnutrition lay the same burden of fatigue on life.

I am not without some knowledge of adolescents wild about physical training and contests. It is for them I am concerned when – as is common – they persist in muscular expenditure which they are unable to make good. Their present nourishment does not even meet the needs of growth. Others, older, add to the length of a regular job, increase still further an ill-satisfied appetite, by abandoning themselves to violent gymnastics. Where they seek euphoria they find exhaustion and its accompanying mental depression. In more prosperous times, that was how the delicate young women behaved who were sent to the snows to rest there on a *chaise-longue* in the sun. They hastened to inter-pret rest as agitation, and *chaise-longue* as skis. Fine young people, our hope, who voraciously attack a hunk of bread or a sliver of meat; I find it hard to think and write: 'Gently, gently . . . take it easy.' Rest is hateful to you. Never have you

rejected it so forcefully in its most demanding form, immobility.
I see you running in teams and throwing a ball in the Tuileries
gardens. In the intervals many of you, instead of being generously flushed, are pale, you have the hollow heaving flanks of
greyhounds, and I prefer not to know what that signifies. Who
is there who can usefully preach to you, restrain you, tell you : 'A
warm terrace, the *Bois*, a bed of lush grass and – save for the
movements of your lungs – a relative laziness of your entire
body in its travail of growth . . .'?

The future ripens despite apparent set-backs; a caterpillar
stiffens when it has to be reborn. But the adolescents of today
have known a period when the entire world lost patience and
resignation. The motor and its fuel have disappeared. The wear-
ing-out or loss of a bicycle tyre are now barely rectifiable dramas,
man must settle to managing his beast of burden. Even when
they are agile, a man's legs don't go far. . . . All this will change,
one demands of youth only what is most difficult : to be patient.
Looking straight ahead without a windscreen, it glimpsed only its
objectives; and these were deformed and hazy like the landscapes
the cinema unwinds beside a train. Presently humiliated, pensive,
will it not consent to drop its gaze? It is the very attitude of
meditation. At its feet life flows more slackly, a burdened
wave. . . .

In the Ile-de France, before the war, I had some connections
with a man who could not read or write. I don't offer his ignorance as an example but I did have occasion to delight in all this
illiterate knew. Because school was distant and his path rich in
temptations, he had learned only what is taught by the sharp
senses : nests, lairs, the forest and patient observation. He refused
to quit his parish and collected marvels without stirring, assured
of their arrival.

The villages of those days were not short of these sedentary
types, who were never bored. They carried out refinements of
grafting, took many cuttings, were proud of their choice vegetables. Without knowing it they were the little rich, content with
little, of a great nation. The peasant, their neighbour, saw more
of the country than they did, merely by visiting the fairs. Ah,
those small stick-in-the-mud Frenchmen, may their like never
die out! . . . I believe that they possessed the art of fruitful
silence. Confined, they long remained without any desire for the

retreat of the limits of a horizon which they varied and peopled with an exact knowledge of the past and present. From his threshold one would extend an arm to indicate the extent of his gaze : 'There, in that little patch of barley, a man once had himself buried seated on his horse. . . . Where you see those willows you could uncover a spring without too much difficulty. Between the wood and a red roof there's a bed of clay worth developing for a pottery. . . .'

'Every evil of man arises from the fact that he is unable to stay quietly in his room.' I quote approximately this phrase of Pascal, but without savouring it overmuch because I do not believe that wisdom consists of choosing immobility. But once immobilized, reduced to snapping up the most vivid and most assimilable of what happens within reach, I prefer to apply to our urban existence the phrase of a landowner jealous of his land : 'Love what's on top, love what's beneath.' Not that the 'underneath' of the city has any charms, but, cut off from the exterior, let's enjoy what's within.

Then again, as Paris ceases to be industrialized, it exhales less fumes and mineral poison. The spring assaults the Gates of Paris. A great bank of rhododendrons, on the Champs-Elysées, ranks its pink flowers. The market-garden freshness of salads and bastions of radishes reign in the Rue Montorgueil. Torn up with the head of lettuce, one can see the pendant, still-surviving daisy, a stray cowslip, the scarlet pimpernel's splash of blood, and the closed buds of the small wild pansy.

The *flognarde*, a quickly made and substantial dessert, an excellent snack hot or cold, needs no milk, manages with two eggs for four or even six persons, three or four spoonfuls of sugar or vanilla sugar, and the indispensable pinch of salt. You can even replace the sugar with a more generous dose of salt and some grated gruyère.

The *flognarde* led me to obtain, through the official mediation of *M. le curé* of Flogny (Yonne), its letters patent and certificates of origin, which are not without interest. The *flognarde* was born at Flogny and is at least a hundred years old. The postmaster, M. Flogny, of Flogny, used to keep an inn and a stage for diligences. While the horses were being changed, Madame Flogny would briskly beat up the mixture and place it in the oven, and the travellers waited patiently around 'the *flognarde* of Madame Flogny', washed down with a light wine about which *M. le curé* Gérard has nothing to communicate. But I have reason to know the district, and I believe that Madame Flogny filled her glasses with a charming wine from Treigny, a regional growth, gay and fruity, later ruined by the phylloxera.

Other gourmet-etymologists lay claim to the *flognarde* on behalf of the Limousin. 'How does one refer, in Limousin *patois*, to a lazy and flabby individual?' writes one of these to me. 'He is called a *flognard*.' But I suspect, on the best of information, that the *flognard* may be compared to a crisp brown titbit, still emitting little splutters of laughter as it leaps out of the oven.

What would I not wish to invent, or revive, inexpensively to enrich your menus, and mine, dear readers! Garlic, which is scarce, was never more necessary. It was my habit, in all seasons, to use the *ail fondant* to restore both breath and good temper. I used to put the garlic fully-clothed in the still warm oven, taking care that the transparent covering of the cloves did not brown. When the white flesh of the garlic softens under the finger, one pierces the skin of the clove and empties it by suction, as children do with boiled chestnuts. You recoil, Madame, just to read this? You are wrong. And garlic is almost a panacea for the health.

I rarely see fennel any more. Should it reappear, enjoy its aniseed flavour, eat it quite raw; we have need of raw vegetables. Or cook it, lightly. Remove the tougher ribs, which will flavour a soup. The tender portion we shall dispose of in one of those doughs poor in butter, in sugar and in eggs, which we all know how to knead and which taste good eaten at the oven door. Fennel tart, tart with preserved peas, sorrel tart, tart with swe . . . Oh, I'm due for a forfeit! One of my correspondents has taxed me: five francs for her poor each time I write the word swe . . . well, that word.

While I'm on the subject of dough, let me say – without prejudice – what I know about bread made in a frying-pan. Around 1922 I was in Algiers during a spring which was very un-Algerian but wildly variable and capricious. It hailed on the roses, it thundered on the daturas, and a short-lived snowfall, even; outlined the bougainvillaeas – the colour of fire or violet wine – clinging to the walls of the Hotel Saint-Georges. As I shivered, contemplating a grey Mediterranean covered with chalky spume, an Algerian industrialist whom I knew said:

'I've some business down south; come along in the car with me. We'll go by Bou-Saâda and take the long way round coming back, by Boghari, Mount Gorno . . . Berrouaghia, Djelfa. . . .

Thus I became acquainted with a fair stretch of desert, its sparse vegetation, alfalfa in widely-separated tufts, its pale deceptive horizons, its curtains of sand moving in the air, its reflected heat and its brief violet twilights; and it was thus that I came across frying-pan bread, during a halt in a kind of pink hamlet, the same faded pink as the desert. Far off shone the Mountain of Salt. Naturally, we had our *mechoui* with the *caïd*. I shan't stress too much the succulence of meat done to a turn, washed down with water salted with rock-salt. . . .

But bread was lacking, so they made some on the spot. To the best of my recollection, the fine scented flour was treated with a little yeast, a little salt dissolved in the water for kneading. Instead of using crocks, as in Europe, the dough was divided among two or three frying-pans. . . . I could not detect any other magic. But I relished the bread cooked in the frying-pan, brown on top, brown underneath, more like a crusty girdle-cake than bread. Knack? Quality, management of the brushwood fire? I don't know. But – robbing Peter to pay Paul – I try to use flour to save our bread, which isn't up to much.

I haven't ventured to try making bread in a frying-pan myself. It's not so much that I'm afraid of wasting the flour. . . . It's just that around this bread there gather images with which I am still infatuated : pink sands, a spring gushing in the *caïd*'s own garden and splashing on large pebbles; memories of lilac, black-currant flowers, swallows so familiar that they used to settle on the damp margin of the spring, mixing at our feet the cement for their nests. Nothing withered in the *caïd*'s enclosure because of the miraculous water. Beyond the walls a small fertile trail, green barley, fruit-trees, marked its passage, then the desert drank it up.

Should I fail with my frying-pan bread, I am afraid that my modest mirages, my monkeys from Chiffa, my splendid return-trip, my Djelfa, Berrouaghia, may vanish in a smoke smelling of burnt toast. . . . Perhaps a reader will try, succeed, and let me know.

6

If an epoch engenders the art it deserves, what art is it that is coming to fruition within the bosom of a sombre reverie, that still awaits its dawn. Among two million prisoners, the artists of today and tomorrow, tormented by the fantasies of captivity, hold the secret of what the art of peace will be. Between 1914 and 1918 virile fingers similarly occupied the idleness of the trenches, modelled clay and carved aluminium rings. In the drawers one hardly ever opens, in the lumber-rooms which are the most cluttered corners of a dwelling-place, we still find the ring of dull metal, a naked woman . . . the base of a shell, metal-work chrysanthemums . . . a stick made of twisted wood, with knife-carvings of serpent scales, with its date. . . .

The same period was marked by the development of those painters and sculptors, endowed with a personal genius, who became notorious. The rest of those who dreamed of art under arms have come back to earth and lived there for a rough and hazardous quarter of a century, have met the demands of an everyday art, dispersed to satisfy the requirements of furnishing, mural decoration, costume jewellery. This last, which was once flourishing with us, has made no advance these past two years and its familiar styles wait to give place to new French inspirations.

It's not only the war which paralyses the aspiring spirit and its realizations in every field. Quite apart from blood baths, French art has already passed through deplorable periods when everything, even literature, seemed struck by some minor humiliating curse, which extended from 'La Parisienne', that frightful monument standing at the entrance to a universal Exhibition, to Baroness Deslandes' coal-scuttle in the shape of a gaping toad, studded with pustules, and with bulging eyes.

There can be no redemption for the products of a tiresome epoch festooned with tapeworms. A retrospective of 1900 would evoke only horror, if one excepts certain feminine fashions, graceful, long-veiled, angeliform, and even these arose from the necessity for contrasts: to each monster his own seraphim. I myself used to wear virginal bandeaus which suited me like a ring in the nose, and J.-L. Forain, who had not yet trimmed his hair and his beard, used to call me his 'midnight angel'.

After all, there are worse absurdities. Jean Lorrain had raised to the rank of 'mystic guttersnipe' a certain Mrs Clarke, whose green eyes, red shock of hair and flowing siren's contours went well with spangled green and blue sheaths. With cool regularity this young woman produced daily a pastel representing a severed head floating among water-lilies and black irises. Sometimes the bloodless head opened its mauve eyes, sometimes it kept them closed. . . . 'Don't you ever paint the body?' I once asked this misguided victim of Burne-Jones. She made no other reply than a scandalized 'Oh!'

Where are all those severed heads? Where the beheaded that Mme Jacquemin also used to paint? All that seems more remote, more out-of-date, than the Directoire. The tidal wave which ritually condemns the shoddy manifestations of an epoch has swept out of the shop-windows – devoid of eatables but rich in 'souvenirs of Paris' – all the damned virgins, including, in various forms, a certain 'Melusine' in maleficent white, a fairy with a serpent's tail being strangled by a sombre horseman in bronze. . . . Dare I avow that I do not prefer to her any of the little naked women who lift their spun-glass, porcelain or galalith legs. . . .

I am waiting – oh so patiently! – for our own epoch to produce its vase. To each age unappreciative of a new art, to each difficult blossoming of the *objet d'art*, falls the duty to bring forth its characteristic vase, which itself takes inspiration from the female form. Like woman, the vase has a neck, more or less rounded flanks, a narrow base. It boasts large hips if Venus is lavish and becomes slender as she does. We had the Valloton vase and the Willette vase, round at the base, rather squat and vulgar. The Henner vase was pale and tall, the ambiguity of the sexes created the stupid 'uniflora', made for the stalk of a single flower. Yet 1900, economical in all things, held diamonds in contempt and was delirious about blue stones. It was at that time that I heard a music-hall artiste lamenting the theft of her jewels: 'They were worth more than six hundred francs!' she wept.

The dream of a potter without clay, the image caressed by a ceramist whose kiln is cold, the vase-type of 1940, deserves to have a flat stomach, thin loins, a hint of scoliosis. At least its

narrow shadow, its undernourished flanks, will harbour none of
of those obligatory monsters, foils to *fin-de-siècle* angels.

Decorative horrors do not arise and develop in the mind of
afflicted man, lucid in the heart of his long suffering. I've no
fear of seeing the deformed offspring of an insomnia shaped into
an ashtray. Nor the teapot – it still exists – which vomits the tea
out of its hideous sunfish mouth, its scaly flanks also those of a
sunfish. Prosperity may so behave as to frighten itself, to do itself
some harm, demand a thrill from art, the appeal of the ugly
and its violent influence on the beautiful. But we may be sure
that many of those for whom art is their glorious concern will,
when they emerge from a seclusion whose duration they hardly
dare contemplate, be passionately impelled toward a lucid art,
toward an expression which is the most legible, the most impreg-
nated by the virtues of free air and light regained.

*To tenants and others. Kindly shut the front door because of
the rats that go in and out. Thank you!*

Thus my concierge informed me that Paris was being rid of rats.
'Deratization' may be a good thing, but it's not a nice word.
In my district the purge was noiseless. I expected worse. The
deep and fragile buildings of the Palais-Royal lend themselves
to the most romantic conjectures. Lizards trace forked lightning
on the interior walls and the goodwill of the proprietors can only
prolong for better or worse the existence of a fine monument
hastily and somewhat flimsily erected. Oddly enough, there were
no rats in this quadrangular city, so symmetrically arranged in
compartments for human existence that you can guess, as you
raise your head, under which *entresol* Jean Cocteau sleeps or
stays awake at night, from which window Christian Bérard
requires a good light for his sketches, behind which lowered blind
Mireille used to work out her songs at a sky-blue grand piano,
and Paul Reboux his historical novels. 1939 and 1940 have
somewhat upset the routine beloved of these artistes, these mock-
bohemians. As for the rest of us denizens of the Palais-Royal, we
know still more about our pads, as seen from the outside. 'There,'
we say, 'must be an old and beautiful fireplace; there a room
without windows, fashioned in the thickness of the wall; there a
strange kitchen surrounded by windows like the cashier's desk

in a bank. . . . We imagine that the melodramatic cellars, which would not withstand a bombardment, contain at least an immured bailiff, the exit of an underground passage, the skeleton of an aristocrat run to earth under the Terror. . . .

But rats we have none. Why? I don't know. Perhaps because we've no stores of foodstuffs. Rats don't congregate without a motive. The rat left on the combatants of the last war the impression of a hardy adversary, formidable as much for bravery as for numbers, and a general feeling of horror, evoked less by its paws and teeth than by its cold snake-like tail and by the impossibility of assessing its numbers. Confronted with invasion by ants, termites and rats, man begins to despair from the moment when he can no longer compute the size of the invading forces. I gave ground once before the ants – for that matter, how could I have destroyed them – which had constructed, in two years, a conical anthill six feet high round the trunk of a young birch-tree. And the poet Renée Vivien refused to hear any more of a property in the Midi where the toads, she said, were 'more numerous than the stars in the sea and the sands of the sky'.

Kipling asserts that Asiatics do not tremble with the shudder that shakes Europeans on encountering a snake, even a harmless one. Is the fear of mice also occidental? It's strange to note that the passage of a minuscule mouse between two rows of orchestra stalls excites two reactions among the female public: to climb up on the seats and then to clasp their skirts round their legs with both hands. And what is the woman of today to do, who has only legs but no skirts? I admit, without any pride, that mice and rats don't give me palpitations. Sewermen of my acquaintance have filled me in on the rat, which they consider intelligent, very brave, and capable of solidarity to the extent that if a rat, fallen into a sewer, cannot cling to the brick walls, ten rats, fifty rats will plunge in, support it with paws and teeth, and offer it the rudder of their tail for its jaws to grasp.

I had the pleasure of getting to know the rats that Rachilde had tamed. The novelist formed such a regard for the character of the rat that it took the place, with her, of more familiar animals. White and fawn, brown, some grey like a mole, sleek, her five or six rats used to pass freely in and out of a cage whose door often remained open, as if they had been so many tame parrots. 'Rats suit me,' said Mme Rachilde, 'they're very affectionate and have a proud nature.' And, in fact, they listened to her words and commands joyfully and obediently and, like her, they had a bright fixed stare and sharp intact teeth.

I spent the month of August 1940 in Lyons; I was working there for *Candide* before returning to Paris. What use was 'deratization' against the very small mouse, more fawn than grey, which swarms in the heart of the deep buildings along the banks of the Rhone? From the very first night I recognized the typical gnawing, the teeth wearing away at the woodwork, the woodwork necessarily in its turn wearing down the teeth if the incisors are not to become greatly elongated. Then came the nocturnal escapades and rushing around and the language of mice let loose, the twittering which resembles that of birds. I feared for my precious kilo of sugar, my pound of chocolate. And I deposited in the right place the items of my peace-offering – breakfast crumbs, a few almonds – which were accepted.

With the evening shadows a pair of mice would enter through the french window, pass under my writing-table every day by my motionless feet to make their way to the banquet. If the window was closed against their departure, they left through the worm-eaten skirting-board. One day when the floor-waiter wanted to sweep up my guests' meal, I stopped him:

'Don't touch that! It's for my mice!'

He didn't understand at first and I repeated it. Then he paled, opened his mouth without uttering a sound and left never to return.

I should have found more understanding and support from one of my fathers-in-law, of whom I knew too little, M. Albert Gauthier-Villars, publisher, whose stocks of books were once menaced by mice. Against them, fortified in the unfathomable Quai des Grands Augustins, he first tried an enthusiastic fox-terrier bitch, a dupe of her hallucinations, who saw rats everywhere, attempted to scale the ramparts of books, brought them tumbling down, and was buried under their ruins with hysterical cries. Then there was rat-bane, and traps. Then discouragement and resignation. . . .

One night, one of the Gauthier-Villars' sons – the one who later signed himself Willy – anxious because his father was sitting up so late, went into his study to remind him of the time. On the desk, in the small circle of light outlined by the green lampshade, half a dozen mice were gambolling, nuzzling each other, combing their whiskers and confidently taking crumbs of cake and crushed sugar from the hand of the tender-hearted publisher. . . .

A relapse is worse than the disease. The chill of April is more destructive than the frosts of December. What will the northeast blast which was so severe last week leave of the delicate snow of petals, greenish-white on the plum-trees, creamy white on the pears, pink and white on the first apple-trees, pure white with a small cuff of blue around the branches of the cherries?

The fruit-tree, which flowers in spite of everything, requires a warm calm period when its blossom falls. If the petals, fallen at the foot of the trees, form an even carpet there is a good chance of fruit and the Normandy landowners, when the orchards cease flowering, never fail to go to see if their apple-trees have 'snowed' in a good circle round the trunks. This year every tree is late, except the lilac, and even the nests are not getting on fast. These I watch as best I can, having neither means nor motive for leaving Paris. I am left with the familiar dusty sparrow of the public gardens, the acclimatized thrushes of the Tuileries and the Palais-Royal.

When the time is right, I shall go to the Bois de Boulogne to listen to the song of the nightingales – liquid, starred with long luminous notes, ascending sobs which tumble in roulades. Disdaining the disasters and tumults of human creation, the nightingale has never failed to keep his assignation with me. During the lulls in a severe night bombardment in the spring of 1918 a thousand nightingales suspended from the trees of the Bois that festoon of pure notes which, initially high-pitched, descends to a low note, climbs once more to the peaks of sound, and ends in silence.

In every country where it sings, the resonant harmonious little grey-red bird has left its legends. In Burgundy they assert that it became nocturnal to evade, in waking, the tendrils of the vine which had ensnared it during sleep. In Asia, it turned aside Death, who had come to seek the Emperor of China. Already he was seated on the imperial bed, lifting his sword like a crescent moon. . . . But the nightingale began to sing for Death : 'Abandon this stifling room and follow me, for nothing can compare with the moonlight and my song pouring out over the flowers and tombs. . . .' Death rose from the near-funereal couch and went to dream under the moon to the nightingale's trills. . . .

The place in the Bois de Boulogne which I call the nightingale's is not very big. It occupied, it still occupies, I think, a small territory poor in carriage-ways to the north-east of the large lake. Singing in concert their intermittent song, it happened that the local nightingales momentarily fell silent in concert. But the very silence formed part of their melody, as the wake forms part of the reflection which blazes the water. Silence presaged the song, prepared it, gave it a sudden soaring; and the nightingales, in unison, found voice again. . . .

An adjacent area is beloved of tits. From one couple to another pass, by right of conquest, the clefts of trees, the trunks hallowed by age or debility. Bold as they are in isolated couples, tits in number are marvellously vociferous and brave. Man, war-maker and creator of child-martyrs, asserts that the tit is 'fierce'. It is not a human thesis which gives me pause. But I have seen valorous sprightly tits – the tomtit coiffed in black, the blue tit touched with azure, the great tit with its modest cloak – expel from a road-circle they had chosen a pair of jays whom they literally did not allow to say a word. The jays' powerful and often dirty beaks, their sturdy bodies and usurping habits, all this yielded before the troop of incensed tits, the ravishing faces drunk with anger, the stammered insults and the so-tiny fragile claws.

Similarly, I've often seen the Cat – the Cat who reigns over us – give ground under the attack of a male redbreast, always the same one, established with his family in a thicket of elms. He was no bigger than a nut possessed of wings and his little bulging breast was the colour of red wallflowers. A boundless authority emanated from him. As soon as the Cat entered the wood he announced his presence by furious 'tsk-tsks', descended from branch to branch above his enemy, forgot the danger sufficiently to stab with his beak the mild blue forehead and sacred ears of the Cat. But for our presence, what might she not have done? But she had been brought up to allow the finches to scratch for millet within reach of her paw, and to drop her gaze when a certain squirrel passed, flying in the air. So the Cat tolerated the redbreast's presumption and changed the conversation by pretending to hunt moles.

'A mole! A mole!' she exclaimed, with frenzied scratching at the friable earth, trampled a hundred times by rabbits and, doubtless, by moles. But we only saw the mole announced by our Cat on one occasion, an occasion when the redbreast, in my opinion, went rather too far in trying to nip the end of the Cat's venerable tail.

'It's only a joke,' said the Cat, 'it's only a joke. . . . A mole! A mole!'

And she dug in the earth diligently. . . . So diligently that we perceived in the hole a lilac snout, little pink hands, a pear-shaped belly, eyes afflicted by the daylight – a mole, in fact, a complete and very much alive mole. . . .

'Bravo, Cat! You've caught a mole! Cat, bravo!'

'Is that a mole?' exclaimed the Cat wordlessly. 'God, how horrible!'

Disgustedly, she shook the paws which had touched the monster and fled.

7

The poet, the playwright, the designer, the novelist – it's the same man, you've recognized him – lives in a house close to mine. He dwells in the depths of one of those *entresols* whose windows, arched like the entry to a burrow, earned the women of easy virtue who used to lie in ambush there the name of 'beavers' and 'demi-beavers'. I had a similar *entresol* for years. But they are better suited to a man of the theatre since the clarity of the daylight touches the pavement before reaching them and is reflected under the arch above like footlights.

Bound by friendship to the poet for long years, I don't presume on it to invade him at all hours. But his varied output makes a paper-scratcher jealous, and with good reason. The arched window-pane reveals this. If the passer-by lifts his head he will see on a large panel some heroic crayonned torso, or the portrait of a horse, or the mock-up of some stage-set, or the author himself, his crest of frizzy hair, his greyhound leanness, the sleeve turned back over his sprawling hand. But the passers-by here rarely lift their heads because the place invites them to dream, to slow their pace, and the poet-painter looks rarely at the passers-by. He contemplates some future poem, some future painting, he places on canvas the first sketch of a stage-set, of a white forecourt, of a red curtain; he sketches the first treads of a staircase, the sombre recess from which the evil spell will emerge. He projects a great implacable lamp on some material, touches some coarse canvas with gold. . . .

In everything that subserves theatrical art there resides and imposes itself a material, manual and phalansterian labour which entirely satisfies those who apply it. Artifice being inexhaustible, how can anyone envisage or predict the 'death' of the theatre? The preparation of a theatrical piece involves forces as physical as do ploughing or building. Removed from all intellectual culture, the theatre reinvents itself; the theatre would resurge spontaneously in a band of ignorant children deported to a desert island. Let a platform be erected, an imaginary horizon-bound six feet of boards, and in dashing from the spectator's sight the actor conveys the illusion that a hero has found his death or straddled a charger without saddle or bridle.

An art whose birth did not depend on the aid of genius could not thrive without it. That is why, every quarter of a century or so, it needs its inspired comedian, its unique comedienne. Even if interpretation is lacking, a producer can compel patience in the watching crowd; the play itself rarely suffices to do so. My poet neighbour, who is entitled to everything by virtue of his poetry, does not intend to be deprived of anything. His avidity, his activity, function as required to satisfy the public's yawning appetite. In recent weeks we have seen him adapt and arrange in his own style a masterpiece of the classic repertory, then write a drama and stage it. The preparations took place under my eyes, under my windows, and all resembling those for a play at a prize-giving.

I envy only the privileges of an inexhaustible youth; the comedians who arranged to meet the author, his aides, his friends, were of the same age – the age of exaltation, the age to astonish passers-by without seeing them, an age to allow the growth of a crazy hair-style out of deference for an epoch and a text, to transport armfuls of materials, properties, armour. An intoxicated dog following the troupe rushed headlong with it into the mouth of the metro, knew how to disappear under a coat, travel mute and invisible, also faithful to a role. A young actress, blonde as a lion, strolled under the elms in the garden, repeated a phrase, confessed a childish anxiety, waiting for the leading man, her partner, to return from painting a set. . . .

I thought, beside my window, that these were happy folk. For their happiness did not depend – as yet – on their success. Their happiness was the outcome of a state of collaboration, ardour and innocence; even their presumption was pure, when the actor affirmed: 'I'm the one who knows how to paint the sets,' when the author thought: 'I could play this part better than anyone,' when the dog nursed the desire to burst on stage, to bite the policeman and rescue Gabrielle Dorziat. . . .

Now that the piece is in actual performance, the comedians' only duty is to play in it and do their best for it, the poet's to write another or to meditate a poem. They don't adjust to this immediately. The fire is not yet extinct in the midst of their group, which has become a 'company' of comedians. One looks lovingly at the mark of a hammer-blow on a fingernail, another says: 'How this paint sticks to the skin! . . .' and the dog, in the wings, counts the seconds that elapse between the slamming of the door and the revolver shot.

After which they remain devoted to the work they have created; but it is no longer the same devotion. Each will fall back on a sort of dramatic asceticism, take cognisance of the burden he bears, instead of radiating in all directions like an exuberant vine. Each of them will be obsessed, responsible, in brief an actor. They will enjoy things less, be more nervous. That will be their true glory and the climate of their finest virtues.

'Speak to us,' they write to me – *they* are the women – 'speak to us of pleasant things.' And as they can write freely to me, they don't need to say that it is through what is agreeable that I can be most useful to them.

As much as my readers, I incline toward whatever can tint a sombre background with a bright colour, and I do not forget the mental colour. A child's cry, a laugh rising from the garden beneath my window, fall on my page as vividly as a red geranium. A bunch of wild hyacinths and lilies of the valley from Rambouillet, when I cannot go to pick them, remind me of a raid on lilies of the valley during which my hand encountered a small warm brooding pheasant.

Is not the tits' nest – situated once more in the hollow of one of the pollarded elms – placed there just to remind me of a dark-red bitch who shed her winter coat in great handfuls? Then two pairs of tits followed her and very nearly depilated her, my *beauceronne*, for the benefit of their nests. . . .

Here I am embarking on animal stories. But it's not long since the mice were dancing between my feet, which I was careful to keep still. Today, it is the children who swarm under my window. It is they who draft my stories of children. She would be good to paint, the glittering little girl, all spangles and dark hair like a brand, half fire, half charred. She's a good five and a half years old and has the authority of a savage queen. She reigns over three children smaller than herself. 'Turn the rope, Jojo! Not like that, turn it quickly! Lulu, you can't have the iron seat, the iron seat is mine, you've got your own chair! Watch out for your trousers, Mémaine, do you think I can afford to change them for you every week?' She is as tough as a real mother, as watchful as the leader of a band of chicks.

A man aged seven shouts to another man of eight: 'Are you coming skating at four o'clock?' 'Not on your life!' replies the man aged eight. 'I've done with all that. I've joined a combine for swapping stamps.'

These are local children. They have the sharp expression, the quick glance of the Parisian kids, and often a disconcerting physical agility; witness the bicyclist, plump as a blackbird, who does figures-of-eight round the pillars and twenty acrobatics in the Galerie d'Orléans. I do not miss such an excellent opportunity to be dumbfounded and to interrogate the acrobat's grandfather:

'Good Lord, how old is he?'

'Four and three months.'

'And how long has he been able to ride?'

'Oh, a long time; he learned when he was quite small (*sic*).'

But are they ever 'quite small' in our city? This year I really suspect that they grow only in mischievousness. They are the unfortunate juniors of the charming adolescent girls who lunch beneath the shade of our trees on two chairs, one of which serves as a table.

One would think, etched and graceful as they are, that the worst conditions of existence define and improve the character of their Parisian beauty. I tremble only to see them too acute, too expressive and, like Nouche, a local child, with too much personality. . . .

For Nouche, abusing her condition as an only daughter, still did not know how to read at seven years of age. So that her tender parents finally became concerned. They chose for her, on a hillside at the gates of Paris, the most modern school where a celebrated foreign method is practised which conceals the bars of the cage, appeals to free will and the personal inclinations of each child.

'You see,' said one of the instructresses to Nouche, 'in the same class there are children engaged in reading, others embroidering a little design they have invented themselves, others cutting out cardboard. . . . Choose, and do what you like best. . . .'

Nouche reflected and said :

'I choose to walk all alone by myself in the garden.'

Mindful of their promises, the instructors in good faith left Nouche in the garden until teatime, then between tea and dinner. . . .

'Nouche,' said the instructress next day, 'look, here are children learning their scales, singing songs; here are others rolling skeins of wool into balls, learning knot-stitch, threading necklaces; here are others laying the table for lunch, learning to boil water for tea. . . . Choose your friends and learn what you like best. . . .'

'I choose,' said Nouche, 'to learn to go for a walk all by myself in the garden.'

And so she did. She would be doing so still if her father, disappointed with the result of the celebrated method, had not taken Nouche aside :

'Nouche,' he said, 'the joke's over. If you don't know how to read, write, count in a month, you'll get the biggest hiding of your life. . . .'

'My God,' said Nouche, 'don't talk so much, my head's splitting. I understand.'

She changed, if I may so put it, her opinions, read, wrote, counted within three weeks for the pleasure of being able to say to her parents :

'I do hope that you're going to put me in a proper school and take me away from here. They string pearls here, they sing songs, they serve tea and do the dishes. And they call that work!'

Il pleut. Les arroseurs, arrosant sous la pluie,
Lavent des lacs de boue avec sérénité.

I no longer know – if I ever knew – to whom to attribute these two alexandrines. But I know that serenity is capable of defying, beneath the shower, the impassive humour of the waterer; rather go to witness that of the public which solicits the favour of applauding, at the Théâtre-Français, *La Nuit des Rois*, *Cyrano*, or even *André del Sarto*. An old barrier, a sort of ancient sheep-pen, banks up the wave of applicants between the colonnade and the wall. It's a treacherous spot. Always an active draught, in the form of a Z, comes from the Place du Palais-Royal, dividing into two draughts, one of which hugs the Rue de Montpensier and the other penetrates the Galerie de Chartres. In summer there are eddies of dust; in autumn a maelstrom of prematurely fallen leaves dances in the same place.

Before the war I've seen the respectful queue, assembled by some masterpiece in bad weather, lengthen, seek the shelter of the interior arcades, three hours, four hours before the performance. What faith, and what an example set by a crowd where no one is rich and no one complains about exchanging money hard to come by, for an insubstantial pleasure! The true lovers of the dramatic art who thronged to stand here in prosperous times are here today. I thought, as the frightful winter slowly passed, that the majority were sickly and ill-nourished, that their shoes were thin. But there they stayed, at their post that no solicitude cares to make more comfortable. Some have folding chairs. A woman sits on a camp-stool, takes her daughter on her knees. Another, furnished with a long cloak, keeps a fold of the cloak for herself, spreads the other fold over a neighbour's legs. The hopeful of both sexes take the precaution of bringing a newspaper and make leggings from it, fastened with string, against the cold. Men, tired of standing, pass an arm over the barrier to relieve the weight of their body. The taciturn read, leaning sideways, changing feet like standing horses. . . .

Sad details, which nevertheless constitute a very heartening spectacle. For the waiting is not just gratuitous, it is already rewarded. I'd wager that nearly all of these devotees of the cheaper seats at the Comédie-Française have already seen, already heard, what they have come to see, hear and applaud over again. That's where they differ, in their long wait, from the other queues of spectators, simply curious about a novelty, who will see it only once. The spectator at a new piece kicks his heels bad-temperedly, the frequenter of the modest seats at the Français is hopeful. He smiles at what he waits for, mentally contemplates what attracts him. He is not drowned, anonymous, among intolerant elbows, feet and bodies; he is one of a fraternity capable of lending him, this one a newspaper, this a folding chair. Saint Martin the Sharer frequents the queue of the Théâtre-Français; I've surprised him there engaged in dividing his cress sandwich and fig-paste biscuits! The object of his charity, however, defended herself stoutly and with much ceremony against such largess:

'No, really, you're too kind, but I don't want to deprive you of it, you've got to eat in a rush as it is. . . .'

'Look,' replied Saint Martin, 'you'd be wrong to deny yourself; my wife has done us proud, just look at the bulge it makes in my overcoat! And anyway, when I come here my stomach seems stopped up. The excitement keeps me going.'

Here the basis of the conversation is less alimentary than elsewhere. The bitter wind that blows under these historic vaults peddles only a minimum of economical recipes and of recriminations. Fraternal despite the prevalent mistrust, together despite the season, what do they talk about, these exceptionally sociable people? O wonder, they talk of art! They talk of Racine, of Musset. They discuss Marivaux. Their memory attests a long fidelity; it is plain that the young have begun at an early age to benefit from the terrible draught that leads to these great works. A strong woman, her hands reddened by everyday work, quotes *Polyeucte*, mistakes a verse which an unknown corrects in an undertone; both of them try to get the great lulling rhythm of the alexandrine right; some young girls have brought the text of one piece. Here, before the threshold, one breathes the very atmosphere and exaltation of the noble theatre without anyone making too much fuss about it. The policeman who presides over good order leans on the balustrade, exchanges remarks with the queue it restrains; I hear in passing that he's talking of Marie Bell.

In a racecourse crowd it is inevitable that all those present are race-goers. But in the one waiting for the box-offices of the Théâtre-Français to open, I have seen or heard no ignoramuses. The words I catch in passing would do honour to a dress-rehearsal audience. And what knowledge of the actors! What familiar deference in designating, by their names and surnames, the active and retired. . . . What blazing enthusiasm and preju-dice, especially among the women!

A local public, in fact : the best, the most enlightened of publics, endowed, moreover, to an extreme with a sense of propriety. A very modest old lady with a shopping-basket – our garden's not short of them – was chatting on a bench with an old gentleman provided with an elderly dog – the type's not rare here – and I heard the name of a young recruit to the Comédie :

'You'll see, you'll see. . . . She'll come on,' said the old lady. 'She's got just the style we need. I saw her leaving after the matinée on Thursday. She already makes a very good exit.'

The compliments of these affectionate elders, assembled to see 'their' artistes depart, are as sweet to the comedians as the cries that escape from younger devotees. The public of the Comédie-Française still retains the habit of celebrating the exit of its favourite actors, the custom of the timid little bouquet, of the rose rather faded from having awaited, grasped in a feverish hand, the passage of an idol. . . .

How can I evoke this kind of spontaneous ceremonial – the discreet bravos, the enthusiastic young girls, the students who jostle each other to open the car-door – without recalling your *aigrettes*, your royal progress and your smile, O Cécile Sorel?

I don't know who invented the toy cap-pistol. I am also ignorant of who perfected it, increasing its detonation till it comes to resemble that of a real, small-calibre revolver. Somewhere in the world there exist spheres which, thrown on the pavement, make the sound of a fire-arm. Let us not forget, in the list of childish amusements, the drum and trumpet. The rattle is not dead and the ball-bearing whistle, now that it has been issued to our

policemen, is particularly exploited by infantile lips. . . . I mention
these noise-producing toys merely to consign their inventors to
eternal fire.

My vituperation is more disinterested than it might seem. I
am not merely defending here the right adults possess to a certain
kind of silence. I don't claim, in the spirit of tit-for-tat, 'noise-
for-noise'. For if we submitted the children to the trial of the
tu-tu-tu-tu, of the boumboum and the hui-i-i-i, I think we should
be accused of driving them mad. Why should we not complain?
The excesses of the radio, of piano-practice, have evoked sanc-
tions. But there is no edict that condemns the use by children of
the shrill trumpet and other so-called musical instruments. All
of us, alas, have nerves more fragile than . . . well, than they used
to be.

A great silence extending over our city ensures that isolated
sounds pierce us painfully. Against our will we repeat the experi-
ment tried formerly by one of my friends who, exasperated by
the tumult of Paris, bought an isolated house on the banks of
the Seine. He settled in and witnessed the first twilight fall with
delight. The first moon rose and simultaneously, at intervals,
distinct, irremediably shattering the peace of the night, the barking of the first farm dog, to which the dogs all round soon
responded.

The human voice is the enemy of our repose only when it
makes itself expressive, isolated, meaningful. A crowd beneath
our windows does not always awaken us, but the neighbour who
converses on the other side of the partition is unbearable. The
children, numerous in the garden, mingle their voices with those
of the sparrows and pigeons; sometimes a school arrives, giving
its children an hour's recreation. All this is gay, lively, linked
with the sonorities made pleasing by the bond between man and
nature, like the mill-wheel, the threshing-machine, the great
saw. . . .

But the moment arrives when the children use their whistles
and their cap-pistols and all is spoiled. Spoiled for us who work
or read; spoiled for the children responsible for the whistling and
the explosions. For the whistle forms part of no game. Worse
still, it paralyses the game. Similarly, the cap-pistol forms no part
of any bellicose illusion and that's just what's strange about it.
The child who has a whistle whistles and does nothing else. The

child who wields a cap-pistol slips a cap under the hammer of the weapon, sets it off and begins all over again. When he has exhausted his ammunition he acquires some more and begins all over again. He doesn't run, he doesn't pursue imaginary enemies, he does not laugh or dispose his battalions strategically. He loads and fires his little weapon indefinitely, just as the child with the whistle whistles till he's out of breath. The one and the other, these and those, seem stricken by a sort of hypnosis. Sometimes the whistling children, tired of whistling standing up, sit down and whistle seated.

Nevertheless, astride the rim of the empty lake, the child machine-gunners machine-gun. I see some who leave the gardens without having joined in the good general roystering. They haven't played ball, or climbed, or roller-skated, or made up conversations between doctor and patient, merchant and customer, manager and long-distance walker. Yet they are the ones who seem to be most tired.

I've often wanted to ask one of these vain beaters of the air if, when they're at home, they indulge in the same sad task, as unfulfilled as it is endless.I feel that maternal irritability, which is considerable in these times of anxiety and undependable victualling, would promptly bring it to an end by convincing and rapid means, even though the guilty one is only partly responsible. He was not born with a liking for violent sounds, discord and deflagration. The first drum frightened him, as did the first trick revolver. But a certain kind of perversity grows in children like a green pea in the rain. To set off himself what used to frighten him becomes a pleasure. A mindless pleasure: a sound repeated without variation stupefies the understanding. Mirbeau asserts that the Chinese torturers have raised it to the level of a torment.

Many things change, will change around us, within us. Although I've no inclination to adopt a tardy career as a reformer, and am persuaded that I should have no success if I tried to direct our urban children towards games which make no noise, I do propose it nevertheless. Our partitions are thin, our dwellings confined, and rare and precious the city gardens, those lungs which are the refuges of infants and young mothers. The latter, pushing the small pram and the dozing baby from Valois to Beaujolais and from Montpensier to Chartres, seek in vain a corner without fusillades or whistle-blasts where baby can sleep and its mother relax.

'If I fired off five hundred shots here with a revolver loaded with blanks, what would you say to me?' I asked one of the obliging park-keepers.

'I'd tell you: "This isn't a firing-range." '

'And if I took your whistle to whistle without stopping for hours?'

'I'd tell you: "This isn't a station." '

'Then tell that to the ones who are whistling and using the pistols!'

The keeper only responded with an evasive gesture and the smile of a brave man who finds it entirely natural to take an ill-behaved stroller to task but thinks twice before upsetting a child.

8

I believe that no success in my career as a writer equalled that earned by my recipe for the *flognarde* published in a daily paper last winter. Not a week passes without someone asking me for it again. 'You, who are above all a practical woman, give us a few recipes now the bad weather's setting in. . . .' My dear correspondents, preserve the conviction that I am a practical woman: you may finish by making me believe so myself.

As for recipes . . . I gauge my impotence by that of those 'aunts' and 'cousins' who are, just now, at the end of their tether. Yet they do their best, strive to achieve a roast without meat, cream without milk, and a virtually eggless omelette. But there are currently, at the end of every economical recipe, two little words which upset everything. They should be kept for the end, they might as well be printed in illegible letters, the words: *two spoonfuls of oil* or *thirty-five grammes of butter*.

Our shrinking malnutrition also uses, as a palliative, expressions never so much seen before. The 'scrap' replaces the sirloin, the 'chunks' of rabbit deputize for hare *à la royale*. But whence to take the scrap when one has not had the whole article? With what goodwill do our culinary guides – your modest disciples, dear Curnonsky – suggest that we replace meat by molluscs! But as there are almost no molluscs, what to put and use in their stead? A good conjunction, *if*. 'If you have a little gravy in the bottom of your plate . . .' It's a precautionary tactic. Try to smile at it. Humour is a form of courage.

Having smiled, let's tackle what one knows least about in France. Out of fifty kinds of salad we grow, we eat, whether cooked or raw, four or five. This is not enough in peacetime; it is plainly insufficient today. Rather apply to M. Pierre Chouard! 'Have you never browsed on the tender tops of lucerne, with or without dressing?' he'd say. 'Nor the birds' groundsel?' I don't say that we should adopt the regime of canaries and goats but we might well – I forgot the rampion – sometimes abandon, without too much sacrifice, our eternal and expensive endive and lettuce! The fine weather is not over and summer will return. If I set about it too late this year, I'm not forgetting that there is, on the less salty seashores, a large and soft and tender false sea-lettuce of an emerald green called the ulva. It's visible from far off and is rarely covered by the sea.

But you are creatures of routine like the children, and sometimes as much as the Asiatics, determined to let themselves die beside a pile of corn if they haven't their handful of rice. What housewife now discards milk that's gone off? I mix it with salt, pepper and raw onion and baptize it 'fontainebleau 41' because it's much nicer than most yoghourts. Or else I incorporate it in an omelette, which swells thereby.

I am unable to construct a long eulogy on the ground-nut. It is wild, but avoids certain soils. It is a small wrinkled tubercle, unbeautiful. Its brother, in Spain, is used to prepare the delicious emulsion called *orchata de chufas*. In the Limousin especially, the child shepherds know how to dig them up and crunch them raw.

Having made my way as far as the Bois, on a damp morning of last week, I followed a mushroom-hunter who filled his bag with minuscule mushrooms with pointed caps, born of two hours of dew. But he was much more proud of a plateful of 'violets', as large as the palm of one's hand, of such a pretty blue-mauve that one does not risk, in gathering them, making a fatal mistake. While I was following him a pair of nuthatches – it's the time of their migration – were chattering in the tall pines. With their tails arched in a fan against the trunk, they explored, deloused the scaly bark. Their bluish backs shone in the sun like new slate; they descended familiarly enough for me to be able to see the slight curve of their long tapering beaks. . . .

I worked for a moment for the man with the mushrooms, who did not overlook the wild garlic. But I found another marvel, one of those fly-sized toads, as large as a bee, which are so finely sculpted in an almost black agate, furnished with eyes in which a grain of gold quivers; and I paid no more attention to anything else, even though it was inedible. In fact, I don't eat frogs either. This long and trying time might well turn us away as a people from certain gluttonies, put off by the strong and heady flavour of roast meat, game and cured provisions. Without illusions as to next winter's fare, I await the chestnut, irreproachable nourishment, cerebral succour, and the walnut if possible. My last ration of meat: eighty grammes, difficult to deal with, bony despite its small volume, has disheartened me. I must have recourse to lentils and fruits in season. Why did I not imitate my friend Max – aged thirteen – who is back from the country and whom I questioned on his holiday tasks:

'Good work this summer, Max?'

'I'll say! Thirty pounds of white haricots I've brought back!'

'And what else?'

'Some long green pears. And first apples.'

'And . . .'

'A pot of melted butter. A round of grey bread weighing ten pounds. If you leave it to get dry, you can keep it a long time, to slice into the soup. . . .'

A pot of butter, a large floury loaf . . . Little Red Riding Hood of '41, how farsighted you are! I should like to obliterate those three anxious furrows between your eyebrows. . . . I hope that youth will return to you – I quote Labiche – with age.

The grape is slow in ripening. It will ripen, however, thanks to these September days, of which nothing is lost to the vine, where the sun's face is clear, washed of clouds, from rising to setting. Many a vineyard will be harvested this month under a sky red at dawn, pink at twilight. The sun of these skies soon dries the dew of the chill nights, abundant enough to water the cluster and its juice should the harvesters cut it too early.

We think of wine with the more reverence since it behaves like other foodstuffs: it becomes scarce or goes into hiding. Demand sends up the price of everything. Empty, a good bottle of thick glass becomes a precious vase, which can be used for preserving both tomatoes and runner beans. It constitutes a bait, an object of barter. Full, we lay it down gently in the cellar. When it comes to drinking it, we exercise a sage parsimony. There will always be enough wine in France for its use not to disappear, but it will be moderated. In Provence, for years, at no matter what time in the summer, we used to treat wine like water: 'I'm thirsty, pour me a glass of wine.' For in the Midi there's no drink that goes down better or is gayer than a young wine, a dark raspberry colour, equidistant from the *rosé* or white, which I reproach for being often, between Cassis and Fréjus, a little sticky, and the heavy *vin noir*, which has more colour than bouquet. . . .

I run on about wine and vintaging because it's September, just as in June I evoked the cherry we had to do without, the fine Montmorency with transparent flesh, in red lacquer. Its cousin, the *bigarreau noir*, is in comparison mere insipidity and a flavour of elderberry seeds – with a little white worm near the stalk. Neither have we seen this year that noble form of peach called 'Venus's breast'. To those who don't know it I impart that it is oval rather than round, with a poorly-marked furrow, and that it bears at its velvet apex the jutting navel which gives it its name. In the *Grande Pomologie*, that inexhaustible picture-book, one may admire it painted from nature with an art which imitates even the beauty-spot inflicted on its divine breast by an over-piercing sun or by the bite of a wasp.

We need not be afraid to contemplate that which we lack. Let us blur those features whose every absence wounds us by a more pressing gaze, a deepened imagination. To evoke just now scenes of abundance is not only a rather mortifying exercise, it is a feat, a brave way of reviving memory's records. There's no recollection that does not have its caverns that time obscures; but from which we can unearth some little secret about to escape us. The mind's eye ferrets them out. When I talk to you of vintaging I have just encountered, on a vine of former days, in a tufted fringe of leaves, a large green lizard which I gropingly seized. I exclaimed with the chill shock – a woman always exclaims – but I did not let go of my prize, which was of good size, delicately scaled, furnished with long fingers which tried to loosen mine, a majestic green tail, a blue spot at each temple, the purple gullet of a small gladiolus. . . .

When I did let it go a tomcat of the house leapt on it. But I seized the tomcat by the tail; it turned round, cried out, and let go the lizard, which it could not find again. During the days that followed the cat returned to the same place, searched under the leaves, and sang guilelessly – in its deep modulated tomcat's voice – an appeal to the ungrateful prey; unless it was a nostalgic *vocero* on the theme: 'Once I had a lizard. . . .'

I rediscover this escaped lizard under a pleasant disorder of meridional titbits, cicadas and sticky wasps. We are, most of us, too heedless of those insubstantial benefits with which our memory is overflowing. We don't sweep in the corners. For lack of culinary recipes worthy of my readers, I offer the means of composing tasty mental pictures. Yes, yes, I hear you grumbling about *l'odeur du festin et l'ombre de l'amour* . . . but I don't retract. Sensitive to the seasons – as the little marine animalcule, though carried far from the sea, remain sensitive to the tides, rising and falling in the water according to the time of the original floods – I congratulate myself on having, come June, a mental haymaking; then the ripe corn and its subtle dusty fragrance, and today I proceed to the grape-harvest, which I know best of all. I mount my flying carpet, from Saint Tropez to Toulon, where the punctual ripening of the grape recruits the entire population in the service of wine. For this egalitarian festival the dressmaker comes with her scissors, the innkeeper abandons his cold oven, the fisherman leaves his boat tied up.

The stranger has but one resort, to sign on for the vintaging, and that is what he does. He can earn his day's wages thereby, at least in the shape of one or two pitchers of blue and gold grapes which will give him, if he so desires, a few litres of *vin cuit*. Press the grapes, put the foaming juice on to cook, and don't take it off until reduced to a third, to be put in bottles and firmly corked. Its alcohol and its sugar, come straight from the sun, make it superfluous to add any flavouring. But they don't excuse you from filtering it before putting it into flasks. For these grapes, full of virtues, disgorge their excess in a thick scum which comes frothing to the top, collects in the gully of the press, fills it with clots, manifests the richness, the thick and generous temperament of the vintage. . . .

In these regions where the sun reigns, quickening the heart-beat and fading the cherry in May, I have drunk wine eight days old which behaved like an adult wine. It is not this, nor the jug with flattened belly that it inflames with bright red, that I regret the most. Fine rustic, cordial passer-by, I'll find you again some day. . . .

But shall I rediscover, once the grape is pressed, while it is not yet cajoled to change itself into *eau-de-vie*, shall I rediscover its especial perfume? It rose from the vat with its polished sides, floated above the *marc* composed of grape-pulp, pips, grapeskins, and here I confess that my optimistic evocation deserts me and turns to melancholy. Because, for a few hours, the marc exhales – fugitive, unforgettable – a perfume of mignonette similar to that which wanders, on a spring night, over the vineyard in flower.

9

I can't go for very long without talking about animals. My first *arrondissement* has become – for good reason! – poor in cats, even in dogs, and parrots are a forbidden luxury in the Palais-Royal. But the decimated species cling to life. Our square has a newcomer, a very pretty crow, descended from what belfry, from what sound-screen? It says, first and last, 'tiac', makes its way on foot in the gutters, and settles without repugnance on the head of the 'Latin Genius', a deplorable statue and an enormous affront to the flowerbeds. The Latin Genius turns towards my windows a bare back which is unattractive from top to bottom. But it's no better seen from in front.

A couple has come together in our historic floral quadrangle; but can I call them a couple? Pierrot the cat and Lili the tortoise never leave each other. In eight or nine years the tortoise has not exceeded the size of an average scallop-shell. She is lively, flat, eyes and ears alert, and naturally enough resembles Voltaire.

She bounds joyfully on hearing her name and comes running if she is not imprisoned in her crate. Free, she crosses the threshold of my ground-floor apartment; can I write that she dashes into the garden? Then begins the anxiety of the affectionate cat, who joins her, addresses her, pushes her with his paw into the right path. But she is obstinate, and the cat walks her just as we walk a dog, that is, by following her. When she reaches a dangerous area, too full of children, the cat lies over her, covering her with his black and white body. He gives her to understand that the hour of siesta has arrived and, overcome by her companion's warmth, she allows herself to be incubated. Beyond the white belly protrudes the small reptilian head, covered with scales, regarded lovingly by the tomcat. If he is the first to quit the communal crate, Lili the Tortoise stands erect on her hindlegs, supported against the wall, and pines until some kind soul delivers her. Should she escape, some other kind soul brings her back. The animals of the square are all somewhat communal.

Communal also the beautiful Moulouk, a white, tawny, black, hairy eskimo with a cool muzzle and golden eyes. Has every animal a sense of architecture and ideal dimensions? Our pigeons fly only within the interior of the rectangular edifice. The sparrow, a few pairs of tits, are here to stay, only flutter about and do not depart. The ravishing cat of the concierge at the Comédie-Française contemplates the outside world through a window-light. Its narrow paradise, the lodge, is sufficient to it. The cats of the garden rarely run the risk of crossing the street. The beautiful Moulouk has adopted the behaviour of our enclosure, that is, he goes out, walks and returns alone.

Just as the Society for the Protection of Animals once placed a vigorous outrunner at the disposal of tired cart-horses, so Mitsou, a cat of the Palais-Royal, goes to town for the work of deratization. Born on the Montpensier shore, she crosses to reach the Valois side, which is particularly well stocked with game. White and black, she is Pierrot's half-sister. Short-haired, with short sharp claws, she has a flank that is flatter, a paler nose and tongue, than before the war. Restrictions. . . . So she makes her way to the drives, where she is invited as to a cure. Nothing is more sudden, more effective, than her attack. In times of plenty Mitsou was all for sport, for the honour of victory and racial hate! Nowadays she eats what she kills, leaves only the tips of the wormlike tails, vomits a little rat-skin, and drinks deeply to purify herself. These meals she conceals from the human eye and digests joylessly. Necessity is not *gourmandise.*

A warm autumn enriches our fauna. With the mauve asters appear the last generations of butterflies. This year the peacock butterfly abounds, noticeably smaller than in July, but resplendent in colour, band upon band, marked by signs in the shape of eyes, garnet, bronze, almost black on the underside; an ensemble both active and lazy since it trips 'on foot' on its dark little legs over a bush of flowers, rather than fly over it.

Saturday, in the great heat of noon, on each clump of pale violet asters, there were a good twenty, as many peacocks as little bright-coloured tortoise-shells or vulcans printed with red, black and white. The false-bee, recognizable by its rounded posterior which has no sting, abounded. A gust of air, the sudden passage of a child, fluttered all the wings on the flowers, to settle again a moment later. Can there remain so few lovers of gratuitous beauty then, that I am so often the only one to pay any attention to the red canna lilies, whose every calyx is large enough to swallow the bird that gathers there a sugared drop, to the butterflies which unpetal, then reconstitute, a bouquet?

They've gone back to school. Here, you can see it at once; the Richelieu garden, from two to four, no longer swarms with children like a family beach in August. After four o'clock they return, eager to retrieve the habits of their liberty. Many are marked, in these first days of school, by those violent childhood emotions which ring the eyes, hollow the cheeks. For the youngest the first days of school are days of lost appetite, gritted teeth, of low fever. But how many admit it?

A certain class of confidence is not intended for grown-ups, still less for parents. These, for their part, repress their anxieties. The mothers take stock of the coming season with an eye that dreads and defies it.

Before the appearance of the worst enemy, cold, there are, in fact, many matters to arrange. A child starting at school may suffer in twenty ways; he begins by suffering from everything until he cares nothing, so he says, for anything. His fastidiousness is wounded by a makeshift smock, trousers too large, hair of a colour that leads to teasing. I still recall, when my family was hard up, a little blouse cut from the unworn parts of an old tail-coat of my father's, in Elbeuf cloth. I was fourteen years old. It is not usual for a girl of fourteen to wear a blouse of black Elbeuf cloth, badly cut. . . . I rushed ahead of questions and astonishment :

'Have you noticed my blouse? It's made from papa's old black suit, it's a good idea, isn't it?'

Each of us counts to his credit, thank God, two or three small traits of courage, well camouflaged as frivolity. . . .

The school uniform, insofar as it was limited to the smock, had something to be said for it. It soothed the children's self-esteem. Let's think no more of it. Let's think of warm soles, of warm socks, of anything to retain the warmth. The children – at least those of Paris, from which I don't stir – have made only too much use during the summer of what might have covered their feet in the bad weather. They embark on autumn and winter with small feet which are pale, tender and chilly, which have not benefited sufficiently from light and sun, not sufficiently hardened their bare soles, not splashed about sufficiently, were it only in the pavement hydrant.

It is difficult to concern oneself about children without reviving in our mind the miserable and tormented shadow of the most recent 'child-martyrs'. I detest this appellation, with its almost official imprint. One says child-martyr as one says road-mender. How is it that France, country of spoiled children – that's an ugly word, too – of enlightened education, of common maternal indulgence, can produce so many terrifying parents? After the sentencing to death of a torturer of a mother, of a ferocious father, I receive a letter. It begins with an outburst from savage and vengeful motherhood. 'Death? Is that all? But it's not enough!' Having uttered this outcry the exacerbated mother goes for the others responsible : 'And what about the neighbours who said nothing? The silent teacher who saw daily the marks on a small body in process of dying?'

At another trial the parent-executioners were barely punished. To the reporter who asked me : 'If you had been a member of the jury, what would you have decided?' I replied : 'A month in prison for the neighbours.' For the neighbours, questioned on the long martyrdom of the two children, declared that they were 'used to hearing them cry out'. Used to it, yes, as they were used to the bell of the tram or to the wireless. As they were used to the sound of the angelus.

This sort of monstrous remark once reached its acme on the lips of a rich woman to whom someone was deploring the secret misery of a great artiste: 'How can one leave such distress ignored and unrelieved? Is it possible? Is it really true?' Mme X tossed a disillusioned head: 'There's more of it than you'd think. Look, take me, who's talking to you, I've a relative in the last stages of destitution.'

But what are we to think of the witness who came forward to testify last week, and to describe the spectacle of the little girl *hung by the wrists from the window catch*, who was no longer crying and had 'haggard eyes'. This witness said enough for us to imagine a dialogue between the two mothers:

'And why do you fix her up like that, your little one?'

'Oh well, it's because she's naughty.'

'Yes, children are really maddening sometimes. Well, goodbye then. Thanks for the iron. I'll bring it back tomorrow.'

Tomorrow. . . . The witness did not say whether the little girl was still 'naughty' the following day, or shut up in her folding bedstead, or even dead. One would prefer to know no more about it.

What it would be useful to know are the reasons for the silence maintained by the teacher at the school attended daily by the doomed child as she neared her end. Do not detect in my curiosity any thirst for punishment, rather the reverse. I know too well that the position of a teacher in certain areas is an unenviable one. The life of a young teacher – solitary, a stranger to the district, among families zealous to inspire fear and favouritism – can be compared to a reign of terror. All who approach a child should be of an heroic purity. . . .

Let us consider, too, on behalf of the silent teacher, that a child's mouth is sealed by a surprising self-control. The majority of schoolchildren of both sexes are inclined, in the bosom of their family, to suppress the cares of scholastic hours. How many reveal to an affectionate teacher the atrocious conditions of a family life? An inflexible silence, inspired less by terror than by shame, by a hopeless filial love, forges, prolongs and aggravates the unhappiness of oppressed children. They would rather die than seek our aid.

There are, I'm told, forty-five thousand of them. Forty-five thousand specimens of the most ephemeral kind that nature has been pleased to create, of the most apt to perish from a breeze, a shock, to die of cold, to be obliterated by a drop of rain, to fade away if our finger probes the multicoloured powder of their wings : forty-five thousand butterflies. . . .

It's not the first time that I've been shown this unparalleled exotic collection. I've been here before, seeking asylum from present time, from waiting, from anxious realities. I tell myself that there are forty-five thousand butterflies and insects; that I have, thank God, no chance of getting to know them all even if I visited them often; and, confident in this store of prodigies which I cannot exhaust, I can admire them unhurriedly and ungreedily.

This collection of wings which, immobile, have crossed the oceans, dwells far from the bare halls and chill illumination of museums, places of exile for entomology. Curiosity dies at the threshold of public exhibitions, when these are arranged for treasures of small size and great number. Entrusted to public visitation, what would become of the pristine freshness of a private collection, the down that adheres to the butterfly as lightly as bloom to a fruit? It dwells at present in the trays of a cabinet-work edifice created for it. The female genius who presides over its security and development conceived the idea of giving each handle of each tray the shape of a bronze bombyx.

Nature has decided that the age of an old butterfly – if I am right – is some forty to fifty days; but man declines to subscribe to nature's wastefulness and selects his victim to be embalmed among those creatures which borrow from their environment the minimum of substance and the maximum of brilliance; he kills them subtly far away and brings them back, folded like a love-letter, across febrile marshes, forests scented with wild beasts, tracks barred by snakes, on the back of the sea's swell. . . .

Are the hunters of exotic butterflies ever sufficiently rewarded for their trouble? Yes, if you consider that this trouble is great, the dangers manifold, and that these very perils constitute an attraction, are part of the reward. The orchids and butterflies which haunt our mortal Eden often fascinate the tracker. The man who embarks on the expedition for love of gain, but who

hunts with passion, forgets prudence : he is lured still further
by the wing endowed with green fire, further still by the fleshy
orchid, further still by a butterfly with four unimaginable petals
and by a flower which, winged and rootless, may take flight. . . .

I cannot but regard the hunter of exotic butterflies, the
venturesome trafficker, in the romantic light of a man tempted,
were his temptation limited to the capture of a prey known and
catalogued, but unrivalled for its blaze of colour, its size and
surprising detail, for its glittering monstrosity, for a hermaphro-
dite or albino variation. . . .

I learn here, I discover, that a regression can upset the species
of lepidoptera established with such a wealth of care as to seem
immutable. But a decision made at a very high level, a force
which had not yet said its last word, comes into operation,
decrees that the Agrias, a marvel that seemed eternally decorated
with pure red and incandescent blue, shall lose this red, will trade
it for a hue of dried blood and orange. Then the sovereign whim
thinks anew, improves the splashes of blue mother-of-pearl, the
arabesque recently muddied with ochre, contemptuously informs
the searcher that down below, at the other side of the world, a
part of creation is not yet accomplished and that animal species
are evolving as they did in the malleable period of the planet.

The sun has rotated, touching in its passage the glazed trays in
each of which forty-eight identical butterflies testify that it would
be absurd to imagine that a forty-ninth specimen could be more
richly embossed, bear a completer rainbow or more unimaginable
oxidations. That which was a green jewel an hour ago turns to
violet, let's call it violet since it's necessary, in the poor nomen-
clature of colours, to bestow a name on this changing glimmer
which, at one edge, still inclines to purple and, at its other edge,
verges mysteriously on a hint of very pale blue. . . .

Pure contemplation rapidly uses up the time. Momentarily
distanced from the dramas of our epoch, we heard only silence
or else the remarks of a knowledgeable mind which patiently
informed us when we posed some stupid ignoramus question. Our
ponderous 'why's' collapse before the mystery of symbiosis.
'Why? . . .'

The shadow gradually obscures the wings of the butterflies, it's
night already. But, in a glass case, the fluorescent minerals have
not yet surrendered their cinnabar glow, their glacial nightmare

blues, their glow-worm greens. Amorphous, torn from strata that capture limpidity, none of them derive from human art. In this house of marvels we withdraw from our fellow man, gently brush him aside. No one has spoken with hostility in this peaceful jungle dominated by the great portrait of a half-smiling panther, of a tiger-cat which was a faithful friend, and by a bronze python, satiny as a bare arm.

A few cold nights, as many cool days; that's enough to change everything and to make us exclaim, when we descend into the metro to encounter the gust of ascending air which ferries such a deeply human odour: 'Ah, it's good here! . . .' No, it's not good, in the metro. But it is our sole resort. It is omnipresent, it serves and fatigues us, links us to our fellow-creatures, saturates us with them, edifies us as to their degree of misanthropy, sociability, personal hygiene even. A rapid means of transport, a heated coach, it is the tumultuous refuge of silence. No one talks in the metro any more, no one cares for the exchange of unconsidered words at the top of his voice.

But the time is not yet past for needless moving around, favoured by the tepid torpor of the underground. The closure of the french windows of a balcony, of the window opposite, the dormer window of the top floor, means the rupture of many a contact, the extinction of some familiar voice, while well-known faces remain for months behind a drawn curtain.

From an open room, receptive to every echo, haunted by insubstantial presences created by light and sound, exchanged signals, the indiscretions of the birds, we must resign ourselves to the same room sealed, to a universe relegated behind the window. Only work, an accepted infirmity, the care required for a child or a companion, avert a crisis familiar to solitary women and which they deny by dignity. Unconsciously to remedy this, they go out on the least pretext despite the foul weather and the cold. 'I forgot to buy . . . I promised to go . . . I'm told that at such-and-such a place you can get . . . Micheline is always at home just now, I'll take her to drink a cup of something warm. . . .' The coat, the ridiculous little hat, and off we go into the metro to the clack-clack-clack of wooden soles.

Somehow or other, women, we have to organize the bad season, other than by borrowing the dark warmth of the metro, the steam of an infusion in a teashop, and the tonic atmosphere of the shady grocers who adopt a slightly clandestine air to sell you an innocent stick of vanilla, a sachet of pepper and a pound of salt, guaranteed marine. I feel authorized to advise you, who are motivated aimlessly instead of sobered by the cold, now the worst weather has arrived, to adopt a less agitated or shall we say less external rhythm of existence. You have solid arguments in favour of your mobility? I, too, to argue against you. It's not your absence but your presence which will expel that black and symbolic animal: I refer to the *cafard*. No, your doctor has not advised you to pace the asphalt after your midday meal, in an eastern blast. No, the staircase of the metro, scaled like a sports-field, does not increase the heart's endurance. No, the anxiety to rush to catch the last train does not constitute a performance worthy of interest. . . .

I could go on. But it makes me breathless to follow you even in imagination, O infantrywomen who spare your bicycle tyres. I'd like to see you back in your home. I'd particularly like this home to deserve more care than you devote to it. The arrangement of your apartment dates from a happier or at any rate a peaceful time, but now you harbour resentment towards it. Why haven't you turned it upside-down? Why haven't you made better use of its resources? You limit its potential in the name of a debatable economy or a sentimental fetishism. A slightly worn armchair is an old friend, but is spoiled by its loose cover. Get rid of the cover. If you own a carpet, don't stow it away, rolled up, at the back of the wardrobe.

On the other hand, you who nourish yourselves on little, and in little time, what do you need with a non-dining-room? Change it into no matter what else: into a sewing-room, a friendly work-circle, a design-room for young girls, a do-it-yourself sanctuary. . . . You can take your meals on a tray, in the largest and warmest room of your house.

You own books, and even love them. Books are expensive nowadays and difficult to replace. Why leave them ranged in that dark corridor, from top to bottom of a panel that you thought too dark to hang pictures on? So that when you look for a book you have to climb on a chair and pass the pale halo of your pocket torch along the shelves. Do your books proud. If you treat them well, they will keep you homebound and occupied, with warm brow, astonished not to have noticed the hours pass. Prolong their lives, dress their wounds, you who know so well how to camouflage a garment, to unpick an old pullover to re-knit it in the shape of socks and gloves. Books, pictures, furniture also form part of your line of defence against physical and mental ills.

And again, don't be ashamed of feeling chilly. You weren't so very plump, even before the war. Now you're minus the under-garment of soft tissue interposed between skin and flesh. And as you are brave little ones, you bravely lie: 'Me, I'm never cold. . . . Me, I'm dressed the same in winter as in summer. . . .' Keep this honourable swagger for the outside world. You've no fire at home? Resort to the dressing-gown. Play the cab-driver, rolled up like a sausage in a travelling-rug. You're engaged in reading, correspondence, a somewhat lengthy task? Settle down, and better than on one . . . half of your backside, if you don't mind. . . . Choose the armchair, the cushion, the best lighting, keep your knees and feet covered. This kind of selfishness, which constitutes an economy of strength and warmth, will render pleasant the hours you had intended to devote to the fine rain, the wind hostile to uncovered ears and short gathered skirts, to the stifling metro. . . .

One more piece of advice: avoid the mirror. Turn your back to it when writing, sewing or reading. Generally, it will have nothing good to tell you. You are not always capable of appre-ciating the beauty impressed on feminine features by slackness, enveloping silence, a profitable resignation, melancholy, and the pride of enduring for several hours without seeking the aid of others.

It is perhaps in the feminine soul, in its primitiveness and attach-ment to the marvellous, that gold has regained an esteem which in no way corresponds to reality. My readers need not fear to find here any general considerations on the yellow metal, the forbidden feelings it inspires, the covetousness its glitter engenders. Let's reassure them by speaking of gold as if it existed only in fantasy, as talismanic substance, ranking with the legendary carbuncle.

I often think of gold, aimlessly and agreeably, because I often hear it spoken of, its adventures and its misdeeds. In tales of yore the devil and his imps used to glide invisibly, on watch-nights, between the sleeping cat and the fearful young girl. They would listen to the pious maledictions of the village story-tellers and, to spice the watch-night, change the *louis d'or* into dry leaves, into glowing firebrands, into owl's eyes. Deceptive wallets, magic parchments signed with ink taken from a wrist vein, fatal pacts. . . . Then matins sounded from the nearby steeple and order was restored. . . .

My acquaintance with gold is superficial and longstanding. Born among fields, having lived among fields for my first twenty years, I've always known that the country worships gold. But I did not know to what extent, or in what manner. I knew only that gold and water, wherever they appeared, received in my riverless country the same devotion, that one leaned over a new and generous well as if the round mirror right at the bottom was a fabulous coin. . . .

I remember that, at fair grounds, bargains were settled in pistoles, that if the simple pistole was worth three francs, the gold pistole was equivalent to two pieces of one hundred sous. . . . I saw little gold, save for a watch of my father, my mother's brace-let, a snake with chestnut hair whose golden head and tail shone with chased scales. Even the most modest in that far-off time had, at the bottom of a chest, what used to be called 'the box with the gold odds and ends'. Its name sufficiently described its contents. Broken links, the warped ring of a watch-charm, part of a propelling pencil, the useless clasp of a necklace, sometimes one of those minuscule five-franc pieces in gold that I found so pretty – the box with the gold odds and ends held nothing that was considered negotiable. The parents merely taught the child-ren that 'that's not to be thrown away because it's gold.'

While I was growing up gold seemed to me gradually to lose its innocence. Whispers about a business of mean thefts disturbed the house where we dwelt with my elder brother, the country doctor. I saw my mother, her cheeks purple with indignation, I heard the servant sobbing, I made out the words : 'A gold-headed pin . . . your father's collar-stud, which is gold . . .' This *malaise* came to a head one day at the end of summer after storms which peeled the tiles from the roof. There were loud exclamations : 'Is it possible! Good people! *Quel butiau que c'te bete!*' and the domestic magpie circled above the roof. . . . The mason had just discovered the treasure of the sole thief, the *ziasse*. Nothing was missing, from the collar-stud to the little gilt spoon and a ten-gramme copper weight. The *ziasse* loved yellow metal and protested with loud grating cries against its retrieval. . . .

Since then, like everyone, I have heard the stories, enhanced by fantasy and immorality, which attach to a gold pebble or a stream of gold. Legends of nuggets, of pirates, of beggars lying on a pallet of gold . . . Gold in news items, gold in sensational events . . . I have seen that a man can love gold for itself, with a strange disinterested love. I have known a rich man – he died not long ago – who used to carry a score of well-polished louis in his pocket. 'Why?' I asked him. He pulled a handful from his pocket, inhaled them : 'Don't you know that gold smells good?' he asked me. I quote a further phrase, which escaped the other day from the lips of a young woman who adorns herself, daily, with a magnificently worked gold cross. 'My dear,' a friend reproached her, 'you can't wear such an . . . obvious . . . jewel just now!' 'Maybe,' said the young woman, 'but the fact is that gold keeps one warm.'

Do such remarks derive from neurosis? But neurosis is as ancient as immemorial gold, that generator of psychosis. I think of a real madman, shut up for years, who night and day never abandoned his fetish, a gold coin. He made the visitors he trusted sniff the gold piece : 'Can't you smell anything? I knew it! You've a coarse sense of smell. A very agreeable odour, slightly oniony, under a perfume of Russia leather. I can detect every odour. Look, for instance, my shower has a nice smell and is curiously reminiscent of the perfume of gold. Perhaps the subsoil which conducts the water here is auriferous?'

Someone showed me an ingot one day. I found it sad and less attractive than a brick, which would have been at least pink. But I admit that minting improves gold and that, alloyed, coined, it rolls with a sound that is, dare I say, silvery. Simple souls expect it to be yellow, whereas human malice now knows how to decolourize it and render it as dreary as platinum. 'Why do you like gold?' a great-grandmother asked a great-granddaughter, aged six, who was playing with the rings and bracelets on her old hands. 'It's because it's yellow, grandmother,' replied the little one, unconsciously sibylline.

Yellow, varying from very pale yellow to marigold yellow,

so heavy that its weight is enough to identify it, it persists through wars, instigates and pays for them. Doubtless it's in the leanest times that women delight in its solar glitter, exhume an unfashionable pendant, clasp round their wrist a thick family band about as artistic as a saucepan. They say, of the brooch which represents a golden pansy enamelled here and there in black, that 'it has a certain antiquated charm'. I don't deny this. But I believe that our brave provisioners, our courageous housewives, do not clearly discern the point and nature of their disposition towards the solar and despotic metal. They barely understand it – and who does understand it? We know that it's terribly heavy, that it is apt to descend to the bottom of the sea, to sleep forgotten beneath the earth, only suddenly to reappear, burdened with ancient crimes. . . . We know that women have always loved its warmth on their breasts. . . .

'It's a pear for one's thirst,' said one of them to me, touching under her dress, between her breasts, a large antique coin at the end of a chain.

But I had already seen her sell a diamond, an old piece of furniture, some rare books, and she has kept the gold piece.

10

'Are you doing anything with your two copper hinges?'

'Nothing, actually.'

'If you'll let me have them, I'll exchange them for you for some solution to stick rubber so that you can repair your hot water bottle. And you know, it's the pre-war solution, the one that smells of chloroform!'

'How much will you give me?'

My astute friend reflects, weighs the two hinges in his hand:

'Three cubic centimetres.'

'Measured in what?'

'In a small salt-spoon, which is just one cubic centimetre. Perhaps a drop or two more. Think about it. I must rush. I'm on the track of some wood,' he says with an important air.

'Lucky devil! Is it sawn wood?'

'Not sawn exactly . . . carved. . . .'

'Will you share it?'

'That depends. Are you catching the *râble* or the train before?'

'The train . . . how d'you mean?'

'Look: I know of two bargains, in a small house at Boulogne – a stag and a Newfoundland dog, both in wood, lifesize. They take up a room by themselves and the tenant wants to get rid of them. The stag alone comes to three hundred.'

'Francs?'

My friend shrugs his shoulders.

'Do we talk about money when we're buying, nowadays? Kilos. Three hundred kilos. The dog is the best, as far as I'm concerned. A Newfoundland, enormous. He's sitting up and begging with a hare in his mouth.'

'A Newfoundland that hunts hares?'

'Artist's licence. Next to the dog there's a thick tree-trunk, in wood. . . .'

'In what wood?'

'In dogwood – I mean the same wood, and a rifle.'

'A real one?'

'In real wood, thank God. Above the dog there's a branch of flowering hawthorn spreading gracefully, in wood. The wood that's wasted nowadays! All in oak. I buy the dog, the stag, I chop them up, I burn them in my oven. I lose on the stag's legs, which are thin, but I gain on the dog's coat, which is done in solid wood curls. Ah, if the Second Empire sculptor had had a taste for elephants, my winter would be assured.'

'And what are you going to give her in exchange, the woman who's selling off her menagery?'

'A complete harness for a pony.'

'Has she got a pony?'

'No, she's got a couple of parrots.'

'That'll never work, even if it's a very small harness. A parrot rarely exceeds six centimetres at the withers.'

'So my good woman will palm off the harness on the old corn chandler, who'll saddle up his miniature horse.'

'You don't say so. . . . You wouldn't know anything about ladder-proof underclothes?'

'I do. I've done well out of it. What I wear instead of underpants are really ravishing little ladies' knickers in pink cotton, with a hem in sky-blue machine-made lace, which comes straight from a haberdasher's known only to God and myself. When I undress at night, I'm like Barbette.* But my wife says she doesn't like me as a transvestite. By the way, if you've got any woollen articles . . .'

My sole response was an ironic glance at my handyman friend. But he persisted:

'. . . any very small woollen items, I'd make you up a pair of Harlequin slippers. Suppose you give me plenty of little bits of wool. . . .'

'It's only a supposition.'

'In my hands that's a superimposition. I join them end-to-end, I quilt them on each other, I stitch them on my slipper pattern. Red, green, yellow, violet. Harlequin slippers. They're comfortable and gay.'

'And the soles?'

'I was waiting for you to say that,' says my mischievous friend. 'For the soles I've a wine-strainer.'

'A wine-strainer? Wouldn't a sock be better?'

'A strainer to filter *eau-de-vie*, a genuine Charentais strainer, in felt! I'll leave you dazzled and go off for my wood by way of the Bois.'

'Is that shorter?'

'No, but it's softer. In the Bois I walk only on grass, it saves one's shoes. It bears thinking about!'

One has to admire them, those whose perpetual challenge to inconvenience, scarcity, the season's rigours, excites resistance, humour and invention. My old godchild of the Great War, an aged legionary, retired to a part of the country already toughened by the cold, writes to me that the habit of carrying about with him, for no particular reason, a satchel or a bag creates the itch to fill them, at least not to bring them back empty. Bring back what? 'The forest is nearby, but beaten in all directions. Some chestnuts have escaped the searchers; they have to be picked out of the clay where they are bogged down, where they would be spoiled. I've pressed beech-nuts here: half a litre of oil: do you know what I dry round my fireplace when I have a

---

* A well-known French female impersonator.

fire? Bits of rotten wood worked by insects which shreds like asbestos. Well dried, light as sponge, it only needs a match, whereas firewood that's too green smokes and goes out. You can't imagine the queer smell that fills my little hut, doors and shutters closed, when the fire warms the steam that comes out of my rotten wood and from the plaited reeds that I've woven myself to make mats and cushions!'

It's moving, the human will not to die. . . . Let's make fun of it quickly, as is our duty. Let's make fun of my friend, who walks so industriously on soft ground. Let's also make fun of the exchanges proposed in this small newspaper, of which I shall soon be the oldest subscriber: *Will exchange fine signed mandoline for boy's shoes in good condition. . . . Any valuable object given in exchange for millet for birds. . . . Good upright piano for small stove burning all fuels, and honey.* I trust that the amateur pianist finds himself properly provided with a superfluous omnivorous stove, that the signed mandoline excites the envy of the owner of the shoes. We are no longer ashamed to barter, to offer, instead of money, its approximate equivalent:

> Give me what you've got,
> You take what I've got.

used to sing one of the stars – Thérésa? Judic? – of an epoch which liked its breasts exuberant and every feminine beauty rounded. No more roundness, let's not talk of that, but let's praise the barter that keeps us all on our toes, in suspense over preposterous hopes, on the alert for the covetousness that may be aroused by a naturalized toucan or by an authentic uniform of a prefect of the Restoration.

Little bits of string no good for anything . . . The poet of the *Hortensias bleus,* Count Robert de Montesquiou, once assured me that one of his female relatives, and not one of the other persons to whom this economical trait has since been attributed, used to label, out of her hundred drawers, the drawer where she kept little useless bits of string. But are there any useless bits of string nowadays?

When I receive a parcel of vegetables from the country, more careful hands than mine undo the worn string that binds the bars of the crate, itself precious and made of wood as light as card-board. Isn't it rather a miracle that these slats of wood have not been detained *en route* for a fireless hearth? All the same, my patience becomes exhausted when it comes to certain knots, and I cut. . . . The little sacrificed ends soon disappear and I did not always realize that they had a use: untwisted, teased into a short strand of hemp, you can imagine a woman treating them like kapok and feather, stuffing what needs to be stuffed. A kind of mish-mash of hemp and paper makes up the interior of counter-panes, which render a great service. And when all string consists of twisted paper? We'll see then. The present state of affairs dispenses us from looking ahead and only determines us to let nothing get lost.

But where are the cupboards of yesteryear? Profound burrow-ings in the attic have left me with only a blue crinoline skirt, prettily embroidered with white garlands in chain-stitch. Made of fine linen material, narrow-waisted, with a wide sweep of skirt, this skirt comes to me from 'Sido'. That is to say, I shan't cut it into artistic tray-cloths or a loose cover for a tub easy-chair or a shirt-blouse.

The other treasures inherited from a provincial mother – 'Don't throw anything away, everything has a use' – have dis-appeared, frittered away by disrespectful hands. The cashmere shawl from India glowed its last fire of colour in the form of a handbag mounted on light-coloured imitation tortoise-shell. At least it escaped the sorriest destiny of cashmere, which is to end up as a table covering.

If I had a good look, mightn't I find one of those blouses in real lace in which the taste of 1900 incorporated some florets of real Irish lace, insertions from Cluny, bonnet-backing in valen-ciennes and satin-stitch, panels in Brussels lace? I shan't look. Such a jigsaw-blouse has no place either in our fashions or in this weather. Formerly I also had a nice lot of old material which could be used for furnishing fabric. So much the better – but I reflect: so much the worse – I had to defend myself against the find I made, in a conjugal dwelling, of a batch of repp. . . . A batch? A tidal wave of repp, which reached the centre of France across the catastrophe and exoduses of the Second Empire. . . . A scandal of repp, all in curtains and *portières*, in pelmets and hangings, in the garnet-red that becomes a shade of baleful and venomous chocolate under the light. A yardage, a mileage of repp, enough to make one flee or burst into tears, and I can scarce bear to mention its twisted fringes which no fire could destroy, which no heirs wrangled over after a decease.

For several years I thought myself under a spell. The garnet repp descended in noble folds from the loft, and when we gaily set out to ransack a well-known abode reputed to conceal a treasure, the garnet repp – always that, that everywhere, tied up in bundles, folded in mysterious boxes – decoyed us more than once. Beautiful severe material, I'd find in you now the virtues a pasha attributed to beauty : abundance and immobility. And the market at Saint-Ouen would parcel you out between a chipped crystal glass and a little hat that the market-woman calls a 'sauce-boat'. Materials of other days, materials in handfuls . . .

'You wouldn't have an oilcloth in poor condition?' interrupts one of my friends.

'Yes. Go and have a look at the one on the kitchen table and let me write.'

'When you've finished with it give it to me, and I'll make a substitute floorcloth out of it.'

'? . . .'

'I'll remove the outer waxed coating in bits and pieces, and underneath I'll find a cotton tissue still good enough for wiping or washing. Not so stupid, eh?'

No, certainly not ! Not so stupid. Emulation and improvisation often go a bit too far. Witness the woman, elegant despite everything, who refused a mauve carnation for her buttonhole because it cost ten francs. . . . She found in her bedroom a silk fancy handkerchief, cut it and crumpled it stunningly into the shape of a carnation, stuck it on the lapel of her jacket and congratulated herself. . . . Then she sighed and fell gloomy : 'It's stupid. The handkerchief cost me twenty francs.'

'But,' I protested, 'it's a flower that'll last long time.'

'No one likes flowers that last,' she said.

It was a feminine response, and a wise one. We all like to cherish and prolong the life of a rose, but we set little store on an imitation rose. We mourn only what is ephemeral.

'What a beautiful tea-rose !' I said to a young woman with a flower.

'I stole it !' she replied, laughing.

Perhaps she boasted, though many of us maintain a precarious balance on a gangway connecting resourcefulness with scrounging.

'Why do you write on only one side of the sheets?' the stripper of oilcloth asked me.

'Because at the newspaper printers the type-setting requires . . .'

I stop. What was true is no longer true, since a stenographer types my manuscripts. I obey, we all obey, a bungling habit which is almost a necessity. To scratch out widely, to draw feet, wings and moustaches around a blot, and always to tear up, tear up, tear up, that's our indulgence. But it's quite true that our flimsy material is becoming exhausted. Anyway, why should I noisily crumple up the condemned sheet for the cat to chase? What's the point of rolling it up and throwing it a long way off when she who used to chase after the paper ball, the cat, is no longer of this world? . . .

'If you possessed unlimited power, children, what would you like to give to her who never fails to give you everything from your birth onward?'

The replies to such a referendum, which also asked for a drawing of the intended object, were not lacking, nor the rewards. In their hundreds, on a sheet from an exercise book, on a piece of cardboard, on packing paper, children of six to thirteen years have painted, drawn, used crayons, ink, watercolour. A grave jury of painters, men of the theatre, writers, has gathered round multicoloured children's work and judged it without laughing. In any case, there was nothing to laugh at. More likely there was occasion, at times, to hide a tear.

Whenever a child, as much a marvel of dissimulation as of spontaneity, thinks himself shielded from our observation, he relaxes and reveals himself as he is, without mental age, passionate, zealous, accomplished. But these moments are brief. He is promptly repossessed by his duty to be a child, a willingness to dwell in his stage of growth and artlessness, from which there escape words that surprise us, avowals of a maturity like to disquiet us. Thank heaven, he also displays his naïvety, and we find this the more charming because it lingers and rejuvenates him.

'If you possessed unlimited power, children . . .' The suggestion offered them an unrivalled opportunity to dream, to digress even. . . . What saddened us, the jury, is that among so many children of both sexes we encountered so little unreason, such timid extravagance. Resignation is not a virtue of early life, and aware of the long habituation that makes them well-behaved, we would prefer to find our children somewhat frivolous. . . .

Some two hundred coloured drawings gaily deck the wall. Boys on one side, girls on the other, as at catechism. The care taken to separate the sexes makes it plain – we weren't expecting this – that boys are more emotional than girls and more poetic. A twelve-year-old offers his mother, 'so that she may relax', peace between all nations. He knows what he's talking about and depicts it in bright colours. A simple and industrious little boy, he conceives of peace only as represented by work. His miner mines, his mower tosses the hay, his fisherman pulls at the drag-net, and the very hens, devoted to their duty, lay with zeal around a woman idle at last, seated at last in a wicker armchair. Two great unrealized dreams float above her in the sky : a winter coat and a summer coat. When I told you there was nothing to laugh at . . .

Another poet takes his pinkest crayons and claps a fat pig on four short legs, with knotted sky-blue tail, and dedicates it to 'My dear mummy, who has seven children'. I've not done with rousing your emotions and being moved myself : here is a large heart, which fills a whole page. At the centre of the heart a steeple, a house under the trees, flowers, and these words : 'For when your hair is white.' There's also a boy who offers 'A magic house where there's no need to sweep, where the food cooks itself, where the children are always good.' Another boy is not too good with his crayon but his text touches us to the quick : 'Mummy, I'd like to give you daddy, who's a prisoner. But I don't know how to draw a camp.'

The utilitarians, the practical little boys, organize a happy state where they take their place beside the maternal flank. A handful of pioneers, all brothers, declaim : 'We are seven boys and we want a Provençal manor-house !' They delegate to the artist of the septet, who comes out of it very well, the task of giving a definite form to their desire. Perhaps the best painter of all is the little lad who makes a mountain of snow out of a white page, merely by tracing the winding paths, dotted with

small green fir-trees. Up above, in the full icy oxygen, he wants
to hoist a mother who is exhausting herself merely keeping alive.
Another gives his parents the countryside. He sees them as so
happy that he pictures the whole family in Pierrot garments,
doing a round dance beneath a sun filamentous with long
rays. . . .

The little girls' coterie is not devoid of interest, thanks to their
allowing themselves to be dominated by a spirit of fashion and
coquetry. A trap, offered to a mother 'because her bicycle is worn
out', shines with both naïvety and art, and its pony makes the
sparks fly. The pony is pink, the trap is blue, the painter is seven
years old, and the jury, rejuvenated, stops smiling only when it
bends over the next drawing: a small suburban villa, pebble-
dashed, neat and new, underlined by three words: 'The lost
house'. . . . Quick, let's pluck up courage again, looking at the
blue and green trees, the meadow, paradise of two fat pigs! A
threatened paradise, since from the height of a cloud stuffed
with victuals there falls a knife, skilfully constructed of tinfoil,
which is aimed at the throat of one of the piglets. . . .

Let's leaf rapidly through the series of pigs, the series of villas,
the series of radios and tea-tables; let's linger over the more
touching litany of model stock-farms, experience surprise that so
many little girls have come up with only a handbag, a pair of
gloves, and even a sewing kit, as panaceas to cure the fatigues
of a devoted mother.

Let's turn to the poignant evocation traced by an orphan;
inspired, visionary, he brings his young mother from the tomb,
a pale and graceful corpse, evokes around her the scenes and
attractions of her earthly existence, and wishes to repay what he
has received from her: life. I hope that such a child will succeed
in growing up without losing touch with this strange lyricism,
derived from the great sorrow that guides his hand. Does he not
already borrow the tricks of colour and design, the lofty, slow and
difficult path of art? Doubtless the only way for a small boy to
be reunited with what he wishes always to cherish is by the use
of this dreaming and as yet inexperienced pencil.

'You've a very nice portrait at the Salon d'hiver,' a friend says
to me.

'Yes, isn't it?'

And I give myself airs, thinking that friends and strangers have been dreaming before the profile of a young woman of twenty-five, laden with a chestnut coil of hair, a red poppy under one ear. . . . However, I stress:

'A talented officiant, evidently, Father Ferdinand Humbert; but this unfinished portrait is one of the nicest things of my youth. . . .'

'Your youth? Where d'you put your childhood, then? A portrait in which you look a good three years old!'

We were not on the same plane. It's all to do with a small pink and white gouache, signed by an obscure painter beginning to be successful in 1941. It's true that at eighteen months – the age of the portrait – I *was* very nice. No one talks to me about the other portrait. And yet it dates from the period when 'Father Humbert', as he was called, painted statesmen, the wives of great industrialists embellished with children and dogs, against the background of a park or a Louis XV *salon*. I was very proud that he was pleased to paint me as I most often was, that is with eyes downcast and rather sad. Between the two portraits the palm goes to an effigy of eighteen months, fresh and polished as if it dated from 1830. . . .

Further on, a lithograph by J.-L. Forain attracts little attention. It is graceful, but I've only one eye. Intimidated by Forain, young, bearded, mocking, I yet dared to ask him:

'Why have you only give me one eye?'

'Probably because you only had one eye that day,' he replied.

He worked in a studio whose disorder resembled the chaotic commencement of the world, as dark as if it had always been raining on its grey window-panes. The few sittings during which I watched him trace a marvellously curving and broad line on the stone – he destroyed several – left me isolated. His brilliant agile glance ran over me disdainfully. Very young women are not resigned to being treated as still-lifes.

Between so many assembled portraits and myself as spectator there interposes the memory of the place which saw their birth. Their painters are not all dead. From the time when Jacques-Emile Blanche painted the great portrait now in the Barcelona Museum, I struggled against afternoon drowsiness to cast a glance at the enviable garden, the stream of forget-me-nots, the arbours of a shady Passy I've lived in and seen destroyed, where

René Boylesve had already dreamed *La leçon d'amour* beneath
the chestnuts of a centennial park. While J.-E. Blanche was working, the lines of his face all sloped to the same side, as if drawn
by the pressure of a migraine. . . .

Léandre's studio, which I've entirely forgotten save for the
Montmartre cats which eyed each other in the garden, lashing
their tails and parading with great strides as if they were playing
Cyrano. . . . Boldini's studio, encumbered with portraits of
American millionairesses choked with pearls. But on the lid of
a cigar-box, the cover of a book, on a dusty page torn from an
album, one, two, ten skilful little sketches were worth more than
the pictures. . . .

Pascau's studio : presented on a large canvas, Mme Rosemonde
Gérard smiling, the angle of the eye stretched toward the temple,
the eyelashes like arrowheads. Finally, the studio of Antonio de
La Gandara, glittering with a glossy display composed of a flooring of polished oak, a dark cheval-glass, some vast easy-chair of
a dead white. An almost empty studio, but the person and the
personality of the artist filled it most formidably. From the
summit of an unequalled physical prestige, La Gandara, as if
condescendingly, painted women, always women. The Princesse
de Caraman-Chimay sheathed in pink satin; her sister, the
Comtesse de Noailles, in pale blue; Polaire in pink, Polaire erect
on her slender feet, waist belted; Polaire, a graceful compromise
between the human species and a gentle animality; Polaire, as
quivering and restless as a captive antelope. . . .

Studio of Fix-Masseau, and the beautiful white marble from
which he extracted my likeness, a grey floor plastered with clay,
the smell of cellars and damp earth . . . I ran no risk of being
bored with an artist, young for his age and taken with everything, who would abandon a statue to model an inkwell after a
water-chestnut, a teapot inspired by the sunfish. . . . I enjoyed
meeting these artists on their own ground : one badgering his
work with brusque touches and words; another bemused and
silent; another singing like a shepherd and forgetting me; another
fussy and full of doubt. . . .

What is not erased from my old portraits are the faces of their
painters. The later ones, where I belong almost allegorically to a
landscape, represent not so much my own features as those, for
instance, of Segonzac and Luc-Albert Moreau. I see the green

eye in a vine, the ruddy cheek in a manor house. Does anyone speak to me of the melancholy felt by a woman looking at her youthful portraits? If regrets there be, mine are for the painters, who have disappeared or departed. But as briefly as we may have known an artist, he has always been ours insofar as we have watched him at grips with his work, preoccupied with giving birth.

II

I don't know whether we ought to accord our various attitudes the name of bravura. But I do believe that a foreigner – I mean someone who hailed from a country foreign to the war – would carry away some astonishment if he chanced to be here at the time of an alert followed by a bombardment. He would be struck, first, by our diversities and then by our resemblances. We need not discuss the behaviour of the children, which is only a manifestation of their inconscience and their Parisian pertness. They respond to the wail of the sirens by imitating the noise, after which they leap and run about as if under a sudden shower; some affect fear in their behaviour, then they think no more about it, return to their marbles and their frayed skipping-rope. If a keeper at the Palais-Royal is ordered to empty the gardens because of guns and passing aeroplanes, the children renew their interest in what's going on but only to react against the ukases and the wearers of the pacific red-striped black uniform: 'No, what's up then, we're not doing any harm, where do they expect us to play then, it's only aeroplanes, it's not as if you could actually hear them. . . .' etc., etc. . . .

The adults, especially the women, give them an example, not of bravado, but of indifference. I've never seen a young woman stop sewing until the intervention, yellow armband on sleeve, of one of the Passive Defence wardens. Even if she is accompanied by a very small child lying in its pram, none does better, or worse, than momentarily lift her gaze to the clouds or the blue sky, then resume sewing or reading. None seek the official shelter – I think it's in the Rue de Valois – it suffices for prams, children and young mothers to gather under the arcades to which the public of the gardens attribute a boundless security. . . . 'We're not outside, we're under the galleries!'

It sometimes happens, if there is an alert, that I shelter momentarily under these same arcades for the pleasure of looking and listening. Our pleasures are not numerous just now. Pleasure to recognize myself in those around me, who are at once loyal and irreverent, attached to the same trivialities, scorning the same essentials. After three years of war we parade – the least possible! – the same privations. Old or young, burdened or not with progeny, we aspire to the same unattainable treasures. 'What I'd really like is some little trousers in woollen jersey. Mine is linings for the sleeves of a man's jacket. Once the lining's gone the outside's not long in following. . . .'

New and deplorable signs appear: men have the right elbow of their garments whiter than the left. Nearly all the handles of the carry-alls, worn out, are mended with string. Many navy-blue outfits are still to be seen on slender women; but we needn't expect that the blue of the skirt has been dipped in the same blue as the jacket. . . . To the clacking of wooden soles I can dream that I am still at Belle-Isle-en-Mer, at the hour when the tide, bringing back the boats, fetches the sardine women to the quayside. But it's nothing more than a covey of young girls, clattering under the galleries at the exit from the Comédie-Française. . . .

Young women and young girls are still very pretty this year despite the hats, despite the absence of hats, the indiscreet uncovered locks, the Savoy cake in curls on the head – return of that frightful crimping! – over-long ringlets: 'Golden hair on your shoulder . . .' and side-hair swept back à la petite fille. Still very pretty, but their style has changed since 1941 and '42. They have grown tired, if not of their virtues, at least of the appearance of virtue. The terrible rage to live – which is what they call the need to experience pleasure – which set the prisons of the Terror ablaze is on them, especially the youngest.

Girls and boys, barely adolescent, take advantage of the metro to make contacts which begin at the lips and finish at the ankles in the obscure pitching of the coach. In the gardens I see them collapse, fused and overcome under my windows like dragon-flies by a lake shore, motionlessly embracing one another.

The most shameless are possibly those who are still encumbered with an awkward innocence and await, coupled under the pink chestnut trees, the miracle of sensual pleasure. Scandalous, they stay locked together, by the grace of bewildered youth. Their long kisses, learned from the screen, make a great thing of their avidity; mouth to mouth, they seem to be swallowing. It is not nice. But one takes pity on them.

Two by two, they stroll along the galleries where there used to saunter, one by one, the last streetwalkers of the Palais-Royal whom I have watched, grave and circumspect, and reserved to the point that I could not believe that a degraded profession directed their steps. Mature, clothed in black, and so unengaging . . . Fatigue, cold, the dog-days drew from them rare terse remarks concerning the temperature or the news. Where, now, is the one who used to embroider standing up, changing from one leg to the other, propped against a pillar? The approach of a male silhouette wrenched her back to her proper task and she promptly hid her work in her pocket. A daily encounter is sufficient justification for the greeting one exchanges in a glance. The clandestine embroiderer replied to mine by holding out the collar she was embroidering:

'Look, isn't that exquisitely done?' she said to me with an enraptured air.

And, while I enthused, she continued in a confessional tone:

'And if you could see my satin-stitch doily to go under my goldfish-bowl!'

I said nothing to discourage the confidences of this seamstress, who remained standing up like a cab-horse. But she proved discreet, timid, enigmatic even.

'Those women, they beat me yesterday,' she whispered one day.

'Beat you? Who are they?'

She indicated the gallery opposite with her chin.

'Those over there.'

'But why?'

On her still fresh, forty-year-old face there appeared a little girl's roguishness:

'Ah, that's it . . . they're jealous. And with reason. Just think, I've no man in my life.'

Because of the duration of the war and an existence whose conditions worsen daily, many children are losing the sweet of their life. That is, alas, inevitable. So many inexorable glances under tossing curls, so many words that make no child blush, so much callousness in the very tactics of being winning! The small girls are not deprived of screen heroes. But there are ways of admiring and cherishing. . . .

One of the leading stars of the cinema lives quite near here, under the arcades. The young girls and the little girls are well aware of it. They congregate beneath the arched window of the *entresol* and demand 'cards' and 'autographs' in the shrillest voices until a frizzy ash-blond head shows itself, the well-known head of a big simple boy, much more shy at heart than his admirers. . . . These call him 'Jeannot' at the top of their voice, but he is not enamoured of such familiar popularity. The little ones lift their fresh piratical faces towards him, menacing with enthusiasm. They climb the stairs, sit on the steps, squeal, exclaim: 'No, we shan't go away! We want photos! And signed photos, not with the name printed! That's what everyone else does! Marie Bell gave us some, in the courtyard! What, aren't you better than Marie Bell!'

Jeannot – you've recognized Jean Marais – tells me about his state of siege, tosses his blond curly crest:

'They're not nice. They're often pretty, but I'd rather they were nice. . . . They need to be gentle, to have a feminine, flexible, restrained tone of voice, instead of this caterwauling. . . . The other day, one was so exceptionally sweet. . . . I didn't know her, but I talked to her for a long time, she looked up like this when I spoke because I'm much taller than she is. She called me "Sir" instead of saying, "Hi Jeannot!" Except once . . . I said to her as I was leaving: "But won't you be told off for getting back so late?" She looked up again like this and said:

"Oh no, sir! I'll tell mummy: 'I was with Jeannot' ".'

It's a fact that the niceness to which my handsome young male neighbour aspires is becoming rather rare. . . . A ring at the bell tears the same Jean from his easel, where he is passionately engaged in painting, to open the door and see at his feet, on the door-mat, one of those minute Parisian children, five years old by size, twenty in expression. . . .

'What d'you want, little one?'

'A photo. With an autograph on it.'

'I've left some photos with the concierge, you've only got to go and ask her for one.'

A sagacious regard, unsmiling and unintimidated, surveys the length of Jean Marais:

'And you think that'll do?'

'Of course. I'm telling you.'

'And if I offer as much as ten *ronds* to give me one?'

Jeannot bursts out laughing, but the psychologist at his feet gravely shakes his head:

'It's clear,' he says, 'that you don't know anything about life. . . .'

I didn't see much to laugh at in this story either. Children don't make us laugh any more. It's too fragile a commodity, and one exposed to too many different fatalities with us now. I'd rather listen to an account of the doings and behaviour of Moulouk, the Eskimo dog, almost as much a star as his master.

At his first film contract, in Italy, Moulouk, who was desolate from having to leave Jean Marais, reached, as they say, the limit.* Even symbolically, haricots do not constitute a menu worthy of a leading four-footed star; but it was objected that Moulouk was untrained. His beauty, his dumb and lively intelligence, the fanatical attachment which bound him to his idol, were better than training. In Paris he already knew how to slip invisibly into the metro, to disguise himself in the lining of a lumber-jacket. In the studio he learned to jump on the back of his master on a bicycle, then to hold his master round the neck launched on a galloping horse. To follow across obstacles, fetch, swim, be silent, obey, he knew all that, which is easy for a dog of quality. . . .

Ever since *Carmen*, since *L'Eternel Retour*, Moulouk has seen his fame increase. As to his prerogatives, at the Palais-Royal these are entirely personal and more or less unlimited. He escapes the rigour of the controls imposed by the leash. And once when one of our wardens attempted to deal severely with a Moulouk at large, a chorus of young fans arose from among the elms to point out his error:

'But it's Moulouk, Mr Keeper! Leave him alone, sir! I tell you, it's Moulouk!'

* (Fr.) *toucha les haricots.*

And the warden diverted his authority from the dog star, Moulouk of the posters, who continued freely to cock his celebrated leg against the ancient elms, shaped as an arbour, bossed and gnarled, enfeebled, immemorial, which decline to die.

It's inevitable that I should run as many risks in the Gardens as Jeannot and Moulouk. The young girls and young men who accost me often style themselves poets. If I am to believe them, ravaged France can count many poets of both sexes who don't disdain the advice of a prosodist. I listen to them entirely without irony, remembering that the slightest sarcasm grievously wounds anyone who is young, inspired, eager to grow and suffer. I admire the fact that the flower that blooms from an ill-fed, ill-housed, humiliatingly-clothed youth should rise to a poem, as in the time when romanticism found it natural to go without bread and fire. The attic, the hollow stomach, the pallor, even the resignation exhaled in the rhythm, are these what 1830 has to bequeath to 1940? It is poignant, it is almost intolerable, within the ornate walls of a royal enclosure where we could wish to encounter only the happy phantoms of silence and peace. But the war leaps over the walls, crosses them, illuminates them. My little poets gone, and the sun having abandoned its eastern springboard to sink behind the western rampart, it is not the night, the night of our city lacking street-lamps or headlights that succeeds them, peaceful and worthy of them, but clusters of rockets, green sulphurous lanterns suspended immobile from a starry nail, the vast pink throb of distant explosions. The whole luminous apparatus of destruction and defence breaches our walls, throws them into relief out of shadow, turns the sward blue. But for the sound of the sirens and the cannonade, we might think these troubled nights an enchantment.

Indoors we are muffled within our deceptive partitions which, at different epochs, used only glass and thin wood. The air, displaced by the explosions, grips our old salon doors, shakes them in their frames, opens them irresistibly, wrenches a great cough from the decrepit french windows, and the searchlights of the anti-aircraft defences dance crystalline over the slate roofs.

It's the moment for those who prefer risks to cellar shelters, it's the moment when honourable human curiosity verifies its endurance. Curtains closed over the half-open windows ('Watch out for the blast and open a window on the stairs as well!'), some play cards. A writer holds the sheet he has just started in the air: he wants to see if his hands are trembling. . . .

'Is the dog frightened?'

'No more than last time.'

'Comfort him.'

'How?'

'By talking to him, of course.'

'What do I have to say?'

'What you like, it's the tone that matters. Speak to him confidently. Tell him this noise doesn't mean anything. Tell him it's going to be like this every day and that he'll have to get used to it. . . . Give him a lump of sugar. Tell him *huisipisi, huisipisi*!'

'What's that mean?'

'I don't know, but it does the trick.'

A young couple relax reading in the garden; the man reads a tired thick number of a prewar review, the woman a novel, if I can judge the format from my window. The alert bellows. Neither the male nor the female reader is affected by the noise. None of the two has raised a head or cast a glance at the sky. The child with bucket and spade has not interrupted his humming monologue. The reflexes of the alert are blunted. If the warden feels that it's necessary to expel them from Eden, this couple rapt from the present time, this absorbed pair will rise, say: 'What? . . . Ah, yes! . . .' and move off at a slow pace to read standing under the arcades.

To awake the reflex, the sudden start, excite the contraction of the heart which pales the face, the blood must flow now, the eyes see, the urgent alarm deliver us to the logic of the danger. This war, in spite of the exasperated tone we adopt to say: 'That's enough, one can't take any more . . .', this war – I speak for those, with those, who don't stir from Paris – is too old for us.

When it was young, at the time of the first alerts over Paris, I once joined with friends and neighbours who went down into a shelter. I must respect the truth: everyone put on a good show. Playfulness and patience were lacking in no one. And what delightful disdain for inconvenience! The sole funereal Pigeon lamp, the guttering candle? A trifle! The imperious presence of the dustbins? We laughed at them. Some mouldy timbers and two empty barrels in the shape of seats? Camping! Never was ill-fortune met with better faces. The surface of the earth transmitted to us heavy quakes, not very noisy, a restrained tumult, and when it fell silent we were free to go up again. The rising dawn lit our return into the short Rue de Beaujolais. We were not a pretty sight, but very cordial: 'That was very nice . . . didn't seem long to me. – Nor to me. – Nor to me!'

It was then that the concierge, who ascended from the safe depths with us, remembered that she had left the key of our apartment in her lodge, and that we were therefore, she said, 'shut out'. One of us, modestly revealing aerial propensities, penetrated into the yards of the Banque de France by separating the fencing and collected therefrom a long ladder by means of which he restored our access to our homes. . . .

'It's as comic as could be!' we exclaimed in chorus. 'We must do it again! To next time!'

But the next day, or rather night, and all the next that followed, I believed the optimists did as I did and stayed in bed.

O warm bed, refuge of the sick, paradise of the fit, what shelter can match you when the poor human frame, prey to sleep or terror, seeks to tremble or sleep in comfort, bed which receives us horizontally, resigned to live and ready to die?

We recall having been innocent braggarts at the commencement, then at the recommencement, of the periods of alert. Fear, reasonable fear, is composed of different elements within us. An animal acquires its experience by accumulation. With us, it's not bravura but fear that constitutes progress, and the means to ward off or fly the peril. At the same time there intervenes a sort of decorum which gives us, if only in appearance, the attitude of frivolity, a daredevil unconstraint. We are sensible as soon as our fear is far enough out of the unconscious, once the danger becomes intelligible to us, once we escape from those supplications and absurd involuntary prayers which ferment internally, shall I say, in a defeated spirit.

Again, educated by it, we recover too quickly from fear. The garden pigeon which trails part of a broken snare from its foot will never again fall victim to such a trap. It knows. It knows at once what we learn slowly and with difficulty. Four years of war have passed over us starlings, who had no more sense than not to budge from our city. Here we have given ourselves to obstinacy, observances, divers forms of patience, by virtue of which we declare ourselves seasoned warriors, a particularly inappropriate phrase that flatters us.

I once wrote that the French housekeeper, stranded on a desert island, would succeed in recreating, at the scene of the shipwreck, most of the characteristics of the comfort she inflicts on her three little rooms giving on a courtyard. In printing this caprice, it's myself I chiefly deride: 'In my third war I shan't be afraid of anyone for practical purposes.' It's a flat pleasantry. Nevertheless, the routine of my second war, this one, keeps me going and I keep it going. Not to mention that an infirmity always teaches you something – if only how to put up with it; an arthritis of the hip is a good counsellor. Without it, should I not have frenziedly raced along the roads to what we thought a quiet spot?

The very thought of being camped in a county town of the south-west, or breathing the Savoy air, or counting the days and months in the bluish pastures of Normandy, makes me shudder; and I turn a fond eye towards the quadrangular garden. Is it possible, my so-loved provinces, that I can envisage you all dispassionately? But it's just that Paris, during the war, is beyond compare.

What a trench it has driven in our hearts, in four years . . . It is dark, night has fallen, and we rail out loud: 'Black as the Devil's backside!' In secret, we cherish this Shulamite with the darkened face. Who comes to disfigure her wounds us. We no longer distinguish, in the rites of our restricted life, what forms part of the cult rendered to the City and what is demanded by the acts of self-preservation. Before such a masterpiece, such an ancient edifice hitherto immune, we regret that, magically, they cannot descend, when the night is full of menace, into a protective abyss. . . .

For us, inured to the warning of the sirens, we know what to do: if it's daytime, avoid the trap of the metro; if it's night, leave the windows half-open (as in 1916), leave the dressing-gown within arm's reach, the water-jug which does not replace the succulent oranges of before the war, and open the cool asylum of the sheets. A large old volume holds itself ready to bear us into southern Africa, along a venerable journey all festooned with snakes and lianas. . . .

Among our passive defences against the raids, there is also room for *belote*, conversation and . . . my work as a writer? Oh no, not for work! It's difficult enough to write when the heavens aren't thundering. The human organism requires, for the service of its senses, the maximum of vacancy. It has to absorb the flapping flags of light, sounds far and near. Irritated, it eliminates that of the sirens so as to occupy itself with the perfect springy bounds suggested by the guns, the ambitious dry rosary expelled by the machine-guns, the collapse that follows the fall of the bombs. It calculates, it errs. It announces: 'That's on Versailles. That's Juvisy again.' It tries to be clever: 'That's the third wave of aeroplanes, the last,' as if it knew anything about it, taking its desires for reality.

A murmur is born, far off, and already fills the horizon. It is the modulated sound of aeroplanes, so quickly swelling. The heart defends itself by accelerating, a muscle in the calf dances its independent dance. The musical *sostenuto* of the aeroplanes increases, vibrates in a broken windowpane as in the secrecy of our loins, and the combined pursuit – anti-aircraft defences and searchlights – aims at the heart of the clouds, overtakes among the stars the aeroplanes we cannot see above us. . . . We are . . . Yes, we are frightened. I am frightened. Fear is not, thank God, a trial I cannot withstand. It is a solicitation which interrogates every limb, excites the second heart which beats in the tonsils. As long as we can keep our troop of organs under control, as long as they do not scatter to follow the most distracted sheep which wants to flee to the abyss, or that foolish ewe which stupidly braves wild beasts it does not know, all is well. To the companion who, anxious on my behalf, asks: 'Are you frightened?' I am sure enough of myself to reply: 'Yes, be easy, I'm afraid.'

The whole thing is that fear meets something responsive within us, and not an empty room with banging doors, not a desert swept by a furious wind. . . . We shall light a cigarette to demonstrate that the little flame does not quiver in our hand. We shall lift a completed page, we shall fill a glass: the page must not tremble, the glass rattle against the inclined bottle. We must not be less worthy than in 1918, when, under the longest aerial attack, I undertook out of pride to explain clearly to a friend to whom I was giving shelter why one of the eyes of the sole is always placed crossways and all anyhow because, originally situated on the underside of the creature, it makes its way with difficulty through the cartilages of the head and emerges haphazardly, as if no matter where. . . .

Meanwhile, the cottage at Auteuil braced its back, coughed, and lent us its fragile slating. . . . The fury of the attack, its proximity and its explosions were such that, obedient to the instinct that drives the frightened man and animal to a hole, or the earth shaped like a grotto, we sat on the ground in an old alcove arranged as a hanging-closet, where it seemed to us that the uproar became less intense. We were only two isolated women in a deserted district, in the midst of night, attack and war. . . .

It was there that, collecting my wits as they say, I applied myself to assembling ideas and words : 'See if you can follow me : the sole when young is not yet a flat-fish, so it has, like other round fish, li-ke-oth-er-round-fish . . .' I articulated forcefully but could barely hear myself. A pearl trimming, which fringed a dress hanging above us, brushed my cheek. Pushing it aside, I recognized the iridiscent *perlage* of an evening-dress. The unexpected sight of this adornment of a happy evening cost me my words, the story of the sole, and the awareness of the moment. So true it is that a present moment, even terrible, does not always prevail over the delightful past. But how many times does the opportune and tangible relic come to us across the darkness it affronts and dissipates?

The memories we retain of our frightened hours is uneven. A motor-car accident leaves us with nothing, except it be the memories of hospital and convalescence, for we have neither prepared for it nor seen it coming towards us. Fear does not menace – I was about, God forgive me, to write : does not reward – those the mind has not forewarned. I have known beings who, by reason of an exceptional existence, had lost the habit of fear. They were not great captains, far from that, rather the inept. In them a sensibility otherwise capable of nobility had been honed down, together with the extinction of the ageless physical reflexes which impress on the face of a frightened child the pallor, the half-open mouth, the expression of a kind of ecstasy, which one sees in certain tormented individuals. Thus old Furth. . . . My reader can have no interest in knowing who old Furth was, and indeed I don't know myself and he died when I was still young. Old Furth, then, spoke to me about fear on a single occasion. He was in the habit of travelling in distant countries and of remaining silent as to what called him there.

He once found himself face to face, alone together, with a lion. . .

'. . . The lion emerged from a copse. We stopped one in front of the other. I can still see the beautiful dark yellow of his eyes and the hair of his mane, like burnt grass. I don't know what came over me. I fell on my knees. I joined my hands like this. He looked at me with such a . . . such a superior air. . . . And then he passed beside me. He was already a long way off while I was still on my knees with my hands together.'

'You had no weapon, M. Furth?'

'No more than usual, a good toy, perfectly adequate. I didn't think of it for a moment. On my knees, hands together . . . When I got up again, do you know what I asked myself? Instead of telling myself that I'd had a narrow escape, that I was a lucky chap, I asked myself what the lion must have thought of me. . . . You must admit that's unusual!'

I admitted it readily. The piratic eye, the antique reddish-white goatee, the mouth clamped on a pipe, all the evocative apparatus that made up old Furth, had been afraid. But he was unaware of it, remembering only that he had put knee to ground before his master, who had despised him.

'But if the interview had been prolonged, M. Furth, which of the two would have had the better of it?'

There old Furth laughed like a drain, showing his yellow octogenarian stumps. Then he resumed the serenity of an old bandit who had never been intelligent enough to tremble with fear more than once in his life.

Once more a dry spring desolates a year. The short cornstalks will furnish neither straw nor full ears. In vain the pigeons with their thirsty plumage spread first one wing, then the other, to implore beneficent water. We shall have no fruit in June, in July. We shall have no . . . The list of what will be denied to us is a long one.

Beneath my window there pass, each at his time, the familiar neighbours. In four years some, from being passers-by, have become friends : that is to say that the war and my immobility have not entirely bereft me. But others no longer pass, will never pass again. Among those bent on living, many occupy themselves in remaining recognizable. It is an activity admissible in whoever grows old in the midst of such a long affliction. It is also a waste of energy. What else do I do? The determination to keep erect, not to permit the development, below the nape of the neck, of the 'camel's hump', the pad which bows the head and the neck, drags at the shoulders. . . .

'Stand straight, daughter,' the erect mothers of former times used to say.

Today their granddaughters curve their backs and hollow their stomachs. Mauriac asserts that the era when women wore the cruel armour of whalebone and stays was marked by an irrepressible liveliness. . . .

'Ah!' exclaims one of these amiable women, sometimes old, sometimes rather young, 'I've had enough! Once the war's over, I'll really let myself go!'

'At what, my dear?'

'At growing old, of course! During the war I don't dare. I'd be ashamed.'

And she painted for me with delectation her future white hair, her future epidermis – thin, wrinkled, unpowdered – her comfortable dresses to be and her carefree life of tomorrow. . . .

'One year of war,' she says finally, 'is interminable. Two years of war are very long. Three, four years . . . one comes to the end of it. But at the price of adaptations which are like an art of passivity. And throughout the whole of this time, moreover, it's a matter of not decaying physically . . . I'm very tired.'

Listening to her, I sought in her her former self, the champion of feminine activity that she was between 1914 and 1918. What magnificent substitutes she supplied during the Great War! In factories and offices, hospitals and business houses, the women and their initiatives sometimes surpassed what was expected of them. The war virilized them, clothed them with the brief tunic of Eliacin, shore their heads like the knob of a staircase, plastered down their hair like Argentine dancers. . . .

One of the peculiarities of the present war is the exclusively, dangerously feminine role it imposes on women. Is it because of the total occupation of our territory, the omnipresence of an alien and virile multitude, that women are assuming the externals of *gamines* and the manners of pupils? I incriminate none of her ulterior motives, well knowing that she never exposes the best of herself. But the sparsity of her hair, the indiscretion of her curls, the inadequately long skirt open to both the wind and the casual glance, all these are errors in which French charm has committed too many provocations. One is tempted to say to these dishevelled uncovered little girls of all ages : 'Chut . . . we are not alone. . . .'

But then, they are often beautiful and cherish their inexpensive adornments. And they would be no doubt quick to reply that the spring, however ungracious, brings the need to blossom. That there is merit in enhancing beauty, in accentuating it in a hundred ways, and that to adorn it, in however barbarian a setting, is to await and already to honour peace. . . .